Perspectives on Wellbeing

Studies in Inclusive Education

Series Editor

Roger Slee (*University of South Australia, Australia*)

Editorial Board

Mel Ainscow (*University of Manchester, UK*)
Felicity Armstrong (*Institute of Education, University of London, UK*)
Len Barton (*Institute of Education, University of London, UK*)
Suzanne Carrington (*Queensland University of Technology, Australia*)
Joanne Deppeler (*Monash University, Australia*)
Linda Graham (*Queensland University of Technology, Australia*)
Levan Lim (*National Institute of Education, Singapore*)
Missy Morton (*University of Canterbury, New Zealand*)

VOLUME 41

The titles published in this series are listed at *brill.com/stie*

Perspectives on Wellbeing

A Reader

Edited by

Sue Vella, Ruth Falzon and Andrew Azzopardi

BRILL
SENSE

LEIDEN | BOSTON

Cover illustration: *Composition in Blue* by John Martin Borg

All chapters in this book have undergone peer review.

The Library of Congress Cataloging-in-Publication Data is available online at http://catalog.loc.gov

ISSN 2542-9825
ISBN 978-90-04-39415-5 (paperback)
ISBN 978-90-04-39416-2 (hardback)
ISBN 978-90-04-39417-9 (e-book)

Copyright 2019 by Koninklijke Brill NV, Leiden, The Netherlands.
Koninklijke Brill NV incorporates the imprints Brill, Brill Hes & De Graaf, Brill Nijhoff, Brill Rodopi, Brill Sense, Hotei Publishing, mentis Verlag, Verlag Ferdinand Schöningh and Wilhelm Fink Verlag.
All rights reserved. No part of this publication may be reproduced, translated, stored in a retrieval system, or transmitted in any form or by any means, electronic, mechanical, photocopying, recording or otherwise, without prior written permission from the publisher.
Authorization to photocopy items for internal or personal use is granted by Koninklijke Brill NV provided that the appropriate fees are paid directly to The Copyright Clearance Center, 222 Rosewood Drive, Suite 910, Danvers, MA 01923, USA. Fees are subject to change.

This book is printed on acid-free paper and produced in a sustainable manner.

CONTENTS

Acknowledgements		vii
Notes on Contributors		ix
Introduction *Sue Vella, Andrew Azzopardi and Ruth Falzon*		1
1.	Belong and Flourish – Drop Out and Perish: The Belongingness Hypothesis *Paul Bartolo*	7
2.	Emotional Intelligence, Resilience and Wellbeing *Natalie Kenely*	21
3.	Spirituality: The Cornerstone of Wellbeing? *Claudia Psaila*	35
4.	Prosocial Behaviour and Psychological Wellbeing *Mary Anne Lauri and Sandra Scicluna Calleja*	47
5.	Family Wellbeing: A Look at Maltese Families *Clarissa Sammut Scerri, Ingrid Grech Lanfranco and Angela Abela*	65
6.	Literacy and Wellbeing *Ruth Falzon*	81
7.	Voices of the Young So-Called Vulnerable: How Well Is Their Being? *Andrew Azzopardi*	97
8.	The Conceptualisation of Leisure as an Indicator and Component of Social Wellbeing *Joanne Cassar and Marilyn Clark*	109
9.	Dis/Empowerment under Patriarchy: Intimate Partner Violence against Women *Marceline Naudi and Barbara Stelmaszek*	117
10.	Disabled People and Social Wellbeing: What's Good for Us Is Good for Everyone *Val Williams, Amy Camilleri Zahra and Vickie Gauci*	133

CONTENTS

11. Wellbeing: An Economics Perspective　　145
    Marie Briguglio

12. Wellbeing: A Welfare Perspective　　159
    Sue Vella

Index　　173

ACKNOWLEDGEMENTS

We would like to thank all our colleagues at the University of Malta who have contributed a chapter to this book. This collaborative venture among academics across the Faculty for Social Wellbeing would not have been possible without the time and expertise of each author. We extend our gratitude to the anonymous reviewers whose feedback on each chapter was most useful, and to the Faculty's Research, Publications and Scholarship Committee. Thanks are also due to Ms Lucienne Brincat and Ms Marija Grech, two of the Faculty's administrators, for their valuable assistance in checking the references. The staff at Brill Sense have been very helpful throughout the whole process and it has been a pleasure to work with them.

We are particularly grateful to Mr John Martin Borg, one of Malta's leading artists, for his generous contribution of the artwork on this book's front cover.

NOTES ON CONTRIBUTORS

Angela Abela is a Professor and founding head of the Department of Family Studies at the University of Malta. She chairs the Centre for Family Research within the President's Foundation for the Wellbeing of Society. She is first author of the Strategic Policy on Positive Parenting for Malta and currently sits on the inter-ministerial task force responsible for its implementation. Angela worked as an expert of the Council of Europe and published extensively in the area of children and families. She is an Associate Editor on *Clinical Child Psychology and Psychiatry* and an international advisory editor of *Contemporary Family Therapy*.

Andrew Azzopardi is an Associate Professor and Dean of the Faculty for Social Wellbeing and Head of the Department of Youth and Community Studies. His lecturing and research focus on inclusive education, sociology, critical pedagogy, disability politics, youth and community studies. He has contributed extensively in a number of other lauded journals, and has published various texts on disability politics, young people, and inclusive education. He is a Member of the Editorial Panel of the highly acclaimed *International Journal of Inclusive Education*, and co-editor of *Inclusive communities: A Critical Reader* (2012). Azzopardi has also edited *Youth: Responding to Lives – An International Reader* (2013).

Paul Bartolo is an Associate Professor in the Department of Psychology, Faculty for Social Wellbeing, University of Malta where he is coordinator of the MPsy training of psychologists. He was recently President of the International School Psychology Association. He has coordinated national and European groups in inclusive education and is currently advisor to the project 'The Changing Role of Specialist Provision in Supporting Inclusive Education' of the European Agency for Special Needs and Inclusive Education. He has published widely on inclusion and professional school psychology including *Inclusive Early Childhood Education: New Insights and Tools – Contributions from a European Study* (2017).

Marie Briguglio is a resident academic at the University of Malta, lecturing in the fields of Behavioural Economics, Environmental Economics, Economic Research Methods and Social Marketing. She holds a Ph.D. and M.Sc. in Economics from Stirling University and University College London respectively, and an Honours degree from the University of Malta. She is Principal Investigator on several international and national research projects, has held various senior civil service positions and was an award-winning screen-writer/broadcaster. She is highly active in outreach, including as Chairperson of the Forum for Active Community Engagement with the President's Foundation for the Wellbeing of Society.

NOTES ON CONTRIBUTORS

Amy Camilleri Zahra is an assistant lecturer in the Department of Disability Studies at the University of Malta. She is currently reading for a doctorate at the same university on 'The intersection between disability and gender: The social representations of disabled women in Malta'. Prior to joining the University of Malta, Amy worked at the National Commission Persons with Disability and was in charge of the monitoring, protection and promotion of the United Nations Convention on the Rights of Persons with Disabilities. Her current research interestes are: disability and gender, the experiences of disabled women and the implementation of the UNCRPD.

Joanne Cassar is a senior lecturer at the Department of Youth and Community Studies at the University of Malta. Her research interests revolve around youth studies; in particular gender, young people's sexualities and the construction of sexual identities. Her academic publications examine the notion of young people's sexualities as social, discursive and material constructs. She has presented papers in numerous international conferences and is also an author of children's books. Dr. Cassar has carried out various research studies about young people, on a local level as well as in collaboration with other European research partners.

Marilyn Clark is an Associate Professor at the Department of Psychology, University of Malta. She holds a Master degree in social psychology from the University of Liverpool and a PhD from the University of Sheffield. Her main research interests are addiction, criminal careers, victimisation, stigma and youth studies. She has published extensively in peer reviewed journals and in a number of academic texts. In Malta she is a member of the national Addictions Advisory Board, an assistant to the magistrate on the juvenile court and a member of the Centre for Freedom from Addictions, President's Foundation for the Wellbeing of Society.

Ruth Falzon is a lecturer within the Department of Counselling. Her areas of expertise and research interest include personal and social development and specific learning difficulties. In particular, she is interested in how emotional literacy, transversal/soft skills, performance auto/ethnography and counselling affect quality of life of persons with dyslexia in the short and long term. She is very involved in community engagement. Ruth is an elected Board Director and Treasurer of the European Dyslexia Association, an elected Executive Council member of the International Association for Counselling; and an official of the Malta Association for the Counselling Profession and the Malta Dyslexia Association.

Vickie Gauci is an Occupational Therapist by profession and has a Master's degree in neurorehabilitation from Brunel University, London. She is an assistant lecturer with the Department of Disability Studies, Faculty for Social Wellbeing, at the University of Malta. She is a disabled researcher and is recently completed her doctoral thesis with the University of Leeds, entitled 'Enabling Technology and

Employment: Exploring the Dis/ability Assemblage'. Vickie is also an occasional reviewer for the journal *Disability & Society*. Her current research interests include disability activism, assistive technology and universal design.

Natalie Kenely is Head of the Department of Social Policy and Social Work within the Faculty for Social Wellbeing. She teaches on personal and professional development, macro-practice, management and leadership. Natalie coordinates social work placements for students and supervises social workers in the field. Her research interests include management, leadership, emotional intelligence, resilience and reflective practice. Her doctoral research, Emotional Intelligence and Transformational Leadership in Social Work, explored issues of organisational climate, human resource functions and leadership in the light of their effect on relationships within a major social work agency. She has presented her research in conferences both locally and abroad.

Ingrid Grech Lanfranco is a Counselling Psychologist and Family Therapist in clinical practice. She is also an academic within the Department of Family Studies at the University of Malta, where she co-ordinates the Master in Family Therapy and Systemic Practice. She is currently reading for a PhD titled 'Early co-parenting programmes with parents of infants with a highly reactive temperament: A randomised study using 'Parents as Partners' (PasP). She co-authored the National Strategic Policy for Positive Parenting Malta 2016–2024, and is also a member of the Faculty Research Ethics Committee within the Faculty for Social Wellbeing.

Mary Anne Lauri studied Psychology at the University of Malta and at the London School of Economics. She joined the University of Malta in 1992 as a member of the Department of Psychology, and between 2006 and 2016, was appointed Pro-Rector. Professor Lauri has authored several works published in both Maltese and international journals. She won a national book prize awarded by the National Book Council (Malta) for the book *Exploring the Maltese Media Landscape* co-authored with Rev. Dr. Joe Borg. Mary Anne is actively involved in political, media and voluntary organisations.

Marceline Naudi, B.A., M.A. (Bradford), Ph.D. (Manchester), is a social worker and a Senior Lecturer within the Department of Gender Studies, at the University of Malta. She lectures and supervises student research on gender issues, violence against women and other anti-oppressive issues at all levels across various Faculties. She is active on issues of gender equality and violence against women, LGBTIQ, as well as wider human rights issues, both in Malta and in Europe. She is Regional Editor of the *Journal on Gender Based Violence*, and is the Scientific Director of the European Observatory on Femicide currently hosted by the University of Malta.

NOTES ON CONTRIBUTORS

Claudia Psaila is a Senior Lecturer in the Department of Social Policy & Social Work at the University of Malta where she lectures on undergraduate and postgraduate programmes. She also lectures on Master programmes in the Departments of Psychology and Counselling. She is a psychologist and social worker. Apart from clinical practice, she provides supervision to practitioners. She has presented and published on the subject of spirituality and practice at international conferences. She has also created and delivered training seminars on spirituality and practice to different professionals in the health, education and social wellbeing fields.

Clarissa Sammut Scerri is a lecturer and Head of the Department for Family Studies at the University of Malta. She is a warranted counselling psychologist and family therapist, and systemic supervisor. Her area of expertise includes the impact of trauma, specifically domestic violence on family members, parenting in adversity, adoption and fostering and qualitative research. She has presented her research at various local and international fora. One of her papers: 'Ethical dilemmas of a clinician/researcher interviewing women about their childhood experiences of witnessing domestic violence', has been shortlisted for the Corinna Seith Award by the WAVE Network, Women Against Violence.

Sandra Scicluna Calleja is a senior lecturer at the University of Malta and an experienced practicing counselling psychologist and supervisor. She has been active in areas of program development, professional development and training. Her areas of interest include psychoanalysis, professional ethics, professional supervision and adult development. She is a founding member of the Maltese Psychological Association and served on the first state licensing board established by the Psychologists' Bill of 2004. She has contributed significantly in other endeavours related to the development of psychology as a profession and as a discipline at the University of Malta.

Barbara Stelmaszek is a Research Officer at the European Observatory on Femicide. In addition, Barbara supports the implementation of the project titled Developing Bystander Responses to Sexual Harassment among Young People. Barbara is a student at the University of Malta working towards her PhD in the Gender Studies department at the Faculty of Social Wellbeing. Barbara's research deals with intimate partner violence, representation of women victims of violence and the violence itself, as well as prevention of lethal intimate partner violence. Previously, Barbara worked as a project coordinator at the European network Women against Violence Europe.

Sue Vella is a senior lecturer at the University of Malta, where she teaches and supervises on social policy from national and European perspectives. Sue holds a Ph.D. and M.Sc. from the University of York and LSE respectively, and undergraduate degrees from Malta. Before joining University, Sue worked in senior management positions in the public sector for almost twenty years, and served on the EU's Employment Committee for seven years. She is currently a member of the National Centre for Family Research, and her research interests include the mixed economy of care, the Europeanisation of social policy, families, migrant welfare, and governance and social cohesion.

Val Williams is a Professor of Disability Studies in Norah Fry Centre at the University of Bristol, UK. She has longstanding interests in carrying out research with disabled people, and has worked in partnership with many people with learning disabilities in inclusive research projects. Val recently led a large research programme called 'Getting Things Changed', co-produced with Disability Rights UK. The research sought to understand how disabling practices may be changed so that we can all enjoy a more inclusive society. Val is an executive editor of the journal *Disability & Society* where she has had the role of Current Issues editor.

SUE VELLA, ANDREW AZZOPARDI AND RUTH FALZON

INTRODUCTION

The study of wellbeing is certainly not new. Over two millennia ago, the Ancient Greeks were already debating different conceptions of the good life, and how it may be fostered, albeit a debate for the privileged in ancient Greek society. In his Nichomachean Ethics,[1] Aristotle speaks of three bases for happiness: sensual pleasure, honour, or true happiness, which results from a philosophical approach to life. For Aristotle, true happiness is a lifelong endeavour and not a fleeting feeling; it is the objective result of rational thought and virtuous action. His eudaimonic vision of happiness is often contrasted with a hedonistic approach, where happiness is seen to lie in the subjective pleasure of satisfying one's desires.

Over the twentieth century, interest in the subjective perspective rose steadily, driven in part by what Inglehart (1977) described as the 'the post-material orientation'. Rising prosperity after the war saw a preoccupation with economic scarcity give way to values such as personal growth, tolerance and democracy. Towards the end of the Second World War, Maslow (1943) pioneered what was to become the humanist school of psychology, which extended the understanding of human motivation beyond the physical, to include the needs to belong and to be esteemed, to actualise and to transcend oneself. The measurement of economic performance, primarily through gross domestic product (GDP), was no longer seen to be an adequate proxy for levels of wellbeing in a country. Social and economic research increasingly turned its focus to understanding the correlates of wellbeing, going beyond the traditional measures like income, wealth and employment. In this vein, prominent economists such as Layard (2011) have brought happiness economics into the mainstream. In a recent paper based on cross-cultural surveys, Clark, Flèche, Layard, Powdthavee, and Ward (2017) find that people's mental health matters more to their happiness than does their income, and that one's emotional health as a child predicts one's satisfaction in later life.

Despite this increased attention to subjective experience, there does not appear to be a conclusive and widely accepted definition of wellbeing except that it is a multidimensional notion. Cooke, Melchert, and Connor (2016) outline four broad categories of approaches to wellbeing. The first, life satisfaction and positive affect, is the modern equivalent of the hedonistic approach, while the second, developing one's potential and functioning well, is closer to the eudaimonic approach. Third, quality-of-life approaches go beyond the psychological to also incorporate the physical and social dimensions of wellbeing. The fourth, wellness, is broader still and encompasses what the authors call a 'holistic lifestyle' approach.

Given these definitional challenges, it is not surprising that the measurement of wellbeing has also generated controversy, raising important issues of validity and reliability. Validity refers to the credibility of data, particularly whether one is measuring what one is supposed to measure, and whether the results can be generalised beyond the context in which they were gathered. Reliability refers to the repeatability of findings, whether an individual would respond in similar fashion if asked the same question at a different time or indeed, whether similar results could be obtained if the study were to be repeated. In respect of validity, it is difficult to ascertain precisely which constructs actually measure wellbeing and whether these should be objective, subjective or a mix of both. Reliability is challenging too. In discussing the 'wicked problem' of wellbeing, Bache and Reardon (2016) note a number of such challenges, including individual differences in respondents' understanding of survey questions; the way in which people sometimes over-rate their wellbeing after resigning themselves to adverse circumstances; or simply, the effect of one's passing mood upon one's responses.

These challenges have not deterred policy makers, at both national and supranational levels, from trying to measure wellbeing[2] with a view to finding ways to increase it. As White (2014) points out, however, this too is a thorny problem. A narrow approach to wellbeing, taking happiness as a policy goal, has come in for particular criticism. Unlike more objective measures of need, people's set points for happiness vary widely. Even if one accepts, for argument's sake, that the state does have the remit to maximise happiness as such, important questions remain about the ways in which happiness is maximised, how it is distributed and whether or not it displaces other important policy goals. White argues that it remains important to address needs, as determined through broad consultation within a democratic process.

This reader draws its inspiration largely from the fields of positive psychology and the capabilities approach. For the first, the work of Seligman (2011) on flourishing cautions against a monist approach to wellbeing, or reducing all human motivation to one single goal such as happiness, wealth, the relief of anxiety, and so on. He views wellbeing, rather, as a construct to which several elements contribute, including the subjective experience of positive emotion and engagement, but also meaning, accomplishment and positive relationships. We share this approach, and believe it to provide a realistic and useful approach to the subject.

For the second, the works of Sen (1989, 2004) and Nussbaum (2011) on the capabilities approach have been particularly inspiring. In the capabilities approach, quality of life is assessed in terms of whether people have the capabilities they need 'to do and to be' in ways they value and freely choose. Freedom, agency and empowerment are foundational to the capabilities approach. Nussbaum defines capabilities as those "freedoms or opportunities created by a combination of personal abilities and the political, social and economic environment (p. 20); when capabilities are actively realised, they result in functioning.

Writing from the perspective of political philosophy, Nussbaum (2011) discusses how focusing upon capabilities (rather than defined functions) allows for a respect for pluralism and for self-determination. She defines ten central capabilities that a life worthy of human dignity and (at least minimal) flourishing would require, including the right to life, bodily health and integrity; being able to use the senses, imagination and thought; having emotional attachments; practical reason; affiliation; living with and relating to other species; play; and control over one's environment. For Nussbaum, social justice requires that all citizens are brought above a threshold of capability in all of these ten areas, which threshold should be specified in every country's constitutional law or principles.

On the other hand, while Sen (2004) cautions against a purely subjectivist approach to wellbeing (as this tends to disguise deprivation), he also cautions against the definition of a single list of capabilities. The capabilities on which we focus must be relevant to the task at hand, and thus, will differ across social contexts and the priorities these contexts present. Further, Sen emphasises the important contribution of public discussion and reasoning to social progress in a given context, and how a forever fixed list of capabilities might limit such debate. This vision of wellbeing, incorporating as it does both process and outcome, both agency and flourishing, provides the orientation for this book.

THE BACKGROUND TO THIS BOOK

There has been increasing interest in wellbeing, in both academic and policy circles in Malta. In 2012, the new Faculty for Social Wellbeing was set up at the University of Malta, bringing within its purview nine different departments. The vision for this Faculty is not only to strive for academic excellence but also to strengthen outreach and activism among its members – a Faculty *for*, and not simply *of*, wellbeing.

In October 2016, the Faculty for Social Wellbeing launched a new undergraduate degree – a Bachelor of Arts (Honours) in Social Wellbeing – where students can choose from a broad array of study units both within and beyond the Faculty. Students are thus able (beyond a few compulsory units) to compose their own degree, helping them to clarify their interests while laying a strong foundation for the later pursuit of postgraduate studies.

The very brief introduction to this book makes it clear that any endeavour to contribute to the enduring, complex and burgeoning literature on wellbeing must be undertaken with a good dose of humility. It is not the purpose of this text to attempt a definitive or exhaustive statement on the nature of wellbeing, nor to propose new measurement methods or to call for any coherent body of policy measures. There is a rich body of literature around these issues which we encourage students to explore. Rather, the objective at hand is to entice undergraduates to embrace and appreciate the many dimensions of wellbeing, some of which feature in this collection of essays which we offer as an undergraduate reader. Through this collaborative venture, we hope that expertise from across the Faculty's departments may serve to help students discern and pursue those dimensions of wellbeing that interest them the most.

THE STRUCTURE OF THE BOOK

The chapters in this text fall loosely into three groups. The first group of chapters addresses diverse aspects of human flourishing and how they contribute to wellbeing; the second group looks at wellbeing through an empowerment lens while the third looks at wellbeing from the perspective of economics and welfare.

Chapter 1 presents the *belongingness hypothesis,* illustrating how self-esteem, so closely linked to our subjective wellbeing, depends to a large extent upon our sense of being accepted and esteemed by others. Recent developments in social neuroscience illustrate how feeling left out actually causes the brain to register pain, and the lack of social connections affects both physical and mental health. Interpersonal skills, as well as inclusive structures and processes at every level of society, are needed to strengthen belonging.

Chapter 2 sets out the contribution of emotional intelligence (EI) to wellbeing, defining the concept of EI, tracing its history and setting out its core elements. The author illustrates how the identification and regulation of one's emotional states help people become resilient in the face of life's challenges, and how the ability to recognise and respond appropriately to emotional states in others enhances one's relationships. This resilience and relational competence are important factors of wellbeing.

Chapter 3 looks at spirituality as an awareness of the transcendent which, though not necessarily linked to religion, may be inspired by it. Spirituality enables our sense of purpose and search for meaning, shaping values and behaviour, and influencing our relationship with self and others. The author argues that adding the spiritual dimension to the biopsychosocial approach to wellbeing may deepen our understanding of wellbeing and our capacity to strengthen it.

Chapter 4 discusses prosocial behaviour, illustrating that helping behaviour which is voluntary and which expresses one's values leads to an increase in various aspects of psychological wellbeing. The chapter explores the internal factors linked to the predisposition to help, such as upbringing and personality traits, as well as external factors such as a readiness to help kin, proximity, expectations of reciprocity, or even prosocial song lyrics or videogames. The authors present the findings of a quantitative survey carried out in Malta which confirms the link between prosocial behaviour and wellbeing.

Chapter 5 looks at family wellbeing from a systemic perspective, noting how the quality of relationships within a family affects the wellbeing of its members. The importance of secure attachments for people's emotional regulation and relationship quality throughout life is underscored. Attention is also paid to ecological theory, which sheds light on how family interactions are also affected by other factors, such as the meso- and macro-systems. These perspectives inform a review of Maltese families which highlights the need for attention to be paid to income adequacy, child health and the quality of the natural environment.

The second broad group of chapters looks at wellbeing from the perspective of agency and empowerment. The first in this part, *Chapter 6*, argues for the importance of literacy to wellbeing in the 21st century knowledge economy. Literacy propels cognitive development and empowers people to access social structures and resources while illiteracy, still a major challenge in many corners of the world, is often linked to higher rates of welfare dependence, crime and poverty. The need for initial teacher training to promote early literacy success is emphasised, as is the use of technology for effective compensatory strategies.

Chapter 7 explores the wellbeing of young people, drawing upon the narratives of Maltese youth to illustrate that youth should not be seen as a homogenous group. Rather, youth is a time of change, and young people's degree of wellbeing is highly influenced by their social context. A good number feel alienated from their community and lack a sense of belonging or the certainty of parental support. Through his research, the author illustrates that vulnerability is socially constructed, and while it takes different forms, its results are broadly the same, and include loneliness, anxiety and sometimes despair. The author emphasises the need to include youth in the planning and implementation of policies that concern them.

Chapter 8 explores leisure as an important constituent of wellbeing. Engaging in leisure activities can reduce stress and enhance health, happiness and satisfaction throughout the life-course. While cultural and gender expectations shape the type of leisure – and the time available for it – in different ways for different groups, the authors also discuss the potential of leisure as a means of social support among marginalised groups resisting their subordinate status. Offering a place of encounter between different social groups, leisure can help to foster shared identities and inclusive communities.

Chapter 9 explores the notion of patriarchy and its disempowering effects upon women. In a patriarchal culture, characterised by unequal power relations between women and men, women face disadvantages in both the public and private sphere. The authors illustrate this with reference to intimate partner violence, which is enabled by patriarchy but also serves to sustain it. However, they note that many women have 'turning points', often becoming empowered through supportive relationships that help them regain their autonomy and work for a better future.

Chapter 10 takes a critical approach to social wellbeing from a disability perspective. The authors illustrate how four different models of disability have evolved over the years. The first three see the disability as arising from one's medical, social or relational realities, while the fourth opposes the 'tragic view' of disability to recognise how a positive view of one's disability can affirm a strong identity and be used for the good. The authors discuss social care discourses to illustrate the tension between protecting disabled people and supporting their autonomy, underlining the need to maximise choice and control over one's care. The vision of autonomy here, though, is not individualistic but one which recognises the relational nature of autonomy, and the importance of equal relationships and reciprocity to the experience of social wellbeing.

The last two chapters in this volume look at wellbeing from a more macro perspective. *Chapter 11* looks at wellbeing from the perspective of economics which, as the author explains, is ultimately concerned with how welfare may be maximised through the best possible allocation of scarce resources. The chapter provides an illustration and critique of different approaches to measuring wellbeing and to identifying its determinants, while cautioning about the possibility of reverse causality. Taking the case of Malta as an example, similarities are found to other countries in that health, socialisation, cultural participation, environmental quality, trust in government and religiosity are closely related to wellbeing. In concluding, the author points out that economics goes beyond the measurement of wellbeing to study what factors cause fluctuations across time and space, thus allowing for policy recommendations that are grounded in evidence.

Chapter 12 takes a welfare perspective on wellbeing, arguing for the objective dimensions not to be sidelined. The chapter illustrates how the birth and growth of the welfare state has helped raise universal living standards in ways possibly unimaginable to any but the wealthiest who lived before the Second World War. The introduction of the welfare state helped to institutionalise solidarity, as people across classes came to accept that the pooling and redistribution of resources helped insure everyone against the worst of life's arbitrary misfortunes. While the welfare state has managed, if imperfectly, to meet universal basic needs, it cannot be taken for granted. The chapter sets out various challenges facing contemporary welfare systems, and argues that clear values, political commitment and careful policy design remain as necessary as ever if the gains in living standards made after the mid-20th century are to be maintained.

NOTES

[1] Trans. Joe Sachs (2002).
[2] See for instance the World Health Organisation (http://www.who.int/healthinfo/survey/whoqol-qualityoflife/en/); the OECD (http://www.oecd.org/statistics/measuring-well-being-and-progress.htm); the United Nations (http://research.un.org/en/happiness); and the EU http://ec.europa.eu/eurostat/statistics-explained/index.php/Quality_of_life_in_Europe_-_facts_and_views_-_overall_life_satisfaction).

REFERENCES

Bache, I., & Reardon, L. (2016). *The politics and policy of wellbeing: Understanding the rise and significance of a new agenda*. Cheltenham: Edward Elgar Publishing.
Clark, A., Flèche, S., Layard, R., Powdthavee, R., & Ward, G. (2017). *The key determinants of happiness and misery* (Centre for economic performance discussion paper No. 1485). Retrieved April 10, 2018, from http://eprints.lse.ac.uk/83622/1/dp1485.pdf
Cooke, P. J., Melchert, T. P., & Connor, K. (2016). Measuring wellbeing: A review of instruments. *The Counselling Psychologist, 44*(5), 730–757.
Haybron, D. (2008). *The pursuit of unhappiness: The elusive psychology of wellbeing*. Oxford: Oxford University Press.
Layard, R. (2011). *Happiness: Lessons from a new science*. London: Penguin.
Maslow, A. (1943). A theory of human motivation. *Psychological Review, 50*, 370–396.
Nussbaum, M. C. (2011). *Creating capabilities: The human development approach*. London: Harvard University Press.
Seligman, M. (2011). *Flourish*. London: Nicholas Brealey Publishing.
Sen, A. (1989). Development as capability expansion. *Journal of Development Planning, 19*, 41–58.
Sen, A. (2004). Capabilities, lists and public reason: Continuing the conversation. *Feminist Economics, 10*(3), 77–80.
White, M. D. (2014). *The illusion of wellbeing*. Basingstoke: Palgrave Macmillan.

PAUL BARTOLO

1. BELONG AND FLOURISH – DROP OUT AND PERISH

The Belongingness Hypothesis

ABSTRACT

This chapter sets out the research evidence that highlights the social nature of human beings. It first describes psychological theory about a positive sense of self-esteem as the foundation of one's wellbeing. It then shows how one's sense self-esteem is in turn based on one's feeling of being accepted and esteemed by others. This human sensitivity to inclusion and exclusion by others is elaborated in 'the belongingness hypothesis'. An account is then given of social neuroscience experiments using fMRI showing how people are highly sensitive to being left out even in simple computer games, and how social pain is registered in the brain in a similar fashion to physical pain. Similarly, research shows how human wellbeing is enhanced while the impact of stress and illness is reduced through connections with others. In conclusion it is suggested that a community that aims to enhance the wellbeing of its members needs to promote inclusive structures and processes.

Keywords: self-esteem, belonging, social neuroscience, inclusion, wellbeing

INTRODUCTION

This chapter sets out the research evidence that highlights the social nature of human beings and that human wellbeing is enhanced through positive relations with others. It first describes how psychologists have argued that our search for wellbeing, in terms of being the best that we can be, is founded on a positive sense of self-esteem. It then shows how one's sense of self-esteem itself appears to be founded on our feeling of being accepted and esteemed by others. This need to be accepted by others has been formulated as 'the belongingness hypothesis'. This human sensitivity to inclusion and exclusion by others has been supported by social neuroscience experiments using fMRI, that show how people are extremely sensitive to being left out even in simple computer games, and how social pain is registered in the brain in a similar fashion to physical pain. This is supported by research on how human wellbeing is enhanced, and the impact of stress and illness is reduced, through connections with others. Finally, an account is given of how the sense of belonging and self-worth is also influenced by one's social identity and the way and the status of the groups with which one categorises oneself and is in turn associated with by others. In conclusion it is suggested that a community that aims to enhance the wellbeing of its members needs to promote inclusive structures and processes.

SELF-ESTEEM INFLUENCE ON WELLBEING

Recent research on wellbeing has moved from a *hedonic* to an *eudaimonic* perspective: the *hedonic* view ties well-being to a subjective condition of getting what one wants and the pleasure of such enjoyment; the *eudaimonic* approach equates well-being with living well in the sense of being the best that one can be or actualizing one's potentials (Ryff & Singer, 2008; Schueller, 2013).

The enjoyment of eudaimonic wellbeing has in turn been strongly linked to how we feel about ourselves – often termed as our level of self-esteem. A search under 'self-esteem and well-being' 'in the title' on the Web of Science core database yielded 95 articles (February 2017) published in the last seven years. At a more popular level, a search for books under 'self-esteem' on the Amazon website yielded 87,598 items. A healthy sense of self-esteem means you feel good about yourself as you are, that you are a worthy individual (Mruk, 2013). This gives one a sense of subjective wellbeing. Self-esteem is understood to affect not only one's wellbeing and life satisfaction, but also one's emotions, motivation, thinking, behaviour, social relations and achievement throughout life. Positive self-esteem has been argued to be a basic human need (Greenberg, 2008). Low self-esteem, that is seeing yourself as not acceptable to yourself and others, has been found to be related to much human misery such as higher rates of teen pregnancy, alcohol and drug abuse, violence, depression, social anxiety, and suicide (Guindon, 2010).

The concept of self-esteem was first raised by two humanistic psychologists. Alfred Adler had been among the inner circle of Freud, but he clashed with Freud's main theory that the root of human motivation was the libido or sexual drive. Adler proposed instead that each individual person's life was motivated by a struggle to overcome a "feeling of inferiority" – a fear that he or she 'may be hurt or trodden upon' (Adler, 1930, p. 10). He emphasized the uniqueness of each individual "engaged in a constant struggle to develop … with an unconsciously formed but ever present goal – a vision of greatness, perfection and superiority" (p. 5).

Self-esteem was later addressed more explicitly by Abraham Maslow (1943, 1971). Maslow too suggested that human beings were innately motivated by basic needs and drives towards personal growth. He researched mostly what he saw as the highest human need which he called 'self-actualisation', that is the human tendency to seek to actualise one's potentials, capacities and talents. However, in a hierarchical pyramidal metaphor, he suggested that this '*higher*' or '*growth*' need could only be addressed if other more *basic* needs at the bottom of the pyramid were satisfied. He listed four such needs that had to be met before one could engage in the search for self-actualisation, namely, in bottom-up order, '*physiological needs*', '*safety needs*', '*love*' or '*belongingness needs*', and '*esteem*' needs. Maslow actually distinguished two types of 'esteem needs': one is our sense of competence, self-efficacy and confidence which Maslow describes as 'self-respect' or 'self-esteem'; and the other is the recognition of our achievements by others, which Maslow calls 'self-esteem from others' (Maslow, 1943).

There are debates as to whether one can have self-esteem or self-respect without esteem from others. Adler had linked the human motivation to improve oneself as a struggle to overcome a feeling of inferiority which in Maslow's terms can be seen as the search for 'esteem from others'. Adler had linked this sense of inferiority to evolution, arguing that human beings are among the weaker animals in terms of physical strength, and each individual, during the developmental period, also carries a feeling of inferiority in his or her relations both to adults and the world at large (Adler, 1961). He also noted as further evidence of the human need to depend on others the fact that human infants required a much longer time to grow into maturity and independence than any other animal (Adler, 1964).

A similar human need to be esteemed by others has also been proposed by sociologists through 'Social Comparison Theory'. Its originator was the sociologist Leon Festinger (1954) who saw human motivation and behaviour as determined by social pressures. He made no reference at all to Adler. However, the two theories do overlap as Festinger had suggested that social comparison serves the two related human motivations of self-evaluation and the search for self-improvement. Social comparison theory later added a third motive, namely self-enhancement. This refers to using or avoiding comparisons in order to enhance one's self concept or self-esteem (Gibbons & Buunks, 1999). Thus, both Adlerian and Social Comparison theories underlined first of all that human motivation is primarily social (Buunk & Nauta, 2000). Both also imply that a person's wellbeing is negatively affected if one feels inferior to others. And both imply that this leads to a striving for superiority (Adler) or search for status and prestige (Buunk et al., 1999). Both make a link to Darwin's theory on the evolutionary competition for survival of the fittest, as stated above and is evident in the following statement of social comparison theorists:

> Engaging in social comparisons is ... a very fundamental aspect of human nature, and an important determinant of wellbeing. ... As many other social animals, humans compete with each other for status and prestige in groups, and social comparison assists individuals in determining their rank in the group, in assessing what others find attractive in them, and, importantly, in providing information on how one should change one's behaviour to obtain favourable outcomes. (Buunk & Nauta, 2000, p. 281)

SELF-ESTEEM AS A SOCIOMETER – MONITORING OUR LEVELS OF ACCEPTANCE

More recently, an attempt has been made to link the above needs of love or belongingness and self-respect and esteem by others to one more fundamental human need: the need to belong. Leary (2003), who himself had initially started studying self-esteem, came to the conclusion that one's feelings of self-esteem were not only associated with the need to belong, but rather that feelings of self-esteem were actually a gauge of one's satisfaction of their need to belong. He suggested that self-esteem might be an internal, subjective 'marker or monitor of the individual's 'inclusionary status. He therefore named it a 'sociometer'. Such a sociometer would raise one's feeling of self-esteem in response to situations that confirm one's acceptance, while any indication of being ignored or rejected will be felt as a lowering of the feeling of self-esteem.

There is an assumption that the sociometer has a neurological basis in the brain but is experienced as a psychological phenomenon. Such an explanation is within the current understandings of cognitive psychology. For instance, when evaluating the correctness of a concept, one experiences a level of psychological confidence based on the balance of physiological positive, confirmatory neurological links in the brain to the features of that concept vis-à-vis links that contradict it. Similarly, while experienced as an internal private sense of self-worth, the sociometer proposal suggests that the feeling of self-esteem is actually a reflection of the neurological registration of perceived feedback from others of the level of acceptance or rejection. The registration of the balance of positive and negative signals of acceptance and rejection is psychologically felt as one's level of self-worth.

The sociometer is also seen to operate in one's overall sense of self-worth. The ongoing registration of one's level of acceptance in any situation is termed 'state' self-esteem helping one to regulate the current situation. We also talk, however, of self-esteem as a characteristic of persons – as a person of high or low self-esteem. This has been termed 'trait' self-esteem. It has been suggested that the self-esteempeople experience as a general trait of their personality is also regulated by the sociometer, consisting of the mind's "compilation of the individual's history of experienced inclusion and exclusion" (Leary, 1990, p. 227; Eisenberger et al., 2011).

It may seem inappropriate to describe self-esteem, usually a positive characteristic, in this way. Seen in this way, it suggests too great a dependence of one's self-esteem on what other people think, which is generally regarded as unhealthy. Indeed, Social Anxiety Disorder is the result of oversensitivity to others' opinions of oneself, with a constant fear that one will not be up to the expectations of others. Such oversensitivity to others' judgement may be severely dysfunctional: "The person, for example, may be so uncomfortable carrying on a conversation that he is unable to talk to others, particularly someone he doesn't know. A person who is anxious over being observed may be unable to go out to dinner because she fears being watched while she is eating and drinking" (APA, 2013, p. 202). It has also been found that those people who tend to engage more in comparisons of themselves with others also score higher on neuroticism, and that social comparisons tend to be made more often when people are in a state of uncertainty or anxiety (Gibbons & Buunks, 1999).

However, the possible misuse of the sociometer mechanism does not make it an unhealthy instrument. Being concerned with what others think about you is usually a way of ensuring appropriate behaviour and collaboration (Leary, 2003). Indeed, friendly cooperative relationships would not be possible unless people take note of how others perceive them and evaluate them. One should not look at such sensitivity as a sign of insecurity, manipulation, or vanity, but rather expect well-functioning individuals to be on the lookout for how other people react to them most of the time, particularly to the degree to which they are accepting and rejecting. Leary suggests that such monitoring by one's sociometer is essential for one's development of appropriate behaviour and personal and social wellbeing. In order to meet one's basic need to belong it is important that one responds accordingly to the implicit and explicit feedback given by others about the acceptability or otherwise of one's thinking and behaviour.

In this sense healthy individuals can regard even the negative reactions of others to them as very useful feedback. For instance, if you have been talking a lot in a small group and see signs of disinterest – less eye contact, people turning to talk to their neighbour – it could make you aware that you are taking too much of the group's time, and so you can repair the situation immediately by starting to listen more, regaining group acceptance in the process. If you think that what you are doing is part of your style of working or being – such as liking to go for country walks but the group you are with always puts down similar suggestions – you might decide to look for opportunities to join other groups that are more accepting of your leisure style. Taking all negative reactions as feedback can thus enhance your group skills as well as enable you to seek those social environments that most promote your wellbeing.

THE BELONGINGNESS HYPOTHESIS

The sociometer theory was developed by Leary at the same time as he was working with his colleague on 'the belongingness hypothesis' (Baumeister & Leary, 1995). This hypothesis states that our desire to belong, to be accepted and recognised by others, is a basic human need that is wired into our being, as is also evidenced in the brain activation during rejection experiments (Gere & MacDonald, 2010).

Baumeister and Leary's (1995) seminal paper has spawned research in this area (see e.g. Gere & MacDonald, 2010), with a staggering 4437 citations in the WEB of Science core collection, and over 12,000, on Google Scholar, and 120,029 citations of all types, of which 14,000 in just 2016. The original hypothesis, backed by a rigorous review of relevant empirical research, was that "human beings have a pervasive drive to form and maintain at least a minimum quantity of lasting, positive, and significant interpersonal relationships. ... Lack of attachments is linked to a variety of ill effects on health, adjustment, and well-being" (p. 497).

It is important to note that the novelty of this hypothesis was the emphasis on 'belonging', or the "fundamental need to be accepted by, valued by other people and to belong to social groups" (Leary, 2013). Baumeister and Leary suggested that belongingness was an innate need that 'presumably has an evolutionary basis. The desire to form and maintain social bonds can be seen as having both survival and reproductive benefits. Group cooperation can better ensure a supply of food, success in hunting larger animals or in protection from predators. It is also easier to find mates in groups, and to protect and care for the young, including orphans. If this holds, then it would be likely that evolutionary selection would strengthen mental systems in human beings that tend to register affective distress when deprived of social contact or relationships, and pleasure or positive affect from social contact and relatedness: "These affective mechanisms would stimulate learning by making positive social contact reinforcing and social deprivation punishing" (Baumeister & Leary, 1995, p. 499). The review of relevant empirical studies was presented in the form of nine predictions about belongingness.

Baumeister and Leary noted firstly how people in all cultures had a spontaneous inclination to form social relationships. Since that paper was written, we have seen the phenomenal uptake of social media like Facebook. It has created another avenue for people's yearning for social connectivity, while it has not reduced our continuing search for personal face-to-face relationships.

People also work hard to maintain their relationships. They resist breaking social bonds even when there are difficulties. The loss of a partner, friend or relation for whatever reason causes great grief to the survivor. Indeed, our thinking and emotions are closely tied to relations with others. We process our experiences and learning within the context of our relationships. One of my students who studied why some children were very much into reading while others saw it as compulsory drudgery was surprised to find that the avid readers in fact were motivated to read books because they talked about them among themselves, had common favourite authors and stories, and indeed were exchanging books much as they share music and games.

Our strongest emotions of happiness and hurt are caused by relationship events. Being welcomed, accepted, and included leads to a variety of positive emotions (e.g., happiness, contentment, and serenity), whereas being ignored, rejected, or excluded generally leads to negative feelings (e.g., grief, anxiety, depression, meaninglessness, jealousy, and loneliness). The distress of divorce is most striking.

Being deprived of stable social connections can indeed be detrimental to physical and mental health. This can also happen if the connectivity does not include positive affective interactions or if it consists of conflictual interactions. Isolation can lead to both depression and self-harm including suicide as well as to criminality. It has been noted that the perpetrators of gun shooting at schools in the US were mostly young people who had felt ostracised.

While Baumeister and Leary cited evidence for the above predictions, there has been increasing research since then on both the consequences of exclusion in social interaction as well as of breakages in couple and child-carer bonds. The most striking remains the social neuroscience research showing that the social pain of exclusion, is similarly registered in our brains as physical pain (Lieberman, 2013).

EXPERIMENTS REVEAL THE PAIN OF EXCLUSION

As already noted, exclusion has been researched in different ways (Williams & Nida, 2011; Richman & Leary, 2009). These range from face-to-face conversations to mobile text messaging, and laboratory situations where participants are led to think that another research participant (actually the experimenter's collaborator) does not wish to work with them, or that another person preferred interacting with another participant rather than with them, or that everyone in a get-acquainted task chose not to work with them, or that another participant was not interested in what they had to say, or providing bogus feedback that the participants were selected last for a team. Other forms of research included giving participants a prognosis, based on invented answers to a questionnaire, that they will lead a 'life alone'; asking participants to write about a rejection/exclusion experience; or providing participants with an experience of exclusion in a ball-tossing game.

The ball-tossing game involving three players has been the most widely used laboratory situation. Initially it was made up of three real people sitting in a room waiting for an experiment to start, only one of whom was an actual participant. While waiting, one of the experimenter's collaborators picks up a ball from a shelf and starts tossing it to the others. Eventually the tossing either includes, or excludes, the participant. This game was developed into a computerised version known as *Cyberball*, which is now available for use as open source software on https://cyberball.wikispaces.com/.

Consider the following earlier experiment about adults' reactions to being ignored in the Cyberball game (Eisenberger, Lieberman, & Williams, 2003). Participants first watched and then played the computer ball-tossing game by managing a character on the screen. There were two other players that they believed were controlling the two other characters on screen. Each participant went through three activities: (1) They were first told that, due to technical difficulties, they could only just watch the other two "players" play CyberBall while their character just watched the others; (2) In a second activity (Inclusion), participants played CyberBall with the other two players; (3) In a final game (Exclusion), the participant received seven throws and then received no more balls as the other two players continued tossing the ball to each other for the remainder of the game (45 throws).

Participants' brain activation during the experiment was recorded through an fMRI scan. Afterwards, participants filled out questionnaires asking them how excluded they felt and about their level of social distress during the final Exclusion activity. As expected, questionnaire responses showed that participants felt ignored and excluded during the final activity. The fMRI data indicated that during the Exclusion game there was higher activation of that part of the brain which usually registers physical pain – in the dorsal anterior cingulate cortex (dACC) – than during the Inclusion game. The level of activation of the dACC was moreover found to be higher when a higher level of distress was reported by the participant (Eisenberger et al., 2003).

The results of experiments like the above have been seen first of all as clear evidence of the wiring of our brain for recognising signs of threats to one's possible exclusion, even when very brief, and virtual, and from strangers. Secondly, they have provided evidence that the social pain experienced when we are rejected is registered in our brains in the same way as physical pain.

In fact, in normal parlance we often use physical pain terms to describe the hurt of being rejected; for instance: 'My heart was bleeding at every word he said'. 'It was painful to let him go'. 'I could feel being stabbed in the back'. 'I could not overcome the pain of being put down by someone I loved'. 'Her insults opened a wound that cannot heal'. The use of such language is found among all people and languages. What is new is the finding that rejection and loss actually do activate the same areas in our brain that are activated when we hurt physically. This challenges the saying that, 'Sticks and stones can hurt my bones, but words can never hurt me' Words of rejection can indeed activate our brain pain centres as much as a beating with a stick.

These findings have confirmed earlier suggestions of similarities between brain processes for physical and social pain in that drugs that reduced physical pain also reduced social pain. Morphine or codeine are best known for their pain-relieving effects and are commonly prescribed for pain management. It was found that in the case of several other mammalian species, morphine, which increases mu-opioid-related activity, reduces separation-distress vocalizations made by infants when separated from their mothers, whereas naloxone, which inhibits mu-opioid-related activity, increases distress vocalizations (reviewed in Nelson & Panksepp, 1998; Eisenberger, 2012).

This was confirmed on human participants by DeWall et al. (2010) who tested whether Tylenol (generic name: acetaminophen), a medication typically thought to reduce physical pain, could also reduce social pain. Participants were randomly assigned to take either a daily dose of Tylenol or a placebo over a period of 3 weeks. Meanwhile they were asked to fill out the Hurt Feelings Scale each evening where they had to report on how much social pain they experienced that day: they had to respond to items such as 'Today, being teased hurt my feelings' on a scale ranging from 'not at all' to 'a lot'. It was found that initially all reported the same level of hurt feelings. However, over the 3-week period, those who took the placebo continued to report the same level of hurt feelings, while those who took Tylenol showed a significant reduction in hurt feelings.

SOCIAL CONNECTIVITY INFLUENCES OUR MENTAL HEALTH AND WELLBEING

Indeed, there is wide evidence that lack of social support, isolation and conflictual interactions can have detrimental effects on people's physical as well as mental health (DeWall, 2009). Cohen (2004) distinguished between three different types of social connections that can have an influence on one's health, namely *social support*, that is a social network's provision of psychological and material resources intended to benefit an individual's ability to cope with stress; *social integration*, that is participation in a broad range of social relationships; and *negative interactions*, that is conflictual relationships. He reported findings for each of these connections.

Social support buffers one against stress, eliminating or reducing the effects of stressful experiences by promoting less threatening interpretations of adverse events and enabling effective coping strategies. In one of his studies he had found that "both student and adult samples reported more symptoms of depression and of physical ailments under stress but that these associations were attenuated among those who perceived that support was available from their social networks" (Cohen, 2004, p. 677).

He further found that "emotional support worked in the face of a variety of types of stressful events, whereas other types of support (e.g., instrumental, informational) responded to specific needs elicited by an event" (Cohen, 2004, p. 678). A prospective study of healthy Swedish men aged 50 years and over (Rosengren, Orth-Gomer, Wedel, & Wilhelmsen, 1993) found that those with high numbers of stressful life events in the year before the baseline exam were at substantially greater risk for mortality over a seven-year follow-up period. However, this effect was ameliorated among those who perceived that high levels of emotional support were available to them. This effect was not found for those with few stressful events.

Social integration promotes positive psychological states (e.g., identity, purpose, self-worth, and positive affect) that induce health-promoting physiological responses, provides access to information and is a source of motivation and social pressure to care for oneself. This is usually contrasted with isolation and linked to length of life. The first prospective study that found a link between social integration and longer living was carried out in California by Berkman and Syme (1979). They found that healthy adults who were married, had close family and friends, or belonged to social and religious groups at study onset were more likely to still be living at the nine-year follow-up than their more isolated counterparts. The association between social integration and mortality has since been replicated in many prospective community-based studies (reviewed by Berkman & Glass, 2000). Other studies have found that greater integration predicts survival from heart attacks, less risk for cancer recurrence, less depression and anxiety, and less severe cognitive decline with aging (see Cohen et al., 2000). Although both men and women seem to benefit from social integration, there is evidence that men benefit more than women (House, Landis, & Umberson, 1988).

Negative interactions, on the other hand, are themselves a source of stress and in turn lead to behaviours and physiological concomitants that increase risk for disease. For instance, Cohen and his colleagues (1997) had first assessed whether participants were involved in serious, enduring (one month or longer) social conflicts and then exposed each one to a virus that causes the common cold. They found that those with enduring conflicts with spouses, close family members, and friends were more than twice as likely to develop a cold as persons without any chronic stressors in their lives.

As far back as 1897, Durkheim had suggested that a stable social structure was protective against suicide. Several later studies reported other benefits to health for those that were socially connected (DeWall, 2009). When compared to those who have a strong sense of connectedness, people who are chronically excluded have lower-quality sleep (Caccioppo, Hawkley, & Berntson, 2003), poorer immune system functioning (Kiecolt-Glazer et al., 1994), and a higher likelihood of death following myocardial infarct (Berkman, Leo-Summers, & Horrowitz, 1992).

On the other hand, a lack of social connectedness relates to poorer daily health. Lonely people experience higher daily peripheral resistance (TPR) and lower cardiac output (CO) than do non-lonely people (Hawkley, Burleson, Berntson, & Caccioppo, 2003). Simply living alone (as opposed to living with others) is a potent risk factor for mortality and morbidity (House, Landis, & Umberson, 1988).

In a major meta-analytic study reviewing 148 studies (308,849 participants), it was found that people with stronger social relationships had a 50% increased likelihood of survival than those with weaker social relationships. This finding remained consistent across age, sex, initial health status, cause of death, and follow-up period (Holt-Lunstad, Smith, & Layton, 2010). The researchers concluded that the influence of social relationships on the risk of death are comparable with well-established risk factors for mortality such as smoking and alcohol consumption and exceed the influence of other risk factors such as physical inactivity and obesity. They urge health professionals and educators to take social relationships as seriously as the other risk factors that have been found to affect mortality.

BELONGINGNESS THROUGH GROUP MEMBERSHIP – SOCIAL IDENTITY

So far we have looked at belongingness from the point of view of a person's relationships to other individuals. However, it has been found that people's experience of social inclusion and exclusion, and even their sense of self-worth, are significantly influenced also by their social identity, that is how they associate themselves with different social groups (Tajfel, 1981). For instance, one may categorise oneself as a student, a female, a mother, an animal lover, a vegetarian, a middle class person, a supporter of a particular political party etc. If you see yourself as having those social identities, then you will esteem yourself, and be motivated and behave according to how you think members of those groups are regarded in society and how they are expected to behave; the 'I' becomes 'we', and emotions are experienced and perceived from the point of view of 'us' and 'them'. Depending on how much belongingness to a particular group is important to a person, how high or low the group is regarded by society, and how much differences between groups are highlighted, social identity can have a great impact on one's sense of well-being and behaviour (Verkuyten, 2014).

To consider how one's social identity is tied to social wellbeing, it is useful to introduce another term that has often been associated with self-worth, self-esteem and esteem by others, namely human dignity. The concept of human dignity captures both one's subjective feeling of self-esteem as well as society's recognition, inclusion, valuing and respect for one as an individual and member of social groups. These two meanings of dignity are clearly distinguished by Nayef Al-Rodhan, Head of the Geopolitics and Global Futures Programme in Geneva:

> Dignity has at least two meanings. First, it can be understood as a sense of self-worth. To have a sense of dignity implies that one is able to appreciate

oneself to a sufficient extent to withstand pressures or attacks on one's self-esteem. Second, it may also be understood at the community level, in which case inclusion may be seen as endowing people with a sense of dignity. Inclusion may be considered the essence of dignity, because to be included by others implies that one is valued by others and, therefore, considered worthy of integration into a community. ... dignity shall be considered as respect for one's social value, demonstrated through an acknowledgement by others as an equal within a community. (Al-Rodhan & Watanabe, 2007, p. 59)

In the latter sense, one's dignity and well-being are distorted when one is not recognised as an equal member of society and is treated as a less deserving individual or is humiliated. Such misrecognition or humiliation may also be suffered by one both directly as an individual, or indirectly through one's social identity. The latter happens when society stigmatises and discriminates against the group with which one categorises oneself:

The thesis is that our identity is partly shaped by recognition or its absence, often by the misrecognition of others, and so a person or group of people can suffer real damage, real distortion, if the people or society around them mirror back to them a confining or demeaning or contemptible picture of themselves. Non-recognition or misrecognition can inflict harm, can be a form of oppression, imprisoning someone in a false, distorted, and reduced mode of being. (Taylor, 1994, p. 25)

For instance, one marginalised group in many societies is that of people in poverty. It is widely understood that the suffering of such people is ultimately rooted in economic incqualily and that they can best be enabled to afford a decent living through a redistribution of wealth and income and state benefits. However, it has been argued that the challenge faced by the poor goes beyond the lack of resources (Morrison, 2010, p. 6). Another important disadvantage suffered by the poor is the misrecognition, stigma and social exclusion by society leading to 'the inability to participate in the normal relationships and activities available to the majority of people in society, whether in economic, social, cultural or political arenas' (Levitas et al., 2007, p. 9).

From a societal perspective, the misrecognition and social exclusion experienced by disadvantaged groups are described as a loss of an individual's dignity, of being treated as a second class citizen. Such lowering of one's dignity was clearly expressed by one woman's protest in a study on disadvantaged groups in a deprived area of Rio de Janeiro: "Dignity is everything for a citizen – and we have no dignity. We are treated like cattle in the clinics, on the buses and in the shops. Only in rich neighbourhoods are people treated with dignity" (Wheeler, 2004, p. 41). Taking this approach to poverty in a Maltese study, Cardona (2010) focused on the need to raise the voice of the poor by publishing what they actually said in their interviews instead of writing about them:

Unless and until this phenomenon of poverty is seen as a direct violation of the dignity of the person, this reality will worsen, as we see it doing all around us .... In order to be able to do this, we all need to learn to listen to the voice of the poor and to understand the reality that pushed them into poverty. In doing so together, we might identify new ways of assisting poor families to determine their goals and to move towards achieving them. (Brincat, 2011)

This need for social inclusion in the wider sense applies to the members of other disadvantaged groups in society. Social movements such as those for disability rights, feminism, and multiculturalism, have highlighted that the unjust distribution of material resources is intertwined with the social exclusion and unjust social and cultural processes suffered by these groups. Thus, human rights conventions, such as the UN Convention on the Rights of Persons with Disabilities (2006), highlight as one of their general principles, the right to 'Full and effective participation and inclusion in society' (Art. 3c). In this sense, human wellbeing can be enhanced if society is truly inclusive, that if all individuals and groups are equally valued and respected and provided with equal opportunities to participate with dignity within the common activities of the society.

This consideration of the impact of the social environment on one's dignity, one's sense of self-esteem and sense of belongingness shows the complexity of the phenomenon highlighted in the belongingness hypothesis. The satisfaction of the need to belong is a complex phenomenon that is not only influenced by the availability or lack of one's personal relations to others, but also by how one is accepted or rejected as part of the groups one associates oneself with and is associated with by others, as well as the status of acceptance or rejection of the groups themselves within society.

CONCLUSION

It has been argued that the newborn brain is wired in the first place to maintain connections with others as the most important need for survival, being also the main assurance of the baby's access to food and safety (Lieberman, 2013). It seems that the satisfaction of this need to be connected, to belong, remains profoundly bound to our wellbeing throughout life. As has been argued in this chapter, our sense of self-esteem, of wellbeing, appears to be closely linked to how we are accepted or rejected by others.

This clearer understanding of the human development need for belongingness has important implications for both the individual and society. From an individual perspective, the development of interpersonal skills that enhance one's ability to engage in positive social interaction is an essential developmental task. The development of a person's social intelligence, such as communication, empathy, friendship and teamwork skills is an essential challenge for individuals (Goleman, 2016), and should also be a main concern of families and education (Cefai, Bartolo, Cavioni, & Downs, 2018).

At the same time, the emphasis on the need for one to be accepted by others raises a challenge from the societal perspective. Societies aiming to promote people's wellbeing need to work towards the reduction of exclusive systems and the development of inclusive structures and processes that enable all people and groups to participate, be accepted and belong. Inclusion has to be promoted at the political level (e.g. Bartolo, 2015) as well as in families (e.g. Satir, 1988), educational settings (e.g. Bartolo et al., 2002; Flecha, 2015; European Agency for Special Needs and Inclusive Education, 2017), work settings (e.g. Carberry & Meyers, 2017), leisure (Dashper & Fletcher, 2013), and neighbourhood settings (e.g. Mackay, 2014).

REFERENCES

Adler, A. (1930). *The education of children.* New York, NY: Greenberg.
Adler, A. (1961). The practice and theory of individual psychology. In T. Shipley (Ed.), *Classics in psychology* (pp. 687–714). New York, NY: Philosophical Library.
Adler, A. (1964). *Problems of neurosis.* New York, NY: Harper & Row.
Al-Rodhan, N. R. F., & Wartanabe, L. (2007). *A proposal for inclusive peace and security.* Geneva: Slatkine.
American Psychiatric Association. (2013). *Diagnostic and statistical manual for mental disorders* (5th ed.). Arlington, VA: American Psychiatric Publishing.
Bartolo, P. A. (2015). *Winning people's hearts: How inclusion and exclusion informed the Malta general election campaign of 2013* (Education Research Monograph Series, Vol. 1). Malta: Malta University Press.
Bartolo, P. A., Agius Ferrante, C., Azzopardi, A., Bason, L., Grech, L., & King, M. (2002). *Creating inclusive schools: Guidelines for the implementation of the national curriculum policy on inclusive education.* Malta: Ministry of Education and Employment.
Baumeister, R. F., & Leary, M. R. (1995). The need to belong: Desire for interpersonal attachments as a fundamental human motivation. *Psychological Bulletin, 117*(3), 497–529.
Brincat, R. (2011, October 17). Maltese living in poverty. *Times of Malta.* Retrieved August 20, 2017, from http://www.timesofmalta.com/articles/view/20111017/opinion/Maltese-living-in-poverty.389492
Buunk, B. P., & Nauta, A. (2000). Why individual needs are not enough. *Psychological Enquiry, 11*(4), 279–283.
Carberry, E. J., & Meyers, J. S. M. (2017). Are the 'best' better for everyone? Demographic variation in employee perceptions of fortune's 'best companies to work for'. *Equality, Diversity and Inclusion: An International Journal, 36*(7), 647–669.
Cardona, M. (2010). *You will always have the poor among you, John 12 v 8: A report about poverty in Malta.* Malta: Jesuit Centre for Faith and Justice.
Cohen, S. (2004, November). Social relationships and health. *American Psychologist, 59*(8), 676–684.
Cohen, S., Doyle, W. J., Skoner, D. P., Rabin, B. S., & Gwaltney Jr, J. M. (1997). Social ties and susceptibility to the common cold. *Journal of the American Medical Association, 277*(24), 1940–1944.
Dashper, K., & Fletcher, T. (2013). Introduction: Diversity, equity and inclusion in sport and leisure. *Sport in Society, 16*(10), 1227–1232.
DeWall, C. N. (2009). The pain of exclusion. Using insights from neuroscience to understand emotional and behavioural responses to ostracism. In M. J. Harris (Ed.), *Bullying, rejection, & peer victimization: A social cognitive neuroscience perspective* (pp. 201–224). New York, NY: Springer.
DeWall, C. N., MacDonald, G., Webster, G. D., Masten, C. L., Baumeister, R. F., Powell, C., … Eisenberger, N. I. (2010). Tylenol reduces social pain: Behavioral and neural evidence. *Psychological Science, 21*, 931–937.
Eisenberger, N. I. (2012). Broken hearts and broken bones: A neural perspective on the similarities between social and physical pain. *Current Directions in Psychological Science, 21*(1), 42–47.
Eisenberger, N. I., Inagaki, T. K., Muscatell, K. A., Byrne Haltom, K. E., & Leary, M. R. (2011). The neural sociometer: Brain mechanisms underlying state self-esteem. *Journal of Cognitive Neuroscience, 23*(11), 3448–3455.

Eisenberger, N. I., Lieberman, M. D., & Williams, K. D. (2003). Does rejection hurt? An fMRI study of social exclusion. *Science, 302*, 290–292. Retrieved from http://www.sciencemag.org

European Agency for Special Needs and Inclusive Education. (2017). *Inclusive early childhood education: New insights and tools – Contributions from a European study* (M. Kyriazopoulou, P. Bartolo, E. Björck-Åkesson, C. Giné, & F. Bellour, Eds.). Odense, Denmark.

Festinger, L. (1954). A theory of social comparison processes. *Human Relations, 7*, 117–139.

Flecha, R. (Ed.). (2015). *Successful educational actions for inclusion and social cohesion in Europe.* London: Springer.

Gere, J., & MacDonald, G. (2010). An update of the empirical case for the need to belong. *The Journal of Individual Psychology, 66*(1), 93–115.

Gibbons, F. X., & Buunks, B. P. (1999). Individual differences in social comparison: Development of a scale of social comparison orientation. *Journal of Personality and Social Psychology, 76*(1), 126–142.

Greenberg, J. (2008). Understanding the vital human quest for self-esteem. *Perspectives on Psychological Science, 3*(1), 48–55.

Guindon, M. H. (2010). What is self esteem? In M. H. Guindon (Ed.), *Self-esteem across the lifespan: Issues and interventions* (pp. 3–24). New York, NY: Routledge.

Leary, M. (2013). *Mark Leary on the need to belong.* Retrieved October 16, 2013, from http://vimeo.com/34785200

Leary, M. R. (1990). Responses to social exclusion: Social anxiety, jealousy, loneliness, depression, and low self-esteem. *Journal of Social and Clinical Psychology, 9*, 221–229. Retrieved from http://www.dsm5.org/Documents/Social%20Anxiety%20Disorder%20Fact%20Sheet.pdf

Leary, M. R. (2003). Commentary on self-esteem as an interpersonal monitor: The sociometer hypothesis (1995). *Psychological Inquiry, 14*(3–4), 270–274.

Levitas, R., Pantazis, C., Fahmy, E., Gordon, D., Lloyd, E., & Patsios, D. (2007). *The multi-dimensional analysis of social exclusion.* Bristol: Department of Sociology and School for Social Policy, University of Bristol

Lieberman, M. D. (2013). *Social: Why our brains are wired to connect.* New York, NY: Crown Publishers.

Maslow, A. (1943). A theory of human motivation. *Psychological Review, 50*, 370–396.

Maslow, A. (1971). *The further reaches of human nature.* New York, NY: Viking.

Morrison, Z. (2010). *On dignity: Social inclusion and the politics of recognition.* Melbourne: The Centre for Public Policy.

Mruk, C. J. (2013). *Self-esteem and positive psychology: Research, theory, and practice* (4th ed.). New York, NY: Springer.

Nelson, E. E., & Panksepp, J. (1998). Brain substrates of infant–mother attachment: Contributions of opioids, oxytocin, and norepinephrine. *Neuroscience and Biobehavioral Reviews, 22*(3), 437–452.

Richman, L. S., & Leary, M. R. (2009). Reactions to discrimination, stigmatization, ostracism, and other forms of interpersonal rejection: A multimotive model. *Psychological Review, 116*(2), 365–383.

Ryff, C. D., & Singer, B. H. (2008). Know thyself and become what you are: A eudaimonic approach to psychological wellbeing. *Journal of Happiness Studies, 9*, 13–39.

Satir, V. (1988). *The new people making.* Palo Alto, CA: Science and Behavior Books.

Schueller, S. M. (2013). Review: Understanding our best: Eudaimonia's growing influence in psychology. *Quality of Life Research, 22*, 2661–2662.

Tajfel, H. (1981). *Human groups and social categories: Studies in social psychology.* Cambridge: Cambridge University Press

Taylor, C. (1994). The politics of recognition. In A. Gutmann (Ed.), *Multiculturalism: Examining the politics of recognition* (pp. 25–73). Princeton, NJ: Princeton University Press.

UN Convention on the Rights of Persons with Disabilities. (2006).

Verkuyten, M. (2014). *Identity and cultural diversity.* London: Routledge.

Wheeler, J. S. (2004). New forms of citizenship: Democracy, family and community in Rio de Janeiro, Brazil. In C. Sweetman (Ed.), *Gender, development and citizenship.* Oxford: Oxfam.

Williams, K. D., & Nida, S. A. (2011). Ostracism: Consequences and coping. *Current Directions in Psychological Science, 20*(2), 71–75.

NATALIE KENELY

2. EMOTIONAL INTELLIGENCE, RESILIENCE AND WELLBEING

ABSTRACT

Emotion is a key part of what makes us human. We are indeed "creatures saturated by feelings" (Howe, 2008, p. 1). This chapter explores the relationship between 'emotional intelligence', 'resilience' and 'wellbeing' – three concepts that are closely intertwined. This chapter describes the three concepts individually and then looks at the link that exists between them. The literature provides ample evidence that emotional intelligence is conducive to wellbeing (Bezzina, Falzon, & Muscat, 2015, p. 153). This chapter shows how emotional intelligence, most particularly the abilities to recognize emotions and to regulate them in self and others, contributes to resilience and provides the necessary tools that allow us to face adversity confidently and with courage. Emotional intelligence contributes to our ability to appraise situations in a constructive way, resulting in better outcomes and heightened wellbeing.

Keywords: emotional intelligence, resilience, emotional regulation, coping, wellbeing

INTRODUCTION

The reason we weren't executed was because I changed the way he felt about us.

These are the words of Chris Moon. Moon is a former British Army Officer and is one of the few Westerners to have survived being taken prisoner in the 1980s by Khmer Rouge guerrillas, one of the most brutal terror groups in history, in Cambodia. He negotiated his release and that of his colleagues, thus escaping the threat of execution. On his return to Cambodia some years later to film a documentary on the Khmer Rouge, he met the Commander who had decided not to execute the prisoners. The Commander confirmed that he had taken this decision because Moon had in fact managed to change his feelings towards the prisoners.

Moon had in some way managed to regulate the immense fear he himself admits to having felt in the circumstance, keeping himself calm in the face of severe adversity. When asked by a journalist how he survived that time, he said, "I controlled how I was thinking and how I behaved. It's easy to start thinking there's no hope. You must focus and don't give up. As we were held for longer I knew it was less likely we were going to get out, but you have to keep your head in the right place". In Moon's testimony, I can see a distinctive illustration of an emotionally intelligent person. Moon must have accurately read the emotional reactions of his captors – their frenzy, excitement, and nervousness – and understood the danger that those agitated reactions could pose for him. Being able to regulate his own emotions created by this frightful situation he could calm himself down and express that calmness in his behaviour. The power of emotional contagion probably resulted in his captors calming down, becoming more reasonable and less frantic. His emotion-regulation competence and clarity of thought that this brought with it probably saved his life.

We may not find ourselves in life-threatening situations like Moon, yet we have all found ourselves in situations that presented a threat to us – a threat to our safety, our wellbeing, our relationships, our jobs – situations in which emotions ran high. We may also look back on life experiences and realize that we have become more resilient, stronger and more able to face what life brings with it because of the way we coped with those particular experiences.

I consider the concepts that I have introduced through this story – 'emotion', 'emotional intelligence', 'resilience' and 'wellbeing' – as being intertwined. In this chapter I will explore the relationship between them. I begin by exploring these concepts separately.

A SHORT WORD ON THE NEUROSCIENCE OF EMOTION

According to Salzman and Fusi (2010), neuroscientists have until now "described cognition and emotion as separable processes" (p. 173) – the brain's amygdala controlling emotion and the prefrontal cortex controlling cognition. However, they propose that "these mental state parameters are inextricably linked and represented in dynamic neural networks composed of interconnected prefrontal and limbic brain structures" (Salzman & Fusi, 2010, p. 173).

In other words, emotion is inseparably intertwined with cognition. It has the capacity to precede and cause particular lines of thought (Franks, 2006, p. 39). It has also become central in brain studies. At the same time, thought processes and cognition are capable of evoking and creating emotional states in return. While this is not a subject that can be developed fully here, it is worth noting that neuroscience frameworks have challenged traditional psychological views on the very nature of emotion, as well as the sociological tradition that emotional brain processes are much more typically unconscious than conscious (Franks, p. 38). As I will explain further on, evidence is growing for the importance of emotion to rational decision-making.

Massey (2002) argues that "evolution has bequeathed us a cognitive structure with two mentalities – one emotional and one rational" (p. 20). He explains how human decisions and behaviours "cannot be modelled solely as a function of rationality" (p. 20). He sums up his analysis in this way:

Because of our evolutionary history and cognitive structure, it is generally the case that unconscious emotional thoughts will precede and strongly influence our rational decisions. Thus, our much-valued rationality is really more tenuous than we humans would like to believe, and it probably plays a smaller role in human affairs than prevailing theories of rational choice would have it. (Massey, 2002, p. 25)

Adolphs and Anderson (2018) argue for the view that emotions cause behaviour. They also acknowledge however, that once an emotion has caused a behaviour, that behaviour can itself trigger further emotional or mental states. Ledoux (2000) shows how emotional states influence one's attention and perception; and affect memory and decision-making. In other words emotional arousal controls and directs brain activity. It is the ability to properly manage this emotional arousal, making sense of it and controlling the subsequent behaviour that emotional intelligence seeks to conceptualise. Salzman and Fusi (2010) suggest that "both the functional and the electrophysiological characteristics of the amygdala and the prefrontal cortex overlap and intimately depend on each other. Thus, the neural circuits mediating cognitive, emotional, physiological, and behavioral responses may not truly be separable and instead are inextricably linked" (p. 174).

We can therefore conclude the same way we started this section – that while on the one hand, emotional processes can influence cognitive processes, on the other hand cognitive processes can regulate or modify our emotions. This leads us soundly into the discussion of emotional intelligence that in very lay terms has been described as the ability to allow both emotion and cognition to inform and shape our decision-making.

UNDERSTANDING EMOTIONAL INTELLLIGENCE

One thing we can agree on is that when dealing with people, we need to remember that we "are not dealing with creatures of logic but creatures of emotion" (Carnegie, 1998, p. 13). Emotion is a key part of what makes us human. We are indeed "creatures saturated by feelings" (Howe, 2008, p. 1). We are emotional beings just as much as we are social beings, capable of experiencing strong feelings, and it is within relationships that we experience and live most of these emotions. Therefore, the more able we are to understand ourselves on a level of feeling, the more skilled we can become in our social interactions.

Imagine this: you've been offered a well-paying job with ideal conditions, and opportunities for growth. Yet something inside makes you feel apprehensive about resigning from your current job. What would you do? You could ignore the feeling and choose what appears to be the logical path, or go with your gut feeling and risk losing a great opportunity. You might otherwise consider both the logical thoughts going through your head, and the feelings about the job offer. With that information in hand, you could then manage the apprehension itself and use it to make a decision that you would be serene about. Solving problems and making wise decisions using both thoughts and feelings, or logic and intuition, is a part of what we refer to as emotional intelligence (Mayer & Salovey, 1997; Salovey & Mayer, 1990).

Salovey and Mayer (1990) first described Emotional Intelligence formally and defined it as "the ability to monitor one's own and others' feelings and emotions, to discriminate among them and to use this information to guide one's thinking and actions" (p. 189). Linking emotions and intelligence was relatively novel when first introduced in a theoretical model in the 1990s (Salovey & Mayer, 1990). Questions people ask about emotional intelligence include: Is emotional intelligence something you are born with? Is it something you either have or you don't? Can emotional intelligence be learnt? Can it be measured reliably and validly? What does emotional intelligence mean in everyday life? How does emotional intelligence affect mental health and wellbeing, relationships, performance? They are questions researchers too, have been seeking to answer in these twenty-five years or so. And they are questions I will attempt to answer through this chapter.

Conceptualising Emotional Intelligence

'Emotion' and 'intelligence' have since time immemorial been viewed as two opposite constructs which do not go well together. Emotion has been seen as something that derails individuals from achieving their goals. Yet, "the theory of emotional intelligence suggested the opposite: emotions make cognitive processes adaptive and individuals can think rationally about emotions" (Brackett, Rivers, & Salovey, 2011, p. 89). As early as 1960, Mowrer maintained that emotions "do not at all deserve being put in opposition with 'intelligence' ... they are it seems, a higher order of intelligence" (pp. 307–308). However, it was only until much later "that the idea that there was such a thing as emotional intelligence" was beginning to crop up in a variety of different fields including literary criticism and psychiatry (Howe, 2008, p. 11).

The 1980s saw the emergence of two important areas of psychological research. The first area, cognition and affect, involved how cognitive and emotional processes interact to enhance thinking (Brackett et al., 2011). Emotions like happiness and anger seemed to influence strongly how people think, make decisions and perform. The second was an evolution in models of intelligence itself. "Rather than viewing intelligence strictly as how well one engaged in analytic tasks associated with memory, reasoning, judgment, and abstract thought, theorists and investigators began considering intelligence as a broader array of mental abilities" (Brackett et al., 2011, p. 89).

The term 'emotional intelligence' was first coined in 1985 when Wayne Leon Payne published his doctoral thesis *A Study of Emotion: Developing Emotional Intelligence*. In 1990, Salovey and Mayer, gave a conceptually clear idea of the fact that people who could appreciate and understand the role of emotions in their own and others' psychological life seem to be socially very skilled. And their paper

Emotional Intelligence set off an era of avid research and writing on the concept, which was further popularized by Daniel Goleman in 1995 with his bestselling book "Emotional Intelligence: Why it can Matter more than IQ". Goleman described how emotional intelligence could be "as powerful and at times more powerful than IQ" in predicting success in life (Goleman, 1995, p. 34). He also described how researchers were linking emotional intelligence to pro-social behaviour in young people. Unfortunately, having been popularized in a rather non-scientific, augmented form by Goleman, the concept of emotional intelligence has been criticised as a 'fad' based on unreasoned and unreasonable claims (Murphy, 2013, p. 353). And the greatest criticism has been thrown at the claim that emotional intelligence is more significant than IQ when predicting success in life.

The noughties, then, saw the study of emotional intelligence being approached through two main models: the ability model and mixed models (Mayer, Caruso, & Salovey, 2000). On the one hand, the ability model views emotional intelligence as a standard intelligence that can be measured as a mental ability with performance assessments that have a criterion of correctness (i.e., there are better and worse answers, which are determined using complex scoring algorithms). On the other hand, there are the mixed models. Cary Cherniss (2010) describes these as ones that mix the ability conception with personality traits and competencies such as optimism, self-esteem, and emotional self-efficacy. Proponents of this approach use self-report instruments as opposed to performance assessments to measure emotional intelligence (i.e. they are measures that ask people to judge and report how good they are at perceiving others' emotions accurately).

It is well known that self-report measures are problematic because respondents can provide socially desirable responses rather than truthful ones, or respondents may not actually know how good they are at emotion-based tasks. As they apply to emotional intelligence, self-report measures are related weakly to performance assessments and lack discriminant validity from existing measures of personality (Brackett & Mayer, 2003). In fact, Van Rooy, Viswesvaran, and Pluta (2005), carried out a meta-analysis of 13 studies that compared performance tests (like the Mayer, Salovey & Caruso Emotional Intelligence Test (MSCEIT), 2002) and self-report scales (like the Bar-On, 1997). They reported that performance tests were relatively distinct from self-report measures ($r = 0.14$). Even when a self-report measure is designed to map onto performance tests, correlations are very low (Brackett & Geher, 2006). And as such, any self-report measures (including those on emotional intelligence) are more susceptible to faking than performance tests. This was also one of the main criticisms directed at the proponents of emotional intelligence.

For these reasons the ability-based definition and performance-based measurement of emotional intelligence are widely preferred when researching the concept. Murphy (2013) asserts that at the scientific end, measures of EI 'abilities' are shown to be closely related to general measures of ability (in other words, IQ), with the best test said to be the MSCEIT version 2 (Mayer, Salovey, Caruso EI Test). I myself have taken a positivist epistemological stance by using the MSCEIT in my doctoral research on Emotional Intelligence and Transformational Leadership, in order to measure the emotional intelligence of my research participants (Kenely, 2008). This viewpoint is supported by researchers not associated with any of the established measures of emotional intelligence (e.g., Matthews, Zeidner, & Roberts, 2002). This rather positivist epistemological stance towards measures and viewpoints has served to temper some of the earlier wilder assertions about emotional intelligence. In fact "we are now in possession of a more measured understanding of the undoubted importance of emotional intelligence in human affairs" (Howe, 2008, p. 11).

Mayer, Salovey, and Caruso (2008), in an article responding to major criticisms of emotional intelligence as a construct, have argued that there exists a "valid and conceptually important new variable for investigators and practitioners" (p. 512). They argue that the acceptance of the construct is threatened less by its critics, perhaps, than by those who are so enthusiastic about it as to apply the term indiscriminately to a variety of traditional personality variables (Daus & Ashkanasy, 2005; Murphy & Sideman, 2006).

Emotional Intelligence Models

In 2004, Mayer, Salovey, and Caruso building on Mayer and Salovey (1997) devised a general working definition of emotional intelligence based on the four discrete mental abilities or 'branches' that comprise emotional intelligence:

> the capacity to reason about emotions and of emotions to enhance thinking. It includes the abilities to accurately perceive emotions, to access and generate emotions so as to assist thought, to understand emotions and emotional knowledge, and to reflectively regulate emotions so as to promote emotional and intellectual growth. (Mayer et al., 2004, p. 197)

This is now known as the four-branch model of emotional intelligence, and comprises of a number of abilities that build hierarchically (Schneider, Lyons, & Khazon, 2013). *Perceiving emotions* includes the ability to accurately identify and express emotions. This in turn, helps to discriminate between hospitable and hostile situations. The *ability to generate and use emotions* to enhance thinking includes adjusting emotion to redirect cognitive, rational processes, obtain new perspectives, and improve problem solving or creativity. *Emotional understanding* includes the ability to understand emotional information, the manner in which emotions combine, their causes and consequences. *Emotional management* includes the ability to be open to feelings and regulate them to enable growth, even when under pressure.

In an extensive review of the literature on Emotional Intelligence, Dulewicz and Higgs (2000) identified the core common elements in the overall construct. These are: self-awareness, emotional resilience, motivation, interpersonal sensitivity, influence, intuitiveness, conscientiousness and integrity.

Emotional intelligence involves an individual's ability to be aware of their own emotional reactions in differing situations and their abilities to manage their responses accordingly (Mayer et al., 1997). This awareness coupled with an ability to control or manage one's emotions, allows individuals to make more appropriate decisions with confidence. On the other hand, not handling emotions well can harm our health, wreak havoc with our confidence and render us ineffective or dangerous.

UNDERSTANDING WELLBEING

Wellbeing is a complex and multidimensional construct that concerns optimal experience and functioning. There is, as yet no unanimous definition of wellbeing, and different researchers speak of physical, economic, social, emotional, and psychological wellbeing (Diener, 2000). However, there is general agreement that at minimum, wellbeing includes the manifestation of positive emotions and moods (for example, contentment and happiness), the absence of negative emotions (for example, depression and anxiety), satisfaction with life, fulfillment and positive functioning (Frey & Stutzer, 2002). In simple terms, wellbeing can be described as judging life positively and feeling good (Diener, Suh, & Oishi, 1997).

Di Fabio and Kenny (2016) describe wellbeing as a construct of long-standing interest in the field of psychology, and as such it deserves additional attention for its primary prevention potential for fostering health and wellbeing. They maintain that while psychologists recognise the importance of systemic change to remedy modern-day social and economic problems, they are also interested in identifying individual factors that foster wellbeing and can serve as assets that protect individuals from psychological harm and ultimately foster wellbeing.

Hedonic and Eudaimonic Perspectives of Wellbeing

Current research on wellbeing reflects two general perspectives, a distinction first made by Aristotle. The hedonic approach focuses on happiness and defines wellbeing or happiness as being fundamentally about maximising pleasure and avoiding or minimizing pain (Ryan & Deci, 2001). The eudaimonic approach, on the other hand, focuses on meaning in life and self-realization, and the extent to which a person fully integrates this into his or her life (Burrus et al., 2012, p. 154).

Burros et al. (2012) explain that hedonic wellbeing has typically been studied in the Subjective Well-Being tradition – an expansive term encompassing both a cognitive component (people's satisfaction with their lives in general, as well their satisfaction with specific domains of life, e.g., work, family life); and an affective component (the frequency with which people experience positive and negative emotions). People with high subjective wellbeing tend to report high satisfaction with life in general and also experience frequent positive and infrequent negative affect.

Conversely, eudaimonic wellbeing has been studied using several approaches, the most prominent of these being the Psychological Well-Being approach, which states that wellbeing includes six dimensions of functioning: self-acceptance, positive relations with others, environmental mastery, autonomy, purpose in life, and personal growth.

More recently, Seligman (2011) introduced a new understanding of wellbeing or 'flourishing'", and described it as having five important pillars or elements: positive emotion, engagement, relationships, meaning and accomplishment. He describes them as the permanent building blocks for a life of profound fulfilment. In this definition, we can see how both hedonic and eudaimonic aspects of wellbeing are brought together in one integrated approach.

A short word on social wellbeing is also called for. A number of studies cite a rich and fulfilling social life and a network of close social support with family and friends as being strongly correlated with subjective wellbeing (Diener & Seligman, 2002). We cannot deny that healthy social networks and a sense of belonging or social connectedness contribute towards a person's wellbeing. In fact, social wellbeing is often described as the extent to which a person feels a sense of belonging and social inclusion in a particular group or community. Social wellbeing is the basis for social equality, social capital, and social trust. It is the antidote to racism, stigma, violence and crime. It depends largely on the quality of government, the quality of services and provision of support for those in need, and the fair distribution of resources. However it also depends in part on the sum of individual mental wellbeing, and on the quality of interpersonal relationships in a group, community or society, including respect for others and their needs, compassion and empathy, and authentic interaction.

UNDERSTANDING RESILIENCE

Resilience is another complex and multi-faceted construct (Grant & Kinman, 2014). We may say that resilience is a person's ability to recover from adversity, react appropriately, or bounce back when life presents challenges. Resilience to certain events has been likened to elasticity in metals (Lazarus, 1993). Howe (2008) describes it as "people's ability to deal with stress, pressure and the demands made of them" (p. 106). He emphasises however that resilience is not "just a matter of some naturally given inner strength or the possession of a robust temperament" (p. 107). Resilience depends on how well people "perceive, appraise, approach and tackle stresses and challenges" (p. 107).

Buckner, Mezzacappa and Beardslee (2003) found that good emotional regulation (one of the key components of emotional intelligence) contributes to resilience as well as to sound mental health. Thus, resilience may be viewed as one very important factor of wellbeing. In fact, Kinman and Grant (2011) highlighted the importance of inter- and intra-individual emotional competencies in promoting resilience and enhancing wellbeing (p. 261).

This takes us back to Chris Moon and his incredible story of survival. His story did not end with his release from captivity in Cambodia. In 1995, while volunteering with an organisation (Halo Trust), clearing landmines in Africa, he was blown up in a supposedly safe area of a minefield, losing an arm and a leg. He survived initially by treating himself and arrived in a South African hospital, fourteen hours later, having lost so much blood that doctors were astonished he was still alive. Back home, he recovered three or four times faster than was expected and after intensive rehabilitation, within a year after leaving hospital he ran the London Marathon, raising funds to help disabled people. He also went on to successfully complete a Masters degree. Moon taught himself to run and is believed to be the world's first amputee ultra-distance runner.

When interviewed about this episode in his life, Moon speaks about surviving by "maintaining the ability to reason" and resisting what he calls the "death mechanism" – where giving up was at that moment, the most attractive option. His ability to regulate his fear and distress, his decision to remain in control, once again undoubtedly contributed to his survival after the accident. His ability to bounce back and to react after this horrendous experience is testimony to the power of emotional intelligence and its contribution to resilience. Shneider et al.'s (2013) study, in fact demonstrated that aspects of emotional intelligence confer benefits during the stress process by promoting resilient psychological and physiological responses (p. 5). Moon goes on to say that he "worked on making a choice, focusing on what I had rather than what I had lost. It required a great deal of mental discipline".

LINKING THE THREE CONCEPTS

A growing number of studies have provided evidence for the positive relationship between emotional intelligence and indices of wellbeing such as greater life satisfaction, higher self-esteem, higher self-acceptance, positive affect, positive social interaction, and better health (Koydemir & Schutz, 2012).

Saarni (2000) too believes that "important consequences of emotional intelligence are *a sense of subjective wellbeing* and adaptive *resilience* in the face of future stressful circumstances" (p. 78). Howe (2008) also sustains that emotional intelligence has "close links with the 'coping and stress' literature *(and)* suggests resilience" (p. 22). Schneider et al. (2013) found that emotional intelligence conferred stress resilience (p. 4).

Thus, the thread that connects emotional intelligence, resilience and wellbeing is certainly there. In fact, Bezzina, Falzon, and Muscat (2015) confirm that the literature "provides ample evidence that emotional intelligence is conducive to wellbeing" (p. 153). They go on to refer to major authors like Austin, Saklofske, and Egan (2005) who found that emotional intelligence is positively associated with life satisfaction and social network size and quality, thus contributing to our social wellbeing too.

Emotional intelligence, most particularly the abilities to recognize emotions and to regulate them in self and others, contributes unquestionably to resilience and provides the necessary tools that allow us to face adversity confidently and with courage. Emotional intelligence contributes to our ability to appraise situations in a constructive way, resulting in better outcomes and heightened wellbeing.

Several new assessments have been developed in recent years, to explore the link between emotional intelligence and wellbeing, often with reasonable validity evidence. Burrus et al. (2012) used one such measure – the Situational Judgment Test of Emotion Management STEM (MacCann & Roberts, 2008) – to study this phenomenon. The STEM is an ability-based, rather than self-report, situational judgment test measure of Emotional Intelligence. It is moderately correlated with intelligence, independent from personality, and predicts outcomes such as alexithymia (difficulty identifying and describing emotions), depression, stress, and anxiety (MacCann & Roberts, 2008). This study provides direct support for the hypothesis that emotional intelligence is related to wellbeing. Burrus et al. (2012) found evidence that the key component of emotional intelligence, emotion management, was related to both hedonic and eudaimonic wellbeing. Specifically, those with high emotion management tended to have higher psychological wellbeing, and *like* people who reported high subjective wellbeing (referred to earlier) frequently experienced positive affect, and infrequently experienced negative affect. This reinforces the link between emotional intelligence and wellbeing.

In a review of existing literature pertaining to emotional intelligence, health, and wellbeing, Zeidner, Matthew, and Roberts (2012) suggest that emotional intelligence influences subjective wellbeing by fostering adaptive methods of coping with social challenges, social stress and interpersonal conflicts; promoting the development of supportive social networks; decreasing negative and increasing positive emotions; and enhancing emotional regulation. Emotional intelligence is also conceptually related to the psychological wellbeing focus on personal growth and self-actualisation (Zeidner et al., 2012). Skills in interpersonal (social) and intrapersonal (emotional awareness and internal self-regulation) emotional intelligence should contribute to positive relationships with others and the capacity for mastery over one's environment that allow for personal growth, a sense of meaning in life, and self-actualisation. Sanchez-Alvarez, Extremera, and Fernandez-Berrocal (2016) show that these conceptualisations of the pathways between emotional intelligence and wellbeing are supported by studies documenting relationships between emotional intelligence and social support, and between emotional intelligence and coping efficiency, stress reduction and emotional regulation.

Emotional intelligence has gained attention as a focus of research and intervention for its promise as a set of skills that can be taught to enhance coping resources and promote wellbeing (Sanchez-Alvarez et al., 2016). The connection between emotional intelligence and a range of positive outcomes across the academic, social, psychological and career domains among adolescents has been well documented too (Di Fabio & Kenny, 2016). Research has also found emotional intelligence to be associated with a variety of individual and social resources, such as resilience, positive self-evaluation, and social support (DiFabio & Kenny, 2012).

"A truly healthy individual has neither thought alone, nor emotion alone, but a functional integration among his or her major psychological processes" (Mayer et al., 2008, p. 513). Indeed, emotions are functional when the information they provide is attended to, interpreted accurately, integrated into thinking and behaviour, and managed effectively (Brackett et al., 2011, p. 98). Bezzina et al. (2015) assert that "emotions are a central component of human reactions and human nature" (p. 164), and their impact on relationships and wellbeing is proven.

Burrus et al. (2012) argue that individuals who possess the skills I have been describing here, may be better able to handle the stress of everyday life, to foster a greater number of meaningful close relationships, and to be more socially competent in general (p. 153). Consequently, they continue, individuals with high emotional intelligence also may be more likely to experience elevated wellbeing, or "optimal psychological functioning and experience" (Ryan & Deci, 2001, p. 142).

CONCLUSION

The link between emotional intelligence and wellbeing emerges very clearly on two levels – mental health and social functioning. Bracket et al. (2011) assert that the skills associated with emotional intelligence, should "help individuals to deal effectively with unpleasant emotions and to promote pleasant emotions in order to promote both personal growth and wellbeing" (p. 95). They also propose that emotional intelligence "promotes positive social functioning by helping individuals to detect others' emotion states, adopt others' perspectives, enhance communication, and regulate behaviour" (p. 96). They reiterate that people with higher MSCEIT scores "tend to be more socially competent, to have better quality relationships, and to be viewed as more interpersonally sensitive than those with lower MSCEIT scores" (p. 96).

This chapter has sought to answer a number of questions about emotional intelligence and its link to resilience and wellbeing. Although research in this field needs to continue, what we have learned thus far is promising: emotional intelligence can be measured objectively, it predicts important life outcomes, and impacts relationships. It appears that the skills that comprise the construct can be learned (Brackett et al., 2011, p. 99), and it contributes to mental health and wellbeing. I would like to make one final reference to Chris Moon and his testimony. He highlights in one statement the incredible mental discipline, resilience and emotional competence he has: "For me the challenge was not to think like a victim … perhaps for all of us in life the challenge is how we think … to not give up, to not be ground down by the incredibly oppressive situation we would be in".

REFERENCES

Adolphs, R., & Anderson, D. J. (2018), *The neuroscience of emotion – A new synthesis.* Princeton, NJ: Princeton University Press.

Austin, E. J., Saklofske, D. H., & Egan, V. (2005). Personality, well-being and health correlates of trait emotional intelligence. *Personality and Individual Differences, 38*(3), 547–558.

Bar-On R. (1997). *The Emotional Intelligence Inventory (EQ-i): Technical manual.* Toronto: Multi-Health Systems.

Bezzina, A., Falzon, R., & Muscat, M. (2015). Emotional intelligence and the maltese personal and social development model. In L. Zysberg & S. Raz (Eds.), *Emotional intelligence.* New York, NY: Nova Science Publishers, Inc.

Bhullar, N., Schutte, N. S., & Malouff, J. M. (2013). The nature of well-being: The roles of hedonic and eudaimonic processes and trait emotional intelligence. *The Journal of Psychology, 147*(1), 1–16. doi:10.1080/00223980.2012.667016

Brackett, M. A., & Geher, G. (2006). Measuring emotional intelligence: Paradigmatic shifts and common ground. In J. Ciarrochi, J. P. Forgas, & J. D. Mayer (Eds.), *Emotional intelligence and everyday life* (2nd ed., pp. 27–50). New York, NY: Psychology Press.

Brackett, M. A., Rivers, S. E., & Salovey, P. (2011). Emotional intelligence: implications for personal, social, academic and workplace success. *Social and Personality Psychology Compass, 5*(1), 88–103. Retrieved from http://ei.yale.edu/wp-content/uploads/2013/09/pub184_Brackett_Rivers_Salovey_2011_Compass-1.pdf

Brackett, M. A., & Mayer, J. D. (2003). Convergent, discriminant, and incremental validity of competing measures of emotional intelligence. *Personality and Social Psychology Bulletin, 29,* 1147–1158. doi:https://doi.org/10.1177/0146167203254596

Buckner, J. C., Mezzacappa, E., & Beardslee, W. R. (2003). Characteristics of resilient youths living in poverty: The role of self-regulatory processes. *Development and Psychopathology, 15,* 139–162. Retrieved from https://www.ncbi.nlm.nih.gov/pubmed/12848439

Burrus, J., Holtzman, S., Minsky, J., MacCann, C., & Roberts, R. D. (2012). Emotional intelligence relates to well-being: Evidence from the situational judgment test of emotional management. *Applied Psychology: Health and Well-Being, 4,* 151–166. doi:10.1111/j.1758-0854.2012.01066.x

Carnegie, D. (1998). *How to win friends and influence people.* New York, NY: Pocket Books.

Caruso, D., & Salovey, P. (2004). *The emotionally intelligent manager.* San Francisco, CA: Jossey-Bass.

Cherniss, C. (2010). Emotional intelligence: Toward clarification of a concept. *Industrial and Organizational Psychology, 3,* 110–126. doi:10.1111/j.1754-9434.2010.01231.x

Daus, C. S., & Ashkanasy, N. M. (2005). The case for the ability-based model of emotional intelligence in organizational behavior. *Journal of Organizational Behavior, 26,* 453–466. doi:10.1002/job.321

Di Fabio, A., & Kenny, M. E. (2012). Emotional intelligence and perceived social support among Italian high school students. *Journal of Career Development, 39,* 461–475. doi:https://doi.org/10.1177/0894845311421005

Di Fabio, A., & Kenny, M. E. (2016). Promoting well-being: The contribution of emotional intelligence. *Frontiers in Psychology, 7,* 1182. Retrieved from https://doi.org/10.3389/fpsyg.2016.01182

Diener, E. (2000). Subjective well-being: The science of happiness and a proposal for a national index. *American Psychologist, 55*(1), 34–43. Retrieved from http://dx.doi.org/10.1037/0003-066X.55.1.34

Diener, E., & Seligman, M. (2002). Very happy people. *Psychological Science, 13*(1), 81–84. Retrieved from https://doi.org/10.1111/1467-9280.00415

Dulewicz, S. V. D., & Higgs, M. J. (2000). Emotional intelligence: A review an evaluation study. *Journal of Managerial Psychology, 15*(4), 341–368. doi:10.1108/02683940010330993

Franks, D. D. (2006). The neuroscience of emotions. In J. E. Stets & J. H. Turner (Eds.), *Handbook of the Sociology of Emotions. Handbooks of sociology and social research.* Boston, MA: Springer. Retrieved from https://doi.org/10.1007/978-0-387-30715-2_3

Frey, B. S., & Stutzer, A. (2002). *Happiness and economics.* Princeton, NJ: Princeton University Press.

Gardner, H. (1993). *Frames of mind: The theory of multiple intelligences* (10th Anniversary ed.). New York, NY: Basic Books.

Goleman, D. (1995). *Emotional intelligence: Why it can matter more than IQ.* New York, NY: Bantam Books.

Goleman, D. (1996). *Emotional intelligence: Why it can matter more than IQ*. London: Bloomsbury Publishing.

Grant, L., & Kinman, G. (2014). Emotional resilience in the helping professions and how it can be enhanced. *Health and Social Care Education, 3*(1), 23–34. Retrieved from http://www.tandfonline.com/doi/full/10.11120/hsce.2014.00040

Howe, D. (2008). *The emotionally intelligent social worker*. London: Palgrave Macmillan.

Kenely, N. (2008). *Emotional intelligence and transformational leadership in social work* (Unpublished thesis). University of Malta, Malta.

Keyes, C. L. M. (2002). The mental health continuum: From languishing to flourishing in life. *Journal for Health Social Behaviour, 43*(6), 207–222. Retrieved from https://www.ncbi.nlm.nih.gov/pubmed/12096700

Killian, K. D. (2008). Helping till it hurts: A multi-method study of burnout, compassion fatigue and resilience in clinician working with trauma survivors. *Traumatology, 14*, 31–44. doi:https://doi.org/10.1177/1534765608319083

Kinman, G., & Grant, L. (2011). Exploring stress resilience in trainee social workers: The role of emotional and social competencies. *British Journal of Social Work, 41*(2), 261–275. doi:https://doi.org/10.1093/bjsw/bcq088

Koydemir, S., & Schutz, A. (2012). Emotional intelligence predicts components of subjective well-being beyond personaility: A two-country study using self- and informant reports. *The Journal of Positive Pscychology, 7*, 109–118. Retrieved from http://dx.doi.org/10.1080/17439760.2011.657050

Lazarus, R. S. (1993). From psychological stress to the emotions: A history of changing outlooks. *Annual Review of Psychology, 44*, 1–21. Retrieved from https://doi.org/10.1146/annurev.ps.44.020193.000245

Ledoux, J. (2000). Cognitive–emotional interactions: Listen to the brain. In R. D. Lane & L. Nadel (Eds.), *Series in affective science. Cognitive neuroscience of emotion* (pp. 129–155). New York, NY: Oxford University Press.

MacCann, C., & Roberts, R. D. (2008). New paradigms for assessing emotional intelligence: Theory and data. *Emotion, 8*, 540–551. doi:10.1037/a0012746

Massey, D. S. (2002). A brief history of human society: The origin and role of emotion in social life. *American Sociological Review, 67*, 1–29. Retrieved from https://www.scribd.com/document/30657252/Massey-Douglas-S-A-Brief-History-of-Human-Society

Matthews, G., Zeidner, M., & Roberts, R. D. (2002). *Emotional intelligence: Science and myth*. Boston, MA: MIT Press.

Mayer, J. D., Caruso, D. R., & Salovey, P. (2000). Selecting a measure of emotional intelligence: The case for ability scales. In R. Bar-On & J. D. A. Parker (Eds.), *The handbook of emotional intelligence: Theory, development, assessment, and application at home, school, and in the workplace* (pp. 320–342). San Francisco, CA: Jossey-Bass.

Mayer, J. D., & Salovey, P. (1997). What is emotional intelligence? In P. Salovey & D. Sluyter (Eds.), *Emotional development and emotional intelligence: Implications for educators* (pp. 3–31). New York, NY: Cambridge University Press.

Mayer J. D., Salovey, P., & Caruso, D. R. (2002). *Mayer-Salovey-Caruso Emotional Intelligence Test (MSCEIT) user's manual*. Toronto: Multi-Health Systems.

Mayer, J., Salovey, P., & Caruso, D. (2004). Emotional intelligence: Theory, findings and implications. *Psychological Inquiry, 15*(3), 197–215. Retrieved from http://www.unh.edu/emotional_intelligence/EI%20Assets/Reprints...EI%20Proper/EI2004MayerSaloveyCarusotarget.pdf

Mayer, J., Salovey, P., & Caruso, D. (2008). Emotional intelligence: New ability or eclectic traits? *American Psychologist, 63*(6), 503–517. doi:10.1037/0003-066X.63.6.503

Moon, C. (n.d.). *Chris's story*. Retrieved from https://www.youtube.com/embed/TbaaC9pLSLs

Moon, C. (n.d.). *Toughen your mind*. Retrieved from https://www.chrismoon.co.uk/images/FHM.pdf

Morrison, T. (2007). Emotional intelligence, emotion and social work: Context, characteristics, complications and contribution. *British Journal of Social Work, 37*(2), 245–63. doi:10.1093/bjsw/bcl016

Mowrer, O. J. (1960). *Learning theory and behaviour*. New York, NY: John Wiley and Sons.

McQueen, A. C. H. (2004). Emotional intelligence in nursing work. *Journal of Advanced Nursing, 47*, 101–108. doi:10.1111/j.1365-2648.2004.03069.x

Murphy, K. (2013). Four conclusions about emotional intelligence. In K. Murphy (Ed.), *A critique of emotional intelligence: What are the problems and how can they be fixed?* London: Routledge.

Murphy, K. R., & Sideman, L. (2006). The fadification of emotional intelligence. In K. R. Murphy (Ed.), *A critique of emotional intelligence: What are the problems and how can they be fixed* (pp. 283–299). Mahwah, NJ: Erlbaum.

Payne, W. L. (1985). *A study of emotion: Developing emotional intelligence* (Doctoral dissertation). Retrieved from http://geocities.ws/waynepayne/index.htm

Ryan, R. M., & Deci, E. L. (2001). On happiness and human potentials: A review of research on hedonic and eudaimonic well-being. In S. Fiske (Ed.), *Annual review of psychology* (pp. 141–166). Palo Alto, CA: Annual Reviews, Inc.

Saarni, C. (2000). Emotional competence: A developmental perspective. In R. Bar-On & J. D. A. Parker (Eds.), *The handbook of emotional intelligence* (pp. 68–91). San Francisco, CA: Jossey-Bass.

Salovey, P., & Mayer, J. D. (1990). Emotional intelligence. *Imagination, Cognition and Personality, 9*, 185–211. Retrieved from http://ei.yale.edu/publication/emotional-intelligence-5/

Salzman, C. D., & Fusi, S. (2010). Emotion, cognition, and mental state representation in amygdala and prefrontal cortex. *Annual Review of Neuroscience, 33*, 173–202. Retrieved from http://doi.org/10.1146/annurev.neuro.051508.135256

Sanchez-Alvarez, N., Extremera, N., & Fernandez-Berrocal, P. (2016). The relation between emotional intelligence and subjective wellbeing: A meta-analytic investigation. *The Journal of Positive Psychology, 11*(3), 276–285. Retrieved from http://dx.doi.org/10.1080/17439760.2015.1058968

Schneider, T. R., Lyons, J. B., & Khazon, S. (2013). Emotional intelligence and resilience. *Personality and Individual Differences, 55*(8), 909–914. Retrieved from http://doi.org/10.1016/j.paid.2013.07.460

Seligman, M. (2011). *Flourish – A visionary new understanding of happiness and well-being*. London: Nicholas Brealy Publishing.

Van Rooy, D. L., Viswesvaran, C., & Pluta, P. (2005). A meta-analytic evaluation of construct validity: What is this thing called emotional intelligence? *Human Performance, 18*, 445–462. Retrieved from http://dx.doi.org/10.1207/s15327043hup1804_9

Zeidner, M., Matthew, G., & Roberts, R. (2012). The emotional intelligence, health and wellbeing nexus: What have we learned and what have we missed? *Applied Psychology and Wellbeing, 4*, 1–30. doi:10.1111/j.1758-0854.2011.01062.x

CLAUDIA PSAILA

3. SPIRITUALITY

The Cornerstone of Wellbeing?

ABSTRACT

Recent years have seen an interest in the spiritual dimension of persons' identity, health and experiences with many claiming that this is essential since we are spiritual beings. In fact, the spiritual dimension of care is being studied in disciplines such as psychology, education, health and social work. Moreover, interest has grown in understanding what contributes to one's wellbeing. In this chapter, I explore the relationship between spirituality and wellbeing. I begin by understanding the concepts of 'spirituality' and 'religion' and the relationship between the two. This is followed by a discussion of the concept of 'wellbeing'. Both spirituality and wellbeing are multidimensional constructs that are difficult to define. However, this chapter explores parallel meanings between spirituality and wellbeing and the potential link between the two. I would argue that one's wellbeing rests upon one's spiritual wellbeing such that it is fundamental to one's overall mental, physical and emotional health.

Keywords: spirituality, religion, flourishing, meaning, wellbeing

INTRODUCTION

Many are in agreement that we are spiritual beings and as such, the spiritual dimension is a fundamental aspect of our identity. In the same way as we develop physically, cognitively, emotionally, socially and psychologically, we also develop spiritually (Rowan, 2005). These different dimensions make us who we are and contribute to our wellbeing. However, what do we understand by the concept of 'wellbeing' and how is this related to one's spirituality? In this chapter, I discuss the relationship between spirituality and wellbeing. I begin by examining the concepts of 'spirituality', 'religion', and 'wellbeing'.

SPIRITUALITY AND RELIGION

There are no universal definitions of 'spirituality' and 'religion' although many agree that both are multidimensional constructs (Oman, 2013). Some of the difficulty in understanding spirituality is its relationship to religion.

Spirituality and Religion as Distinct and Opposite

While some might see spirituality and religion as inextricably linked and complementary (Miller & Thoresen, 2003) such that persons consider themselves to be both spiritual and religious, this is not the case for others who may consider themselves as spiritual but not religious. In fact, persons may label themselves as 'atheist' or 'agnostic' while still considering themselves to be spiritual (secular spirituality). Their spirituality is not linked to their religion. At times, such understanding of religion and spirituality is based on an oppositional differentiation where religion is perceived as having to do with the institutional, public, norms and dogma while spirituality is understood as having to do with transcendence, meaning-making, personal beliefs and connection (Sperry & Shafranske, 2005). Furthermore, such oppositional differentiation may lead to a negative evaluation of religion and a positive appraisal of spirituality (Zinnbauer & Pargament, 2005). This disenchantment with the institutional aspects of religion was also evident in a study of Maltese youth who are active members of Catholic religious organizations (Psaila, 2014a). The study shows that 14% of the respondents who attend their religious group on a regular basis reported that they do not attend Sunday Mass. Decline in church attendance is often seen as a measure of disenchantment with formal religion and the rise of a more secular form of spirituality. This is also evident in other countries (Sperry & Shafranske, 2005; West, 2001; Zinnbauer et al., 1997).

Spirituality and Religion as Overlapping

Others, however, have noted an overlap between the constructs, which may further add to the difficulty in arriving at a common definition of both spiritualty and religion. For some, spirituality is subsumed within religion while for others religion is one element or expression of spirituality. When creating an oppositional differentiation between religion and spirituality such that religion is only perceived as dogma, norms, the institutional, ritual and practices, the public (as opposed to it being a personal endeavour), we are devoiding religion of the sacred or the spiritual (Pargament, 2007; Psaila, 2012). Some believe that both religion and spirituality have an existential dimension since both deal with meaning-making and purpose. Furthermore, both deal with the nature of human beings and their destiny together with the meaning of universal experiences such as life and death (Swinton, 2001; Nolan & Holloway, 2014). According to Pargament (2007), both spirituality and religion are involved with the sacred. He explains:

> ... the most critical function of religion is spiritual in nature. Although religion serves a host of purposes – providing a sense of meaning and purpose to life, comfort, intimacy, health and self-development – the most essential of all religious functions is the desire to form a relationship with something we consider sacred. (p. 31)

With regards to spirituality, Pargament (2007) clarifies that:

> The sacred is the heart and soul of spirituality. For many people, the sacred is equivalent to higher powers or divine beings. Others think of the sacred in a broader sense, one that encompasses any variety of objects, from mountains, music, and marriage to vegetarianism, virtues, and visions. Both perspectives are accurate. (p. 32)

The road to the sacred may or may not be through religion. So, for example, a person might make sense of their suffering (Why is this happening to me? What did I do to deserve this?) by referring to their Christian belief and feel strengthened by their faith (religious meaning-making). The person might feel accompanied by and find solace in the image of the suffering Christ on the Cross. Another person may view their suffering as meaningful because they are experiencing support and compassion from others and because they view suffering as an inevitable part of life that leads to growth (non-religious/secular spirituality). Zinnbauer and Pargament (2005) explain that while with religion, the sacred takes place in an institutional context, with spirituality, the context is not restricted. Swinton (2001) agrees, explaining that a distinguishing factor of religion is that it has to do with a system of beliefs and that this system usually centres on a form of perception of God which is shared in a community. He distinguishes between 'religious spirituality' and 'nonreligious spirituality' claiming that they are intimately linked and 'reflect genuine attempts to express the experiences of the spirit' (p. 38).

We Are Spiritual Beings

'Spirit', from which the word 'spirituality' is derived, comes from the Latin 'spiritus' which means 'breath'. Swinton (2001) explains how this refers to the 'enlivening force of a person' such that 'the very being of the person is permeated by' (p. 14) the spirit which 'motivates and vitalizes human existence' (ibid: 14). It is for this reason that many consider human beings to be spiritual beings. Another reason is the fact that the construct of 'spirituality' is often linked to meaning-making and the search for meaning. Zohar and Marshall (2001) explain that 'we are driven by a need to ask 'fundamental' or 'ultimate' questions' (p. 4). Thus, for many, our striving to find meaning and purpose (Frankl, 1964) is what makes us spiritual beings.

Spirituality as a Multidimensional Construct

As discussed, although there is no universal definition of 'spirituality', many agree that it is a multidimensional construct. Some of the dimensions have already been highlighted. Dyson, Cobb, and Forman (1997) elucidate the importance of 'relationship' in understanding spirituality: relationship to self, other persons and God or a higher value. Furthermore, the main themes that they associated with spirituality were meaning, hope, relatedness/connectedness, beliefs and expressions of spirituality. Elkins, Hedstrom, Hughes, Leaf, and Saunders (1988) identified the following nine dimensions to their understanding of spirituality: transcendent, meaning and purpose in life, mission in life, sacredness of life, material values, altruism, idealism, awareness of the tragic and fruits of spirituality.

Moreover, as discussed, for some, spirituality is considered a fundamental dimension of one's identity and development (Rowan, 2005). Furthermore, one's understanding of 'religion' and 'spirituality' is often greatly influenced by one's personal experience that includes one's life journey and familial, cultural and societal contexts. Our spirituality is influenced by the dominant religion of our cultural context (familial, communal or societal) whether one moves away from that religion or not and whether this is done consciously or unconsciously (Psaila, 2014b).

Summary Points: 'Spirituality'

Spirituality is a way of being and experiencing that comes through an awareness of a transcendent dimension (whichever way that is defined by the individual: God or Higher Value)

- It involves meaning-making, in particular, searching for meaning in our journey of life
- It is not necessarily linked to religion: non-religious spirituality
- It may be religiously inspired: religious spirituality
- It has an effect on, and may be experienced through, one's relationships to self, others, and God or a higher value
- Spirituality is a multidimensional construct
- It is a fundamental human dimension
- It is very personal and individual
- It is reflected in one's values and behaviour
- It reveals itself in a number of ways based on personality factors, experience and culture

WELLBEING

'Wellbeing' is also a multidimensional construct and one that is difficult to define (Henderson & Knight, 2012). Both theoretical and empirical understandings of wellbeing are often influenced by whether a hedonic or eudaimonic perspective is taken.

Hedonic and Eudaimonic Perspectives of Wellbeing

From a hedonic perspective, wellbeing is focused on maximizing happiness or pleasure and avoiding pain. Ryan and Deci (2001) explain that from this perspective, wellbeing is made up of 'subjective happiness and concerns the experience of pleasure versus displeasure broadly construed to include all judgments about the good/bad elements of life" (p. 144). Consequently, wellbeing is equated to "the positive emotional states that accompany satisfaction of desire; therefore experiences of pleasure, carefreeness, and enjoyment' (Henderson & Knight, 2012, p. 197). Since such desires and their subsequent emotions are subjective, hedonic wellbeing is measured from a subjective intrapersonal perspective that is, it is the person who evaluates his/her wellbeing. This is referred to as 'subjective wellbeing' (SWB). It is measured in terms of high levels of positive (pleasant) affect (emotions and mood), low negative (unpleasant) affect and life satisfaction (Ryan & Deci, 2001; Henderson & Knight, 2012; Dodge, Daly, Huyton, & Sanders, 2012). Subjective wellbeing is composed of cognitive and affective components. The cognitive component refers to a person's evaluation of his/her life (or elements of one's life, for example, work) and the extent to which he/she is satisfied with it (e.g. What is my perception of my work and how satisfied do I feel about it?) The affective component refers to the dominance of the presence of positive affect over negative affect (Do I experience mainly positive moods and emotions?) (Dodge et al., 2012; Henderson & Knight, 2012). From a hedonic perspective, wellbeing involves persons pursuing their desires so as to experience positive emotional states.

An eudaimonic perspective of wellbeing emphasizes the experience of personal growth, meaning in life and engaging in behavior and experiences that are congruent with one's values and inherent potentials (Suh, Gnilka, & Rice, 2017). With eudaimonic wellbeing, the processes of self-actualisation and authentic living are important. Ryan and Deci (2001) explain that wellbeing 'lies in the actualization of human potentials ... well-being consists of fulfilling or realizing one's daimon or true nature' (p. 143). Persons experiencing eudaimonic wellbeing would be engaging in activities and/or experiences that are congruent with their values (value congruence), are true to who they really are (authenticity) and enable them to reach their unique potential (self-actualisation). Eudaimonic wellbeing is measured in terms of 'psychological wellbeing' (PWB). PWB is made up of the following elements: 'self-acceptance, purpose in life, environmental mastery, positive relationships, personal growth and autonomy' (Dodge et al., 2012, p. 225).

Hedonic wellbeing is not necessarily linked to one's eudaimonic wellbeing. As Henderson and Knight (2012) explain, 'not enough people are functioning well in a life about which they feel good' (p. 200). So, a person may be engaging in activities that may be pleasurable (hedonia) but which do not necessarily promote 'wellness' and healthy personal functioning. Such experiences or desires might therefore not be congruent to a person's values, and do not help in his/her process of self-actualisation and growth, even though they may be pleasurable. Alternatively, a person experiencing pain, such as pain due to loss, and who is engaging with such painful experiences, would be promoting their wellbeing. Such an experience would be important for his/her healthy functioning and personal growth. It would therefore promote a person's eudaimonic wellbeing even though the experience is not pleasurable (hedonic). On the other hand, avoiding such pain would lead to dysfunction and potential illhealth.

More recently, researchers and theorists of wellbeing have acknowledged that both hedonic and eudaimonic perspectives of wellbeing may be important in understanding wellbeing. The concept of 'flourishing' combines both elements of hedonia and eudaimonia in the conceptualization of wellbeing (Henderson & Knight, 2012).

'Flourishing': Integrating Hedonic and Eudaimonic Perspectives of Wellbeing

Martin Seligman, who is the founder of positive psychology, wanted to move away from a paradigm that focuses on the absence of dysfunction and ill health to one that stresses positive, optimal functioning. He explains:

> I used to think that the topic of positive psychology was happiness, that the gold standard for measuring happiness was life satisfaction, and that the goal of positive psychology was to increase life satisfaction. I now think that the topic of positive psychology is well-being, that the gold standard for measuring well-being is flourishing, and that the goal of positive psychology is to increase flourishing. (Seligman, 2011, p. 13)

In explaining the concept of wellbeing, Seligman (2011) identifies five elements which he believes would lead to a flourishing life: positive emotion, engagement, meaning, positive relationships and accomplishment (PERMA). He clarifies that these elements are made up of what a person would freely choose. Furthermore, these components of wellbeing include both hedonic and eudaimonic wellbeing.

Predictors of Wellbeing

Ryan and Deci (2001) discuss research that deals with the following predictors of wellbeing: (a) social class and wealth (e.g. socio-economic status is linked to self-acceptance, mastery and growth; the more people focus on their financial and materialistic goals, the lower their wellbeing); (b) attachment and relatedness (many findings link relatedness to SWB; quality of relatedness fosters wellbeing; positive relationships and increased physical health); (c) goal congruence and goal progress (perceived competence and self-efficacy; autonomy and integration of goals).

Assessing One's Wellbeing

One model that can be used in assessing wellbeing is the Well-Being Model that was developed by the University of Minnesota Center for Spirituality and Healing (Kreitzer, 2012). This model incorporates both hedonic and eudaimonic wellbeing:

> Well-being is a state of being in balance and alignment in body, mind, and spirit. It is a state in which people describe themselves as feeling healthy,

content, purposeful, peaceful, energized, in harmony, happy, prosperous, and safe. (Kreitzer, 2012, p. 707)

Their concept of wellbeing focuses on how content one feels about different aspects of one's life while also encouraging a person to find answers within themselves. The Model emphasizes six dimensions which are central to their conception of wellbeing. These dimensions are interrelated.

- Health: physical, emotional, mental, and spiritual health.
- Purpose: an aim and direction, a direct expression of spirituality that gives life and work meaning.
- Relationships: social connections, networks, and the quality of relationships.
- Community: resources and infrastructure and the extent to which people are engaged and empowered.
- Environment: access to nature as well as clean air, water, and toxin free.
- Security: basic human needs, stable employment, sufficient finances and personal safety (Kreitzer, 2012, pp. 708–709).

SPIRITUALITY AND WELLBEING

There seem to be parallels between 'spirituality' and 'wellbeing'. If spirituality is concerned with the search for meaning, purpose, relationships (self, nature, others, God or Higher Power) and values, then one's spiritual wellbeing may greatly impact one's wellbeing. We have also seen how wellbeing and healthy functioning include being true to ourselves, engaging in experiences which might not necessarily be pleasant but which may contribute to our functioning, growth and the development of our unique potential, being satisfied with our lives, having good relationships with ourselves, being connected to others and the environment. I would argue that one's wellbeing rests upon one's spiritual wellbeing such that spirituality is fundamental to one's overall mental, physical and emotional health. Thus, for example, when experiencing emotional or psychological distress, such as suffering, finding meaning in suffering may help one to cope and flourish. Furthermore, such an experience of suffering may lead one to discover oneself, one's inner resources and potentials. It may also help to make one feel connected to others either because of sharing the experience of suffering or as a result of support and compassion received from others. However, one must note that a person who is alone, for example, who does not have such resources (intrapersonal and/or social) or whose support network is dysfunctional, may have a harder time to achieve wellbeing.

Spiritual Wellbeing

Fisher (2011) believes that spiritual wellbeing arises out of spiritual health which he defined as: "A, if not the, fundamental dimension of people's overall health and well-being, permeating and integrating all the other dimensions of health (i.e., physical, mental, emotional, social and vocational)" (p. 21). He explains that our 'spiritual health is a dynamic state of being, shown by the extent to which people live in harmony within relationships in the following domains of spiritual well-being' (p. 21): personal, communal, environmental and transcendental.

The personal domain focuses on the relationship with self which requires self-awareness and understanding one's meaning, purpose and values. On the other hand, the communal domain is centred on the relationship one has with others, particularly in relation to culture, religion and morality. Fisher (2011) describes the environmental domain as 'beyond care and nurture for the physical and biological, to a sense of awe and wonder; for some, the notion of unity with the environment' (p. 22). Finally, he describes the transcendental domain as the relationship of a person with 'something or some-One beyond the human level (i.e., the ultimate concern, cosmic force, transcendent reality or God)' (p. 22).

Paloutzian, Bufford and Wildman (2014) explain that 'the degree to which a person perceives or derives a sense of well-being' (p. 353) from his/her spirituality is important in dealing with and facing his/her health issues. They clarify that spiritual wellbeing (SWB) is related to both physical and mental health but is not synonymous with it. Furthermore, they explain how studies show that once persons' basic needs are met, they do not necessarily experience more wellbeing or contentment. They clarify that 'higher-order spiritual' values and motives take priority as human strivings. Such values, motives, and strivings are sometimes couched in 'spiritual' terms' (p. 354).

Spirituality and Health

Spirituality is a lens through which we view our world while it may also be a resource in helping us to cope. Paloutzian, Bufford, and Wildman (2014) reviewed a number of studies regarding the use of the Spiritual Well-Being Scale (SWBS) and mental and physical health in relation to spiritual wellbeing (SWB). They reviewed studies that focused on physical health such as stress, heart rate, blood pressure and irritable bowel syndrome. Studies involving mental health issues included: anxiety, depression and suicide. They explain that the way a person makes sense of, understands and handles life may impact a person's physical and mental health and means of coping. They clarify that 'there is no evidence that higher SWB has any causally curative effect on a purely organic disease, but there seems to be ample evidence that SWBS scores predict greater comfort and peace in the face of them' (p. 357). This seems to tally with Koenig's earlier findings. Koenig (2004) analysed over 500 studies that took place over a twenty year span ranging from 1980 to the year 2000 and found that 'religious beliefs and practices are associated with lower suicide rates, less anxiety, less substance abuse, less depression and faster recovery from depression, greater well-being, hope and optimism, more purpose and meaning in life, higher social support, greater marital satisfaction and stability' (p. 1195).

Spirituality and/or religion may be positively correlated to coping and pain. Wachholtz, Pearce, and Koenig (2007) reviewed a number of studies and found that patients used spiritual/religious ways of coping with pain such as prayer, looking for spiritual support, engaging in hope and adopting spiritual beliefs and practices. They found that spiritual/religious coping correlates with spiritual support, spiritual connection, peace, calmness, decreased anxiety and improvement of mood.

A local study that was carried out with patients at Hospice Malta (Baldacchino, Shah, Gauci, & Bonello, 2010) found that persons used religious (prayer, relationship with God) and non-religious (relationships with family and friends) ways of coping with their terminal illness. Such spiritual strategies were found to be used by the majority of clients. Furthermore, a negative significant correlation was found between such spiritual coping strategies and levels of depression.

In other studies, spiritual communities were found to have a positive impact in relation to providing support, approval, nurturance and acceptance (Aten & Leach, 2009; Psaila, 2012).

The Other Face of the Coin

So far, we have discussed the positive impact of spirituality and religion on mental and physical health. However, other studies show that spiritual and/or religious issues and concerns may underlie certain psychological problems including psychopathologies (Exline, 2002; Exline, Yali, & Sanderson, 2000; Exline & Rose, 2005; Lines, 2006; Pargament, 2007; Psaila, 2014b). For example, Exline (2002) found that persons undergoing 'religious strain' experienced greater depression and suicidality. She described religious strain as 'interpersonal strain, negative attitudes toward God, inner struggles to believe and problems associated with virtuous striving' (p. 185). Suicidality was also related to religious guilt and fear.

In another paper (Psaila, 2014b), I discuss how certain religious/spiritual beliefs may lead to increased anxiety, guilt, intrapersonal, interpersonal and organizational conflict. For example, a lesbian woman experiencing anxiety due to a clash between her identity and Catholic religious dogma, her faith, and potential disapproving and judgmental familial and/or social religious discourse. For some others, moving away from their religion in a context (familial, communal, societal) which is highly religious, might also cause confusion, anxiety and conflict within themselves and possibly with others. Lastly, although one's community and/or religious/spiritual leader/director may be nurturant and supportive, they might also negatively affect the person's wellbeing. For example, a woman living in a situation of interpersonal violence being encouraged to stay home and 'bear her cross'.

CONCLUSION

Up until some years ago, practitioners and researchers have only been taking a bio-psycho-social perspective to understanding health and wellbeing. The reason for this is the strong influence of each of these dimensions on our health and wellbeing. Physical illness such as cancer may determine and be determined by psychological ill-health such as anxiety; by social situations such as loneliness; and by economic issues such as financial problems. All these dimensions interact to shape one's perception and experience of wellbeing. Furthermore, as we have seen, wellbeing involves the developmental process of flourishing such that a person's wellbeing includes not only positive emotion but meaning and purpose, value congruence, self-actualisation, engagement and positive relationships. Moreover, it is now being recognised that we are spiritual beings and that this dimension has not being given enough attention in understanding and promoting wellbeing. Our spirituality, whether it is religiously inspired or not, provides a lens through which to view and shape our lives and experiences. Our spiritual wellbeing also strongly impacts how well we feel and function and must therefore be included in the equation. It is for this reason that I, together with others, suggest that it may be time to emphasise more strongly a biopsychosocial-spiritual model of health and wellbeing (Nolan & Holloway, 2014; Unterrainer, Lewis, & Fink, 2012). Such a perspective would have policy and practice implications for our understanding and promotion of wellbeing.

REFERENCES

Aten, J. D., & Leach, M. M. (2009). A primer on spirituality and mental health. In J. D. Aten & M. M. Leach (Eds.), *Spirituality and the therapeutic process: A comprehensive resource from intake to termination*. Washington, DC: American Psychological Association.

Baldacchino, D., Shah, A., Gauci, A., & Bonello, L. (2010). Anxiety, depression and spiritual coping of clients receiving hospice care. In D. Baldacchino (Ed.), *Spiritual care: Being in doing*. Malta: Preca Library.

Dodge, R., Daly, A. P., Huyton, J., & Sanders, L. D. (2012). The challenge of defining wellbeing. *International Journal of Wellbeing, 2*(3), 222–235.

Dyson, J., Cobb, M., & Forman, D. (1997). The meaning of spirituality: A literature review. *Journal of Advanced Nursing, 26*, 1183–1188.

Elkins, D. N., Hedstrom, L. J., Hughes, L. L., Leaf, J. A., & Saunders, C. (1988). Towards humanistic-phenomenological spirituality: Definition, description, and measurement. *Journal of Humanistic Psychology, 28*(4), 5–18.

Exline, J. J. (2002). Stumbling blocks on the religious road: Fractured relationships, nagging vices, and the inner struggle to believe. *Psychological Inquiry, 13*(3), 182–189.

Exline, J. J., & Rose, E. (2005). Religious and spiritual struggles. In R. F. Paloutzian & C. L. Park (Eds.), *Handbook of the psychology of religion and spirituality*. New York, NY: The Guildford Press.

Exline, J. J., Yali, A. M., & Sanderson, W. C. (2000). Guilt, discord, and alienation: The role of religious strain in depression and suicidality. *Journal of Clinical Psychology, 26*(12), 1481–1496.

Fisher, J. (2011). The four domains model: Connecting spirituality, health and well-being. *Religions, 2*, 17–28.

Frankl, V. (1964). *Man's search for meaning: An introduction to logotherapy*. Bombay: The Bombay St. Paul Society.

Henderson, L. W., & Knight, T. (2012). Integrating the hedonic and eudaimonic perspectives to more comprehensively understand wellbeing and pathways to wellbeing. *International Journal of Wellbeing, 2*(3), 196–221.

Koenig, H. G. (2004). Religion, spirituality and medicine: Research findings andimplications for clinical practice. *The Southern Medical Association, 97*(12), 1194–1200.

Kreitzer, M. J. (2012). Spirituality and well-being: Focusing on what matters. *Western Journal of Nursing Research, 34*(6), 707–711.

Lines, D. (2006). *Spirituality in counselling and psychotherapy.* London: Sage Publications.

Miller, W. R., & Thoresen, C. E. (2003). Spirituality, religion, and health. An emerging research field. *American Psychology, 58,* 24–35.

Nolan, S., & Holloway, M. (2014). *A-Z of spirituality.* Hampshire: Palgrave Macmillan.

Oman, D. (2013). Defining religion and spirituality. In R. F. Paloutzian & C. L. Park (Eds.), *Handbook of the psychology of religion and spirituality.* London: The Guildford Press.

Paloutzian, R. F., Bufford, R. K., & Wildman, A. J. (2014). Spiritual well-being scale: Mental and physical health relationships. In M. Cobb, C. M. Puchalski, & B. Rumbold (Eds.), *Oxford textbook of spirituality in healthcare.* Oxford: Oxford University Press.

Pargament, K. I. (2007). *Spiritually integrated psychotherapy: Understanding and addressing the sacred.* London: The Guildford Press.

Psaila, C. (2012). *Spirituality in psychotherapy: A hidden dimension. An exploratory study* (Unpublished thesis). Milton Keynes: Open University.

Psaila, C. (2014a). *Grassroots report.* Malta: Kummissjoni Djocesana Zghazagh and Discern Institute for Research on the Signs of the Times.

Psaila, C. (2014b). Mental health practitioners' understanding and experience of spirituality and religion: Implications for practice. *Journal for the Study of Spirituality, 4*(2), 189–203.

Rowan, J. (2005). *The transpersonal: Spirituality in psychotherapy and counselling.* London: Routledge.

Ryan, R. M., & Deci, E. L. (2001). On happiness and human potentials: A review of research on hedonic and eudaimonic well-being. *Annual Review of Psychology, 52,* 141–166.

Seligman, M. E. P. (2011). *Flourish: A new understanding of happiness and well-being and how to achieve them.* London: Free Press.

Sperry, L., & Shafranske, E. (2005). *Spiritually oriented psychotherapy.* Washington, DC: American Psychological Association.

Suh, H., Gnilka, P. B., & Rice, K. G. (2017). Perfectionism and wellbeing: A positive psychology framework. *Personality and Individual Differences, 111,* 25–30.

Swinton, J. (2001). *Spirituality and mental health: Rediscovering a 'forgotten' dimension.* London: Jessica Kingsley Publishers.

Unterrainer, H. F., Lewis, A. J., & Fink, A. (2014). Religious/spiritual well-being, personality and mental health: A review of results and conceptual issues. *Journal of Religion and Health, 53,* 382–392.

Wachholtz, A. B., Pearce, M. J., & Koenig, H. (2007). Exploring the relationship between spirituality, coping, and pain. *Journal of Behavioural Medicine, 30,* 311–318.

West, W. (2001). Counselling, psychotherapy and religion. In S. King-Spooner & C. Newnes (Eds.), *Spirituality and psychotherapy.* Ross-on-Wye: PCCS Books.

Zinnbauer, B. J., & Pargament, K. I. (2005). Religiousness and spirituality. In R. F. Paloutzian & C. L. Park (Eds.), *Handbook of the psychology of religion and spirituality.* New York, NY: The Guildford Press.

Zinnbauer, B. J., Pargament, K. I., Cole, B., Rye, M. S., Butter, E. M., Belavich, T. G., Hipp, K. M., Scott, A. B., & Kadar, J. L. (1997). Religion and spirituality: Unfuzzying the fuzzy. *Journal for the Scientific Study of Religion, 36*(4), 549–564.

Zohar, D., & Marshall, I. (2001). *SQ spiritual intelligence: The ultimate intelligence.* London: Bloomsbury.

MARY ANNE LAURI AND SANDRA SCICLUNA CALLEJA

4. PROSOCIAL BEHAVIOUR AND PSYCHOLOGICAL WELLBEING

ABSTRACT

Prosocial actions that are freely undertaken not done and expressions of well-internalised values may result in positive emotions in the actor. Various studies have found that helping behaviour such as community service and voluntary work increases psychological wellbeing, self-esteem, life satisfaction and happiness. This chapter will discuss whether the positive relation between helping and wellbeing can be supported in the Maltese context. In this study a questionnaire was administered online. It consisted of two standardised tools, one assesses prosocial behaviour using the Helping Attitude Scale (Nickell, 1998) and the other assesses wellbeing by using the Oxford Happiness Questionnaire (Hills & Argyle, 2002). Four hundred and ninety-one respondents answered the questionnaire. Relationships between prosocial behaviour and wellbeing were analysed. Age and gender were also discussed with regard to this relationship. Results support existing research and shows that there is a correlation between prosocial behaviour and wellbeing.

Keywords: prosocial, helping behaviour, care, meaning, wellbeing

INTRODUCTION

A woman was driving in front of a school and saw two 16 year old boys clearly distraught. She could see from their faces that something was wrong. She stopped and asked them whether they need any help. They told her that they had to sit for a Secondary Education Certificate (SEC) exam and had come to the wrong venue. The woman offered to take them to the right school and as a result the boys could do their exam.

How can one describe the behaviour of this woman? What motivated this woman to go out of her way to help these young teenagers? She did not know them. She did not even give them her name. She asked nothing in return and was expecting nothing. Possibly the woman felt good that she had saved the teenagers' skin. Was this altruism? Social psychologists make a distinction between prosocial behaviour and altruism. Some psychologists, while acknowledging prosocial behaviour, question the notion of altruism (Cialdini, Brown, Lewis, Luce, & Neuberg, 1997). They argue that people help other people because of some intrinsic or extrinsic reward.

Helping behaviour can be motivated by external rewards or internal self-rewards (Unger, 1979). A person may help another because the helper knows that assisting this person will or may in future translate into a reward. In accordance to Lerner's (2002) "Just World Hypothesis" some people have the irrational assumption that helpfulness to others will translate into helpfulness towards themselves. A person who donates blood is not expecting a reward but may experience a good feeling or positive emotions which in themselves are rewarding. This positive emotion, argue some researchers is still a reward and the helper is still getting something in return for his action of helping.

In his early research, Batson argued that when we helped others, our motivation was always and exclusively self-interest and he called this 'Universal Egoism' (Batson, 1998, 2008). He thought that altruism was a myth. He assumed that "everything we humans do, no matter how beneficial it may be to others, is really directed towards the ultimate goal of one or more forms of self-benefit" (p. 2). Over the years Batson recognised that his assumption was wrong. He came to believe that altruism, like egoism, were motivational states. The difference between the two, he argued, is that while egoism was a motivational state with the ultimate goal of increasing one's own welfare, altruism had the ultimate goal of increasing another person's welfare. By ultimate goal Batson meant an end in itself. He argued that prosocial behaviour could be altruistic even though some prosocial behaviour could be a subtle form of egoism (Batson, 2008). In this chapter we will be using the terms 'helping behaviour' and 'prosocial behaviour' interchangeably and will not go into the merits of whether an action was altruistic or prosocial because to do this one must know the real motivation behind the behaviour.

From a psychoanalytic standpoint, Alfred Adler calls prosocial behaviour 'Social Interest'. He says that this interest in the wellbeing of others and the desire to collaborate with others is nurtured in us in childhood by our parents, teachers and significant others. In the end it serves the function of enabling us to live collaboratively in a collective (Adler, 1927/1998). Therefore it is essential for our social order. Social interest is also an instrument by which we improve ourselves and therefore serves an egoistic function. In his description of styles of life, Adler talks about the 'Socially Useful' style of life which he considers as one of the healthiest styles of life. In Adler's theory the egoistic motivation and the altruistic are integrated.

In this debate, motivation and the voluntary nature of the action plays an important role (Weinstein & Ryan, 2010). 'Autonomous Motivation' involves helping others because the person believes that this is good. Helping actions are experienced as coming from within and congruent with one's self. They reflect one's values. Thus for an act to be termed prosocial, the person chooses to act in that way freely, out of personal choice (Weinstein & Ryan, 2010; Ryan & Connell, 1989). However 'Controlled Motivation' is a result of either self-imposed pressures such as feelings of guilt or shame or else they are a result of some form of external pressure such as the wish to please others, maintain self-esteem or even obeying orders (Deci & Ryan,

2000; Ryan & Connell, 1989). In the latter case, the act of helping may not produce a sense of satisfaction or wellbeing.

Another distinction in helping behaviour is whether helping is carried out with the intention of deriving personal benefit (exchange orientation) or whether it is characterized by less concern for immediate benefit than for the quality of the relationship and the wellbeing of the person being helped (Clark & Mills, 1993). This distinction is not always clear in the mind of the actor and is difficult for the observer to ascertain.

Helping Behaviour

The term prosocial contrasts with antisocial which applies to aggressive and violent behaviour. There are many definitions of prosocial behaviour. In this chapter, prosocial behaviour will be defined as "voluntary actions that are intended to help or benefit another individual or group of individuals" (Eisenberg & Mussen, 1989). The studies on altruism and prosocial behaviour (e.g. Bateson, Van Lange, Ahmad, & Lishner, 2003; Post, 2005; Cialdini et al., 1987, 1997) centre around the question '... do people help because they enjoy helping or care about others (altruism) or is their helping instrumental to some other goal (egoism)?' (Weinstein & Ryan, 2010, p. 225).

There are many factors that explain why people help others. Some theories focus on the personality of the helpers while others concern the situations that inspire helping. Why and when do people help?

Internal Factors

Some people are more prosocial than others. There are various reasons for this. It could be that a person has grown up in an environment where helping others is encouraged. Parental modelling and upbringing play a crucial role. If a child grows up in an environment where helping is a social norm, he or she is more likely to be helpful to others (Grube & Pilliavin, 2000; Pilliavin & Callero, 1991; Hoffman, 1981). Lauri (2009) found that family members who donate organs cite their parents' example of helpful behaviour as their main influence of their attitudes and helping behaviour. Staub (2005) showed that when children are taught to act in a helpful way, they develop values, beliefs and skills related to helping. Even the media can promote prosocial behaviours. Channels like Nickelodeon and Disney Channel show more prosocial acts than general-audience demographic channels (Wilson, 2008).

But it is not only nurture that plays a role in helpful behaviour. Psychologists believe that some people have particular personality traits which make them more helpful towards others (Penner, 2002; Rushton, Chrisjohn, & Fekken, 1981). Although psychologists have not succeeded in discovering a single personality trait that predicted helping, yet researchers are gathering clues to the "network of traits" that predispose a person to helpfulness. These include emotionality, empathy and self-efficacy (Eisenberg et al., 1991; Krueger, Hicks, & McGue, 2001; Walker & Frimer, 2007). Caprara and Steca (2005) found that self-efficacy is crucial to helping. If the person beliefs that he or she has the skills or the ability to do something to help another person, then the likelihood that he or she helps is greater.

Many studies show that there is a gender difference in prosocial behaviour citing that females tend to help more than males (George et al., 1998; McGuire, 1994). However when the type of situation or context is taken into consideration, the relationship is more complex. Social psychologists, in their studies, often used emergency situations which require physical acts of helping. In such situations men are more helpful than women and women receive more help than men (Eagly & Cowley, 1986). In studies where the context involves communal and relational prosocial behaviour, women are more helpful than men (Eagly, 2009).

External Factors Influencing Prosocial Behaviour

Among the most common theories explaining prosocial behaviour are Kin Selection, the Reciprocity Norm, Empathy-Altruism Hypothesis and Social-Exchange Theory.

Blood is thicker than water. It has been established that one is more disposed to help a member of the family or relatives (Hamilton, 1964; Meyer, 1999). This theory, known as Kin Selection, is an evolutionary concept which says that people will help others who are related to them, even at a cost to themselves, more than they will help people they do not know (Stewart-Williams, 2007). This is particularly relevant to the Mediterranean culture where the family is a very important social structure. Similarity to the person in need also influences helping behaviour. If the person identifies with the person in need, the likelihood of helping is greater. A man is more likely to help another man manoeuvring a pushchair, a baby, and a heavy shopping bag, if he had experienced that situation himself. This is referred to as the Empathy-Altruism Hypothesis.

Research has also found that residents coming from smaller or less densely populated communities are more likely to help someone who needs assistance than residents coming from densely populated towns or large cities (Amato, 1983; Hedge & Yousif, 1992). This could partly be explained by the Bystander Effect (Latane' & Darley, 1970). The more people there are in the vicinity of a person in need, the less likely the person will be helped. It seems that the presence of many people inhibits helping. The belief that others will or should take responsibility for providing assistance to a person in need could be the result of a phenomenon known as Diffusion of Responsibility. In Malta the Bystander Effect exists side by side with still strong Catholic altruistic values which implies stronger prosocial behaviour.

Another factor that influences prosocial behaviour is the person in need and the nature of the need. If the helper's attributions of the person in need and his or her predicament are considered worthy and resulting through no fault of his or her own, then helping is more probable (Higgins & Shaw, 1999). Another theory in helping behaviour is that of the Reciprocity Norm. A person helps another as a form of insurance or investment so that when in the future he or she needs help, it will be given. Doing a good deed is expected to be reciprocated in some form. It is considered as a give and take situation. The maxim seems to be that to those who help us, we should return help, not harm (Gouldner, 1960). The Social-Exchange Theory claims that when deciding whether or not to help a person we consciously, or maybe unconsciously, monitor costs and rewards. According to Piliavin (2003) subtle calculations precede decisions to help or not to help.

A different body of research depicts helping behaviour as more impulsive and spontaneous. For example listening to Michael Jackson singing 'Heal the world' made listeners more willing to pick up somebody's pencil from the ground and less likely to say harsh things about a job candidate. (Greitemeyer, 2009, 2011). Mood has also been found to be related to helping. People in a good mood, according to (Isen & Levin, 1972) are more likely to help a person in need. Even playing prosocial videogames seem to increase the likelihood of prosocial behaviour (Gentile et al., 2009). Appearances seem to influence prosocial behaviour. Persons seem to help persons in need who are attractive more than when they are unattractive (Benson, Karabenick, & Lerner, 1976).

Voluntary Work

Several studies show that people who regularly help others out of their own volition and those who do voluntary work on a regular basis are likely to experience less feelings of hopelessness (Miller, Denton, & Tobacyk, 1986), higher levels of mental health (Schwartz, Meisenhelder, Yusheng, & Reed, 2003) and less depression (e.g. Brown, Gary, Greene & Milburn, 1992; Crandell, 1975; Rietschlin, 1998; Wilson & Musick, 1999). They also experience higher levels of adjustment (Crandall & Lehman, 1977).

The voluntary nature of the work and autonomous motivation are core elements in helping behaviour. One of the questions asked by policy makers is whether prosocial behaviour can be taught. Wilson and Musick (1999) carried out many studies, some of which involved adolescents. They found that young people who are involved in voluntary work develop a higher sense of civic mindedness and may later on be involved in political life. They also claim that these adolescents are less likely to engage in antisocial behaviour. Allen et al. (1994) found that volunteer activities must be carefully designed and monitored if they are to have their desired consequence. Programs geared toward encouraging teenagers to volunteer in the expectation this might keep them out of trouble will not work if this encouragement seems to limit the voluntary nature of the work.

There are many studies on the beneficial effect of volunteering on the actor (e.g. Piliavin & Siegl, 2007; Wilson, 2000). Based on this research voluntary work has been promoted in many schools and universities. 'Mandated Volunteering' has been encouraged (Sobus, 1995) and some policy makers have advocated mandated volunteering to be a prerequisite for the forgiveness of loans and the rewarding of grants (Newman, Milton, & Stroud, 1985; Robb & Swearer, 1985). Mandated Volunteering or community work has also been imposed as part of the punishment for a crime and in obtaining parole. Such external and imposed motives for doing voluntary work have however been negatively associated with positive emotions (Finkelstein, Penner, & Brannick, 2005). In such cases helping becomes an imposition and may undermine subsequent helping behaviour (Frey, 1997; Kunda & Schwarts, 1983). The motivation for helping in this case is controlled and there is no personal choice.

Psychological Wellbeing

In the last two decades increasing importance has been given to the understanding of wellbeing and in finding out what makes individuals happy. In their review of nineteen large datasets, Dolan, Peasgood, and White (2008) found that the most common measures of personal wellbeing involved happiness and life satisfaction (Conti-Ramsden & Botting, 2008). The United Nations General Assembly in 2011 invited researchers to help guide public policies and specifically passed a resolution appealing to member countries to measure the happiness of their people. The first World Happiness Report was launched in 2012 (Helliwell, Layard, & Sachs, 2012).

Traditionally wellbeing has been viewed and measured in terms of economic constructs such as socio-economic status, salaries and GDP. However more recent surveys and international reports are widening their definition of wellbeing. Post (2005) says that wellbeing consists of feeling hopeful, happy, and good about oneself, as well as energetic and connected to others (p. 68). Diener (2000, 2006) defines subjective wellbeing is an umbrella term for the different valuations people make regarding their lives, the events happening to them, their bodies and minds, and the circumstances in which they live. Wellbeing captures different perspective of what makes a person feel good. Ryff (1989) evaluates the research on wellbeing and comes up with empirical measures of what she found to be optimal psychological functioning. She sees psychological wellbeing as having six aspects, that is, self-acceptance, good relationships, autonomy, environmental mastery, purpose in life and personal growth.

The Relation between Prosocial Behaviour and Wellbeing

More than half a century ago, Sorokin (1954/2002) in the preface of his classic 1954 treatise, said that unselfish love and altruism are necessary for physical, mental and moral health (p. xi). More recent studies show a positive relationship between wellbeing and volunteering (Piliavin & Siegel, 2007; Thoitis & Hewitt, 2001), donating money for a good cause (Frey & Meier, 2004) donating blood (Piliavin & Callero, 1991) and longevity in older adults (Dulin & Hill, 2003; Liang, Krause, & Bennett, 2001; Levin, 2000).

PROSOCIAL BEHAVIOUR AND PSYCHOLOGICAL WELLBEING

Table 4.1. Ryff's dimensions of wellbeing (adapted from Ryff, 1989)

	High	Low
Self acceptance	Possesses a positive attitude toward the self, including good and bad qualities; feels positive about past life.	Feels dissatisfied with self; is disappointed with what has occurred in past life, wishes to be different from what he or she is.
Positive relations with others	Has warm, satisfying, trusting relationships with others; is concerned about the welfare of others; capable of strong empathy, affection, and intimacy.	Has few close, trusting relationships with others; finds it difficult to be warm, open, and concerned about others; not willing to make compromises to sustain important ties with others.
Autonomy	Is self-determining and independent; able to resist social pressures to think and act in certain ways; regulates behaviour from within.	Is concerned about the expectations and evaluations of others; relies on judgments of others to make important decisions; conforms to social pressures.
Environmental mastery	Has a sense of mastery and competence in managing the environment; makes effective use of surrounding opportunities; able to choose or create contexts suitable to personal needs and values.	Has difficulty managing everyday affairs; feels unable to change or improve surrounding context; is unaware of surrounding opportunities; lacks sense of control over external world.
Purpose in life	Has goals in life and a sense of directedness; feels there is meaning to present and past life; holds beliefs that give life purpose; has aims and objectives for living.	Lacks a sense of meaning in life; has few goals or aims, lacks sense of direction; does not see purpose of past life; has no outlook or beliefs that give life meaning.
Personal growth	Sees self as growing and expanding; is open to new experiences; has sense of realizing his or her potential; changes in ways that reflect more self knowledge and effectiveness.	Lacks sense of improvement or expansion over time; feels bored and uninterested with life; feels unable to develop new attitudes or behaviours.

The examples of helping behaviour mentioned above are validated and recommended by many religions. Ellison (1991) argued that religious certainty has a positive influence on wellbeing. Frederickson (2003) found that 'helpful compassionate acts' allow people to feel good about themselves and also about

53

others. She also found that positive emotions increased psychological as well as physical resilience and interpreted this as a result of the 'undoing' of negative emotions that are physically harmful. It is difficult to be angry, resentful or anxious when one is helping somebody in need (Anderson, 2003). He argues that love of humanity and affirmation of others encourages altruism giving rise to wellbeing, and in so doing pushing aside negative emotions such as sadness/depression, fear/anxiety and anger/hostility (p. 243).

There are several models which explain the positive relationship between prosocial behaviour and wellbeing. Maybe one of the most relevant is Evolutionary Theory. Group selection theory proposes that altruism between groups is a powerful adaptation for group survival. Helping and altruistic behaviour within groups confers a competitive advantage and gives the members of the group a greater chance of survival (Sober & Wilson, 1998). Anthropologists who studied early egalitarian societies found that they practice 'Ecological Altruism' where helping is a social norm. Some contemporary cultures seem to have abandoned this practice with the result of loss of social capital (Putnam, 2001).

The relation between helping behaviour and happiness seems to be supported by a growing body of biological research. Functional magnetic resonance imaging (fMRI) evidence shows that a prosocial actions such as giving money to charity leads to similar brain activity in regions implicated in the experience of pleasure and reward (Anik, Aknin, Norton, & Dunn, 2009, p. 8). They refer to the study conducted by Harbaugh, Mayr, and Burghart (2007) in which neural activity was recorded while participants decided how to split a one-hundred dollar sum between themselves and a local food bank. Results showed that the decision to give the original one-hundred dollar sum to the food bank rather than take part of the money themselves, led to activation in the ventral striatum, a brain region associated with a range of rewarding stimuli, from cocaine to art to attractive faces (Aharon et al., 2001; Vartanian & Goel, 2004; Elliott, Friston, & Dolan, 2000). Other studies show that helping others can produce neurotransmitters such as oxytocin which is also produced during pleasurable experiences. Luks (1988) said that helping can give the helper a sense of wellbeing which is sometimes known as 'Helper's High'. This can be 'addictive' (van der Linden, 2011; Keltner, Kogan, Piff, & Saturn, 2014). These results suggest that helping others is inherently rewarding.

Most of the research cited above regarding the relationship between prosocial behaviour and happiness are mostly correlational and there are few experimental studies. It is difficult to make a strong claim that helping behaviour makes people happy. However a positive relationship between the two can be ascertained. Moreover it is likely that these may operate in a circular fashion (Anik et al., 2009).

METHODOLOGY

The research question being addressed in this chapter is whether there is a relationship between prosocial behaviour and wellbeing. Data were collected by an online survey using QuestionPro. The survey was made up of two standardised questionnaires. One was the Helping Attitude Scale (HAS) by Nickell (1998). This questionnaire measured prosocial behaviour and attitudes towards helping. The other questionnaire was the Oxford Happiness Scale (OHS) by Hills and Argyle (2002). This measured happiness and psychological wellbeing. The title of the questionnaires were not given to the participants in order to avoid revealing what is being measured and in so doing decreasing demand characteristics and bias. Participants were told that the survey was a study about attitudes towards happiness and wellbeing. The link to a survey was sent to 1500 persons who had communicated with the University of Malta through the first researcher's contacts. Of these, 491 participants responded giving a response rate of 32.7%. There were 53 participants who started answering the questionnaire but did not submit while another 25 submitted incomplete questionnaires which were discarded. Non-Maltese participants were not included in the analysis. It was both a convenience sample and a volunteer sample. The age range was between 15 and 87 (M= 30, SD= 15.4). In the sample, 31.7% were male, 63.1% were female while 5.2% did not answer this question. Respondents were Maltese people coming from over 36 towns and villages. Participants were informed that the questionnaire was anonymous and that they could choose to terminate their participation at any point. Ethical clearance for this study was given by the University Research Ethics Committee (UREC).

RESULTS

Correlation between Total Scores on Prosocial Behaviour and Wellbeing

Prosocial behaviour and attitudes towards helping was measured by the Helping Attitudes Scale (HAS) by Nickell (1998). The scale, consisting of 20 items, (alpha =0.879) was very reliable. The mean score on prosocial behaviour was 4.74, (SD=0.65). Happiness and wellbeing was measured through the Oxford Happiness Scale (Hills & Argyle, 2002). The scale, consisting of 29 items, (alpha=0.065), was very reliable. The mean wellbeing score for the whole sample was 3.72, (SD=0.56).

There was a very significant correlation between the scores on prosocial behaviour and wellbeing (r=0.43, p<0.0005), implying that people who have positive attitudes towards prosocial behaviour and who were helpful are more happy and have a greater sense of wellbeing.

Gender and Age Differences on Total Helping Score

Results show that in this sample, females (n=254) are more helpful than males (n=128). The average score for males is 4.6 (SE=0.06) while average score for females was 4.8 (SE=0.04). An Independent Samples T-Test showed that the difference is statistically significant (t=2.78, df=223, p=0.006). The 95% confidence interval of the difference in the helping score between males and females was (0.06, 0.35).

There was a correlation with age, with younger participants being less helpful. The Pearson Correlation Coefficient was significant but low (r=0.12, p=0.017).

Attitudes towards Helping

Four specific areas were selected from the HAS for further analysis. These items were of particular interest because of other research that is being conducted on the topics. These four items were (i) whether participants agree that helping attitudes should be taught, (ii) attitudes towards organ donation, (iii) attitudes towards voluntary work and (iv) intrinsic reward associated with helping others.

Teaching prosocial behaviour. One of the items in the HAS was 'Children should be taught about the importance of helping others'. The respondents strongly agreed that children should be taught about the importance of helping others. The mean score on a range from 1 to 6 is 5.76 (SD=0.71). There was no correlation with age but there was a significant correlation with gender. Males had a mean score of 5.65 (SE=0.08) while females had a mean score of 5.82 (SE=0.04). A t-test carried out on these results show a significant difference (t=1.963, df=192.6, p=0.05). The 95% confidence interval of the difference between means is between 0.00–0.34.

Organ donation. Another item in the HAS was 'I plan to donate my organs when I die with the hope that they help someone else live'. The average score for this item was 4.84 on a scale from 1–6, with a standard deviation of 1.49. The results show that 17.1% of the sample disagreed with this statement while 48.7% strongly agreed and 19.7% moderately agreed. There was no correlation with age and no gender differences. There was however a significant correlation between planning to donate one's organs and wellbeing (r=0.13, p=0.01).

Voluntary work. In the questionnaire there were two items on voluntary work. One item was 'Volunteering to help someone is rewarding' and the other is 'Doing Voluntary work makes me feel happy'. The two items were recoded into one and the mean score was found to be 5.01 (SD=1.15). There was no significant correlation between the compounded score and age. A t-test was carried out to find whether there were gender differences. The results (t=3.59, df=218.8, p < 0.0005) gave a highly significant difference between males (mean score = 4.75, SE= 0.11) and females (mean score = 5.22, SE = 0.07). The 95 confidence interval of the difference of the means between males and females is (0.21, 0.72). The correlation between the score on voluntary work and score on happiness and wellbeing is positive and significant (r=0.33, p<0.0005).

Intrinsic reward. Literature on helping behaviour is divided on the question of altruism, arguing that even when the person does not receive an extrinsic reward for helping, the person still feels good. Researchers consider this feeling as being an intrinsic reward. Three items tapped into this, one being 'It feels wonderful to assist others in need' another 'I feel at peace with myself when I have helped others' and a third is 'I feel proud when I know my generosity has helped a needy person'.

The computed mean score for this variable, intrinsic reward, is 5.29 (SD = 0.9. There was no correlation between age and intrinsic reward however there was a significant difference between males and females. The mean score for females (n=250) was 5.49 with SE = 0.05, while the mean score for males (n=126) was 5.1 with SE=0.09. The t-test for these scores was significant at the 0.02 level (t=3.2, df=2.08). The 95% confidence interval of the difference between means for males and females was (0.12, 0.52)

Age and Gender Differences on Wellbeing Score

There was no significant difference in the average score on happiness of males and females. However there was a significant correlation between happiness and age ($r=0.31$, $p<0.0005$). Young participants had lower scores for happiness than older ones. The literature on wellbeing has found that at least two constructs are important factors of happiness and wellbeing, these being (i) having a purpose and meaning in life and (ii) having a positive outlook on life.

Having a sense of meaning and purpose in life. Having a sense of meaning and purpose in life was computed from two items of the questionnaire. The first was 'I feel life is very rewarding' and the second was the reverse of 'I don't have a particular sense of meaning and purpose in life'. The average score for the sample was 4.46, SD=1.17. The results show that there is a significant positive correlation between age and having a purpose in life and finding life rewarding ($r=0.22$, $p<0.0005$). There are no significant gender differences in these scores.

Positive outlook on life. Having a positive outlook on life is an essential characteristic of feeling happy. Three items tapped into this construct. This score was computed from these three items 'Life is good', 'I am very happy' and 'I find beauty in things'. The mean computed score of these three items is 4.43 (SD=0.75). There was a correlation between this composite score and age ($r=0.50$, $p<0.0005$). The older people tend to see life in a more positive light than the younger ones. There is also a significant difference (t=3.66, df=234, $p<0.0005$) between the average score of males (m=4.63, SE=0.07) and that of females (m=4.32, SE=0.05). The 95% confidence interval of the difference between means is 0.14, 0.47.

DISCUSSION

The results incontrovertibly confirm the positive relationship between prosocial behaviour and wellbeing. Gender effects appear to operate more than age effects when it comes to attitudes toward wellbeing and prosocial behaviour. However, the effects of age predominate in the indicators of wellbeing. Older participants have a more positive outlook on life. This comes as no surprise in a country with a cultural heritage of centuries of staunch Catholicism and a close knit, family based community. Despite the move of the culture towards more individualism and materialism, helping is considered a central virtue especially by older people. Maltese people are renowned for the hospitality they show foreigners which, when not remunerated, is a form of prosocial behaviour. In addition, social order and harmony and hence prosocial behaviour is especially important in a dense population where persons are constantly knocking elbows. Therefore one can argue that prosocial behaviour is an important component of Maltese identity.

The effects of gender show that females are more helpful than males. Their attitudes towards the promotion of helping behaviour and voluntary work is more positive than that of males. Females also perceive more intrinsic reward in helping. Yet males report having a more positive outlook on life than females. There are various implications here.

The higher female scores support Carol Gilligan's Ethic of Care (1993). From a young age women are socialised to be carers and their morality is coloured by considering the needs of others. Despite the blurring of gender roles that has occurred in the past few decades, caring and nurturance is still the recognised domain of women. So when it comes to the attitudes in the study, women are more likely to perceive the necessity of teaching prosocial behaviour and to value voluntary work. From a young age they are exposed to prosocial behaviour by seeing their mothers, more than their fathers, act in a prosocial manner.

This is not to say that males and fathers do not act in a prosocial manner. However this behaviour in males conflicts with the social dictate of career advancement and breadwinning. This could explain why the attitudes examined in the study are also significantly present in males but to a lesser degree.

The higher male scores on positive outlook on life, combined with relatively lower scores on prosocial attitudes suggest that there are other factors besides prosocial behaviour contributing to a positive outlook. Indeed one may also argue that being prosocial also involves opening oneself up empathically to the suffering of others, for example, picking up an older adult's bag in the street brings one in close contact with the weakness and decline of the person. This may affect positive outlook. Age probably contributes towards a positive outlook that takes pain and negativity into account and is therefore more realistic.

When one considers age effects it is surprising that the attitude towards prosocial and helping behaviour are not stronger in light of the literature mentioned above, namely Erikson's (1964) concept of Generativity and the engagement of older adults in voluntary work. One possible explanation could be that with age there is a greater degree of equanimity and realism. Specifically, while the elderly retain firm convictions, their espousal of issues does not contain the passionate intensity of younger persons, and they are more likely to see the other side of the issue, making their judgements less extreme.

Though attitude scores are not distinctive, age clearly is positively correlated with happiness and wellbeing. This corresponds with the literature. Again the implication is that there are other factors besides prosocial behaviour contribute to wellbeing, for instance Ryff's (1989) six aspects of social wellbeing mentioned above.

The attitude towards organ donation merits an individual comment since there were no age or gender effects. One possible explanation for this could be that this taps a different form of prosocial behaviour than the other attitudes: a form of prosociality that is fuelled by a civic duty rather than an emotional urge. This is justifiable in light of the fact that it triggers the unpleasant thought of one's death so the prosocial cognitions are operating automatically and impersonally to defend against the painful imagining of their dead body. Ultimately pro-social behaviour needs to serve the needs of the self.

Limitations

The fact that the survey was online in a university context and that there was a voluntary aspect to it suggests that (a) the sample was most likely more educated, and (b) answering the questionnaire was a prosocial act in itself and the much higher proportion of female respondents support the gender effect in the results.

Moreover, prosocial behaviour needs to be perceived in the wider context of wellbeing. While it contributes significantly, it is one of numerous factors associated with wellbeing. Indeed, the opposite scenario, that prosocial behaviour actually diminishes wellbeing is also a possibility, for example in co-dependent or dependent persons. This relationship needs to be explored further. There is a darker side to pro-social behaviour that runs the risk of being ignored. There have been instances where dedicated persons of trust, in positions of human helping, abused their position for their own ends and created distress or suffering in the very persons they were supposed to help. Pro-social behaviour can be an effective camouflage for abuse. Couched in the guise of altruism, this is a subtle form of exploitation that is difficult to identify and control. Frequently, only the victims perceive this side of the helper and other persons react with disbelief. This phenomenon would not have been captured in this research and could be considered a limitation. The belief that pro-social behaviour results from a generous, altruistic spirit can blind us to a fuller understanding of this phenomenon and needs to be researched for a holistic understanding of pro-social behaviour.

CONCLUSION

Richard Dawkins (1976), the author of the Selfish Gene said 'let us try to teach generosity and altruism because we are born selfish. Let us understand what our selfish genes are up to, because we may then at least have the chance to upset their designs, something no other species has ever aspired to' (p. 3). Yet, we find many examples of altruism and prosocial behaviour in real life. Mother Theresa who worked tirelessly to make people's lives better said that nothing makes you happier than when you reach out to help those in need. Even if Dawkins is right and we are born selfish, a claim to be researched further, we can still nurture helping behaviour. Research supports the association between prosocial behaviour and wellbeing. The question of whether there is a causal relationship between the two remains largely unanswered. It may be the case that helping and wellbeing operate in a circular fashion. More research in psychology and neuroscience can shed light on this question and the findings can inform policy making in the area of wellbeing.

ACKNOWLEDGEMENTS

This study was made possible by bursary PSYRP07-17 – University of Malta.

We would like to thank Mr Chris Baldacchino for his valuable help when writing this chapter.

REFERENCES

Adler, A. (1998). *Understanding human nature*. Centre City, MN: Hazelden. (Original work published in 1927)

Aharon, I., Etcoff, N., Ariely, D., Chabris, C. F., O'Connor. E., & Breiter, H. C. (2001). Beautiful faces have variable reward value: fMRI and behavioral evidence. *Neuron, 32*(3), 537–551.

Allen, J. P., Kuperminc, G., Philliber, S., & Herre, K. (1994). Programmatic prevention of adolescent problem behaviors: The role of autonomy, relatedness, and volunteer service in the teen outreach program. *American Journal of Community Psychology, 22*(5), 617–638.

Amato, P. R. (1983). Helping behaviour in urban and rural environments: Field studies based on a taxonomic organization of helping episodes. *Journal of Personality and Social Psychology, 45*(3), 571–586.

Anderson, N. B. (2003). *Emotional longevity: What really determines how long you live*. New York, NY: Viking.

Anik, L., Aknin, L. B., Norton, M. I., & Dunn, E. W. (2009). *Feeling good about giving: The benefits (and costs) of self-interested charitable behaviour* (Unpublished manuscript). Harvard Business School.

Batson, C. D. (1998). Altruism and prosocial behaviour. In T. Gillert, S. T. Fiske, & G. Lindzey (Eds.), *The handbook of social psychology* (4th ed., pp. 282–316). New York, NY: Oxford University Press.

Batson, C. D. (2008, March). *Empathy-induced altruistic motivation*. Draft lecture/chapter for the 2008 Symposium on prosocial motives and behaviour. Retrieved April 8, 2017, from http://portal.idc.ac.il/en/symposium/herzliyasymposium/documents/dcbatson.pdf

Batson, C. D., Van Lange, P. A. M., Ahmad, N., & Lishner, D. A. (2003). Altruism and helping behaviour. In M. A. Hogg & J. Cooper (Eds.), *Sage handbook of social psychology* (pp. 279–295). London: Sage Publications.

Benson, P. L., Karabenick, S. A., & Lerner, R. M. (1976). Pretty pleases: The effects of physical attractiveness, race, and sex on receiving help. *Journal of Experimental Social Psychology, 12*(5), 409–415.

Brown, D. R., Gary, L. E., Greene, A. D., & Milburn, N. G. (1992). Patterns of social affiliation as predictors of depressive symptoms among urban blacks. *Journal of Health and Social Behavior, 33*(3), 242–253.

Caprara, G. V., & Steca, P. (2005). Self-efficacy beliefs as determinants of prosocial behavior conducive to life satisfaction across ages. *Journal of Social and Clinical Psychology, 24*(2), 191–217.

Cialdini, R. B., Brown, S. L., Lewis, B. P., Luce, C., & Neuberg, S. L. (1997). Reinterpreting the empathy-altruism relationship: When one into one equals oneness. *Journal of Personality and Social Psychology, 73*(3), 481–494.

Cialdini, R. B., Schaller, M., Houlihan, D., Arps, K., Fultz, J., & Beaman, A. L. (1987). Empathy-based helping: Is it selflessly or selfishly motivated? *Journal of Personality and Social Psychology, 52*(4), 749–758.

Clark, M. S., & Mills, J. (1993). The difference between communal and exchange relationships: What is and what is not. *Personality and Social Psychology Bulletin, 19*(6), 684–691.

Conti-Ramsden, G., & Botting, N. (2008). Emotional health in adolescents with and without a history of Specific Language Impairment (SLI). *Journal of Child Psychology and Psychiatry, 49*(5), 516–525.

Crandall, J. E. (1975). A scale for social interest. *Journal of Individualistic Psychology, 31*(2), 187–195.

Crandall, J. E., & Lehman, R. E. (1977). Relationship of stressful life events to social interest, locus of control and psychological adjustment. *Journal of Consulting and Clinical Psychology, 45*(6), 1208.

Dawkins, R. (1976). *The selfish gene*. New York, NY: Oxford University Press.

Deci, E. L., & Ryan, R. M. (2000). The "what" and "why" of goal pursuits: Human needs and the self-determination of behavior. *Psychological Inquiry, 11*(4), 227–268.

Diener, E. (2000). Subjective wellbeing: The science of happiness, and a proposal for a national index. *American Psychologist, 55*(1), 34–43.

Diener, E. (2006). Guidelines for national indicators of subjective wellbeing and ill-being. *Applied Research in Quality of Life, 1*(2), 151–157.

Dolan, P., Peasgood, T., & White, M. (2008). Do we really know what makes us happy? A review of the economic literature or the factors associated with subjective wellbeing. *Journal of Economic Psychology, 29*(1), 94–122.

Dulin, P. L., & Hill, R. (2003). Relationships between altruistic activity and positive and negative affect among low-income older adult service providers. *Aging & Mental Health, 7*(4), 294–299.

Eagly, A. H. (2009). The his and hers of prosocial behaviour: An examination of the social psychology of gender. *American Psychologist, 64*(8), 644–658.

Eagly, A. H., & Crowley, M. (1986). Gender and helping behavior: A meta-analytic review of the social psychological literature. *Psychological Bulletin, 100*(3), 283–308.

Eisenberg, N., Fabes, R. A., Schaller, M., Miller, P., Carlo, G., Poulin, R., ... Shell, R. (1991). Personality and socialization correlates of vicarious emotional responding. *Journal of Personality and Social Psychology, 61*(3), 459–470.

Eisenberg, N., & Mussen, P. H. (1989). *The roots of prosocial behaviour in children*. Cambridge: Cambridge University Press.

Elliott, R., Friston, K. J., & Dolan, R. J. (2000). Dissociable neural responses in human reward systems. *The Journal of Neuroscience, 20*(16), 6159–6165.

Ellison, C. (1991). Religious involvement and subjective wellbeing. *Journal of Health and Social Behavior, 32*(1), 80–99.

Erikson, E. H. (1964). *Insight and responsibility*. New York, NY: Norton.

Finkelstein, M. A., Penner, L. A., & Brannick, M. T. (2005). Motive, role identity, and prosocial personality as predictors of volunteer activity. *Social Behavior and Personality, 33*(4), 403–418.

Fredrickson, B. L. (2003). The value of positive emotions: The emerging science of positive psychology is coming to understand why it's good to feel good. *American Scientist, 91*(4), 330–335.

Frey, B. S. (1997). *Not just for the money: An economic theory of personal motivation*. Cheltenham: Elgar.

Frey, B. S., & Meier, S. (2004). Prosocial behavior in a natural setting. *Journal of Economic Behavior & Organization, 54*(1), 65–88.

Gentile, D. A., Anderson, C. A., Yukawa, S., Ihori N., Slaeem, M., Ming, L. K., ... Sakamoto, A. (2009). The effects of prosocial video games on prosocial behaviour: International evidence from correlational, longitudinal and experimental studies. *Personality and Social Psychology Bulletin, 35*(6), 752–763.

George, D. M., Carroll, P., Kersnick, R., & Calderon, K. (1998). Gender-related patterns of helping among friends. *Psychology of Women Quarterly, 22*(4), 685–704.

Gilligan, C. (1993). *In a different voice: Psychological theory and women's development*. Cambridge, MA: Harvard University Press.

Gouldner, A. W. (1960). The norm of reciprocity: A preliminary statement. *American Sociological Review, 25*(2), 161–178.

Greitemeyer, T. (2009). Effects of songs with prosocial lyrics on prosocial thoughts, affect, and behaviour. *Journal of Experimental Social Psychology, 45*(1), 186–190.

Greitemeyer, T. (2011). Effects of prosocial media on social behaviour: When and why does media exposure affect helping and aggression. *Current Directions in Psychological Science, 20*(4), 251–255.

Grube, J. A., & Piliavin, J. A. (2000). Role identity, organizational experiences and volunteer performance. *Personality and Social Psychology Bulletin, 26*(9), 1108–1119.

Hamilton, W. D. (1964). The genetical evolution of social behaviour: I and II. *Journal of Theoretical Biology, 7*(1), 1–52.

Harbaugh, W. T., Myer, U., & Burghart, D. R. (2007). Neural responses to taxation and voluntary giving reveal motives for charitable donations. *Science, 316*(5831), 1622–1625.

Hedge, A., & Yousif, Y. H. (1992). Effects of urban size, urgency, and cost on helpfulness: A cross-cultural comparison between the United Kingdom and the Sudan. *Journal of Cross Cultural Psychology, 23*(1), 107–115.

Helliwell, J., Layard, R., & Sachs, J. (Eds.). (2012). *World happiness report.* New York, NY: Columbia University, The Earth Institute.

Higgins, N. C., & Shaw, J. K. (1999). Attributional style moderates the impact of causal controllability information on helping behaviour. *Social Behavior and Personality, 27*(3), 221–236.

Hills, P., & Argyle, M. (2002). The oxford happiness questionnaire: A compact scale for the measurement of psychological wellbeing. *Personality and Individual Differences, 33*(7), 1073–1082.

Hoffman, M. L. (1981). Is altruism part of human nature? *Journal of Personality and Social Psychology, 40*(1), 121–137.

Isen, A. M., & Levin, P. F. (1972). Effect of feeling good on helping: Cookies and kindness. *Journal of Personality and Social Psychology, 21*(3), 384–388.

Keltner, D., Kogan, A., Piff, P. K., & Saturn, S. R. (2014). The Sociocultural Appraisals, Values and Emotions (SAVE) framework of prosociality: Core processes from gene to meme. *Annual Review of Psychology, 65*, 425–460.

Krueger, R. F., Hicks, B. M., & McGue, M. (2001). Altruism and antisocial behavior: Independent tendencies, unique personality correlates, distinct etiologies. *Psychological Science, 12*(5), 397–402.

Kunda, Z., & Schwartz, S. H. (1983). Undermining intrinsic moral motivation: External reward and self-presentation. *Journal of Personality and Social Psychology, 45*(4), 763–771.

Latane, B., & Darley, J. M. (1970). *The unresponsive bystander: Why doesn't he help?* New York, NY: Appleton-Century-Crofts.

Lauri, M. A. (2009). Metaphors of organ donation, serial representations of the body and the opt-out system. *British Journal of Health Psychology, 14*(4), 647–666.

Lerner, M. (2002). Pursuing the justice motive. In D. T. Miller & M. Ross (Eds.), *The justice motive in everyday life* (pp. 10–40). Cambridge: Cambridge University Press.

Levin, J. (2000). A prolegomenon to an epidemiology of love: Theory, measurement, and health outcomes. *Journal of Social and Clinical Psychology, 19*(1), 117–136.

Liang J., Krause, N. M., & Bennett, J. M. (2001). Social exchange and wellbeing: Is giving better than receiving? *Psychology & Aging, 16*(3), 511–523.

Luks, A. (1988). Helper's high: Volunteering makes people feel good, physically and emotionally. And like "runner's calm", it's probably good for your health. *Psychology Today, 22*(10), 34–42.

McGuire, A. M. (1994). Helping behaviors in the natural environment: Dimensions and correlates of helping. *Personality and Social Psychology Bulletin, 20*(1), 45–56.

Meyer, P. (1999). The sociobiology of human cooperation: The interplay of ultimate and proximate causes. In J. M. G. van der Dennen, D. Smillie, & D. R. Wilson (Eds.), *The darwinian heritage and sociobiology: Human evolution, behaviour, and intelligence* (pp. 49–65). Westport, CT: Praeger Publishers.

Miller, M. J., Denton, G. O., & Tobacyk, J. J. (1986). Social interest and feelings of hopelessness among elderly patients. *Psychological Reports, 58*(2), 410.

Newman, F., Milton, C., & Stroud, S. (1985). Community service and higher education: Obligations and opportunities. *American Association of Higher Education Bulletin, 37*(10), 9–13.

Nickell, G. (1998, August). *The helping attitudes scale.* Paper presented at the 106th Annual Convention of the American Psychological Association, San Francisco, CA.

Penner, L. A. (2002). Dispositional and organizational influences on sustained volunteerism: An interactionist perspective. *Journal of Social Issues, 58*(3), 447–467.

Piliavin, J. A. (2003). Doing well by doing good: Benefits for the benefactor. In C. L. M. Keyes & J. Haidt (Eds.), *Flourishing: Positive psychology and the life well lived* (pp. 227–247). Washington, DC: American Psychological Association.

Piliavin, J. A., & Callero, P. L. (1991). *Giving blood: The development of an altruistic identity*. Baltimore, MD: Johns Hopkins University Press.

Piliavin, J. A., & Siegl, E. (2007). Health benefits of volunteering in the Wisconsin longitudinal study. *Journal of Health and Social Behavior, 48*(4), 450–464.

Post, S. G. (2005). Altruism, happiness, and health: It's good to be good. *International Journal of Behavioral Medicine, 12*(2), 66–77.

Putnam, R. D. (2001). *Bowling alone: The collapse and revival of American culture*. New York, NY: Simon & Schuster.

Rietschlin, J. (1998). Voluntary association membership and psychological distress. *Journal of Health and Social Behavior, 39*(4), 348–355.

Robb, C., & Swearer, H. (1985). Community service and higher education: A national agenda. *American Association for Higher Education Bulletin, 37*(10), 3–8.

Rushton, J. P., Chrisjohn, R. D., & Fekken, G. C. (1981). The altruistic personality and the self-report altruism scale. *Personality and Individual Differences, 2*(4), 293–302.

Ryan, R. M., & Connell, J. P. (1989). Perceived locus of causality and internalization. *Journal of Personality and Social Psychology, 57*(5), 749–761.

Ryff, C. D. (1989). Happiness is everything, or is it? Explorations on the meaning of psychological wellbeing. *Journal of Personality and Social Psychology, 57*(6), 1069–1081.

Schwartz, C., Meisenhelder, J. B., Ma, Y., & Reed, G. (2003). Altruistic social interest behaviors are associated with better mental health. *Psychosomatic Medicine, 65*(5), 778–785.

Sober, E., & Wilson, D. S. (1998). *Unto others: The evolution and psychology of unselfish behavior*. Cambridge, MA: Harvard University Press.

Sobus, M. S. (1995). Mandating community service: Psychological implications of requiring prosocial behavior. *Law and Psychological Review, 19*, 153–182.

Sorokin, P. A. (2002). *The ways and power of love: Types, factors, and techniques of moral transformation*. Philadelphia, PA: Templeton Press. (Original work published in 1954)

Stewart-Williams, S. (2007). Altruism among kin vs nonkin: Effects of cost of help and reciprocal exchange. *Evolution and Human Behaviour, 28*(3), 193–198.

Straub, E. (2005). The roots of goodness: The fulfilment of basic human needs and the development of caring, helping and non-aggression, inclusive caring, moral courage, active bystandership, and altruism born of suffering. In G. Carlo & C. P. Edwards (Eds.), *Moral motivation through the lifespan* (pp. 34–72). Lincoln, NE: University of Nebraska Press.

Thoits, P. A., & Hewitt, L. N. (2001). Volunteer work and wellbeing. *Journal of Health and Social Behavior, 42*(2), 115–131.

Unger, R. K. (1979, April). *Whom does helping help?* Paper presented at the Eastern Psychological Association Convention.

Van der Linden, S. (2011). Charitable intent: A moral or social construct? A revised theory of planned behavior model. *Current Psychology, 30*(4), 355–374.

Vartanian, O., & Goel, V. (2004). Neuroanatomical correlates of aesthetic preference for paintings. *Neuroreport, 15*(5), 893–897.

Walker, L. J., & Frimer, J. A. (2007). Moral personality of brave and caring exemplars. *Journal of Personality & Social Psychology, 93*(5), 845–860.

Weinstein, N., & Ryan, R. M. (2010). When helping helps: Autonomous motivation for prosocial behavior and its influence on wellbeing for the helper and recipient. *Journal of Personality and Social Psychology, 98*(2), 222–244.

Wilson, B. J. (2000). Volunteering. *Annual Review of Sociology, 26*, 215–240.

Wilson, B. J. (2008). Media and children's aggression, fear and altruism. *The Future of Children, 18*(1), 87–118.

Wilson, B. J., & Musick, M. (1999). The effects of volunteering on the volunteer. *Law and Contemporary Problems, 62*(4), 141–168.

CLARISSA SAMMUT SCERRI, INGRID GRECH LANFRANCO
AND ANGELA ABELA

5. FAMILY WELLBEING

A Look at Maltese Families

ABSTRACT

Family wellbeing is looked at as a multi-dimensional concept comprising the physical, social, economic and psychological wellbeing. These different elements in families are dynamic in nature and are in turn also shaped by social, economic, political and psychological processes in society. Local research indicates that similar to other countries in the world, heterogeneity in Maltese couple relationships is the mark of the 21st century. What seems to be constant however, is that being in a warm and supportive couple relationship is associated with the highest level of life satisfaction. This also applies to parent-child relationships. Income adequacy is discussed as a major predictor of life satisfaction. Other major wellbeing concerns include public health issues such as obesity, alcohol consumption and the high incidence of circulatory diseases. Finally worry over poor air quality also has an important influence on Maltese families' wellbeing.

Keywords: family, systemic theory, attachment, couple relationship, wellbeing

INTRODUCTION

We are in the midst of great global cultural, economic and social changes which impact couple and family relationships (Abela & Walker, 2014). Malta is no exception to these changes. We are moving towards an egalitarian view of relationships between the sexes. In our society, complexity has increased in respect of living arrangements other than marriage. There is greater disconnection between marriage and procreation, and we live in a context where populations are no longer stationary. These social shifts bring forth other realities including those associated with an aging population, a decrease in fertility and a low birth rate, the challenge of immigrants' integration and adaptation to different cultures, and a critical stance towards all forms of authority including civic and religious institutions. Many of these changes are attributed to our entry into the second demographic transition (Abela 2016; Lesthaeghe, 2014).

DEFINING FAMILY WELLBEING

The concept of family wellbeing is not a term with a precise meaning (Fahey, Keilthy, & Polek, 2012). It can refer to the quality of life of a particular family unit or to the wellbeing of the individuals that make a family, or else to the wellbeing of "the family" in society as a whole. Despite the different definitions in the literature, there seems to be agreement that family wellbeing is a multidimensional concept which should be looked at from different perspectives, namely, the physical, social, economic and psychological (Woolny, Apps, & Henricson, 2010). In addition, scholars look at wellbeing as arising from a complex and dynamic interaction between various factors in individual family members' lives. These interactions are in turn shaped by social, economic, political and psychological processes in society (McGregor, 2006).

A review of the relevant literature by Wollny et al. (2010) also shows that the concept of wellbeing is sometimes used interchangeably with the concept of quality of life or life satisfaction. Again, the definition of quality of life/life satisfaction seems to vary according to specific research purposes and contexts but there seems to be agreement that like the concept of wellbeing, quality of life/life satisfaction can be understood by looking at multidimensional domains such as intimate relationships, economic wellbeing, health, education, housing, the environment the enjoyment of human rights and governance (Eurostat, 2015).

This chapter will review the general wellbeing of Maltese families by considering local research that has looked at the quality of life of families by studying the quality of relationships among family members, namely the couple relationships and the relationships between parents and children. Economic wellbeing will be considered as central to family wellbeing and will include the impact of poverty on children's wellbeing. The health condition enjoyed by family members and the natural environment and its impact on family wellbeing will also be discussed.

CONCEPTUAL FRAMEWORK

Systemic Framework

The systemic framework emphasises the interpersonal relationships between the family members and the interdependance of these relationships. In this respect, relationship quality within families defines to a large extent the wellbeing of the individuals that form part of it. A family can be looked at as being composed of distinct sub-systems such as the parental sub-system, the parent-child system and the sibling sub-system. Each subsystem continually influences and is influenced by the other sub-system in a circular and bi-directional manner. For example, if parents are particularly stressed, their effectiveness as parents within the family may diminish, and this in turn impacts the children who may react negatively to inconsistencies experienced through their parents' ineffective parenting. The children's reaction in turn elicits a particular response from the parents, creating a bidirectional relationship and a dynamic that may at times be harmful to the overall wellbeing of the family (Davis, Schoppe-Sullivan, Mangelsdorf, & Brown, 2009). Such a process is one which inevitably sheds light on a diversity of difficulties within families and helps us to understand the systemic nature of particular situations within the home.

Relationship quality within families also defines to a large extent the wellbeing of the individuals that form part of it. Research shows that the presence of warm interpersonal relationships within families is an important prerequisite of good health amongst the family members. The opposite is also true – when stressful interactions and relationship quality in the family are present, the health and wellbeing of individuals is not only compromised but also eroded (Kravchenko, Stickley, & Koyanagi, 2015). Moreover, research shows that when the relationship quality between a couple is poor, it inevitably spills over onto the parenting relationship and compromises it. This in turn impacts upon the wellbeing of the children as well as the adults themselves (Amato & Afifi, 2006; Belsky, Hsieh, & Crnic, 1998, Casaneuva, Martin, Runyan, Barth, & Bradley, 2008).

A key concept in systemic theory is that in looking at a family as a system, we look at patterns and processes of interactions between parts of the system. This is known as circular causation, and helps one make make sense of relationships and relationship difficulties. It also means that one no longer speaks of linear causation, where A causes B, but looks instead at patterns and processes. This also implies that problems and 'pathologies' are seen as interpersonal in nature rather than emanating from the individual.

One positive aspect of an interpersonal perspective is that family members are not seen as being determined solely by their past experiences and/or by their genes as psychodynamic and/or biological theories would imply. There is also room for resilience and change in the context of safe and supportive relationships (Vetere, 2013). Resilience is here being defined as "a dynamic process encompassing positive adaptations within the context of significant adversity" (Luthar, Cicchetti, & Becker, 2000, p. 543). Accordingly, resilience is neither a trait or quality of an individual but rather a complex interplay between genetic and environmental influences (Rutter, 1999, 2007).

An Attachment Framework

Relationships, by their very nature, require connections to happen, and this can be understood particularly within the context of attachment. Building healthy secure attachments set the foundations for better quality relationships. From the moment an infant is born and throughout the course of his or her life, attaching or forming connections with others is necessary to thrive and remain healthy. Bowlby (1979) states that attachment is not only important at the beginning of life, but is a process which continues throughout life. It impacts to a great extent, feeling, behaviors, thoughts and ultimately relationships. Indeed, the attachment relationship and environment in childhood has a far reaching influence on individuals' wellbeing from infancy to old age (Waldinger & Schultz, 2016).

The environment in which children are brought up will inevitably leave its mark. In fact, the extent of the importance of the environment is apparent in the research and shows that a positive experience of one's family of origin is likely to enhance more secure attachment relationships, and better emotionally regulated behaviours in adulthood (Knapp, Norton, & Sandberg, 2015). On the other hand, when caregivers are unpredictable, or not available or are persistently unresponsive to the children's needs, the children's distress is not relieved, and they do not attain attachment security.

This highlights the importance of supporting environments that are sensitively attuned to the needs of the children. Safe and supportive relationships in adulthood can also give rise to a view that others are helpful and trustworthy. Such relationships also enhance the development of one's capacity to be less preoccupied by one's emotional states, as well as one's capacity to have the space to deal with complex information. This is what is known as "earned relationship security" (Mikulincer & Shaver, 2007, p. 334). It continues to underscore how warm, safe and supportive relationships are an important foundation for wellbeing in families (Waldfogel, Craigie, & Brooks-Gunn, 2010).

An Ecological Theory Framework

Similiar to the systemic framework, an ecological theory framework views interaction as being influenced by factors occurring at different levels of a system – the microsystem, the mesosystem, the exosystem, the macrosystem and the chronosystem (Bronfenbrenner, 1979). Thus, for example, to understand the behaviour of children, one needs to look at these children in the context of their immediate environment, such as their families, schools, religious institutions, neighbourhood and peers. One also needs to look at the interconnections between the microsystems, and the interconnections between the microsystem and other systems to which the children might not be directly linked. For example, a parent's relationship with his or her children might be affected by what happens in the work context especially if the parent has to deal with increased stress or conflictual relationships at the work place. This framework also looks at interactions between systems over time, taking into account the life course, the socio-historical context and the socio-economic context.

On this note, the prevailing socio-economic system and its impact upon the family deserve attention. The contemporary neoliberal context is highly influential on contemporary individuals and families' wellbeing (Wood, 2017), where the underlying primary value is profit and the free market, where competition is maximised (Weinberg, 2016). Individuals are expected to be enterprising, self-reliant, risk-takers and have self-mastery. Human wellbeing is seen to be furthered if individuals are free to direct their lives to both engage in economic activity and also create it, with limited direct control by the state (Sugarman, 2015). Individuals are thus provided with choices and are then held accountable by the state for the choices that they make.

The role of a neoliberal state is seen as one providing greater autonomy to firms and investors so that they may pursue the most profitable outcomes, what has been referred to as 'the new capitalism' (Beck, 1992). The role of the welfare state is diminished and there is less of a concern to protect society's vulnerable members. Values such as fairness, social justice and equality in social and economic relations are secondary to activities that generate wealth. Support to family members is aimed at helping them gain employment – a shift from "welfare to workfare" (Wacquant, 2010, p. 214). There is also diminished appreciation of those factors that are more complex in society (and more costly to address) such as economic, environmental and structural conditions that impact individuals' choices (Crossley, 2016).

If neoliberalism privileges individuals as economic free agents, how does the family feature in this social and economic climate? According to Sennett (1998), the social and psychological costs of these changes are profound. In relation to family formation, the most important impact is that on the labour market. Whilst the production of wealth has helped increase individuals' living standards, other less positive dynamics affect family members. With the production of wealth, there is also the social production of risk (Beck, 1992). If workers wish to have a good economic standing, then they need to devote themselves to the maximization of their wealth, which in turn involves dedication to their employment and less time with their families. Moreover in a context that favours flexibility of employment with technological advances such as teleworking, traditional boundaries between the private and personal, the public and the social are erased, with the potential for the family members to experience stress and tension from being "on call" all the time. In this context, as Sennett (1998) argues, it is not hard to see the challenge of preserving the value of long-term commitments and relationships. Also continually switching jobs, relocating and being preoccupied with personal risk and self interest is also hard on couple and family relationships.

Another outcome of neoliberalism is an increasing provision of intimate care from the poor to the rich. Whilst in the past, there have always been nannies, wet nurses and maids, Stephens (2015) argues that what is different in contemporary society is its global dimensions. In many western countries, very often care is being provided by women from poor countries to rich countries. In Malta for instance, it is not uncommon for women from the Philippines to be employed as child carers and also carers for the elderly.

Beyond intimate care, there is also the outsourcing of the way that traditional caregiving and parenting in families have been done – for example, paying for toilet training your child or paying someone to cook a meal for the family. According to Stephens (2015), these services may be looked at as providing opportunities for different kind of relationships or a transformation in our ideas of parenting. She also argues how current global neoliberal ideas seem to have no limits with regards to the extent that the market infringes the private sphere as to what can be bought or sold.

The impact of neoliberal ideas on the family is a complex one and these few paragraphs only serve as an introduction to the interested reader on family and wellbeing and neoliberalism. In the next section, this chapter will focus more in detail on the wellbeing of families in contemporary Maltese society, informed by the above conceptual frameworks.

The Couple Relationship and Wellbeing

Heterogeneity in couple relationships is a mark of the 21st century and this is also reflected among Maltese couples, mirrored in significant legislative changes such as the introduction of divorce in 2011, and the Civil Union law and the Marriage Equality Act in 2014 and 2017 respectively. Data by the European Commission (2016) show that while in recent decades, the number of heterosexual marriages per 1000 persons has decreased within the EU-28 countries, Malta remains amongst those countries with the highest crude marriage rate in 2014 at 6.7 marriages per 1000 persons, together with Turkey (7.8), Lithuania (7.6) and the former Yogoslav Republic of Macedonia (6.7). However, one needs to keep in mind that the Malta figures also includes wedding tourism. In terms of immigrant families, 4.9% of the Maltese population is non-Maltese and hence this figure includes a number of multi-cultural couples (Abela, 2016).

The EU statistics also show that since the introduction of divorce law in 2011, the crude divorce rate has increased from 0.1 to 1.1 from 2011 to 2012 and has remained at 0.8 for both 2013 and 2014. Marital separations also have been relatively low in Malta – at 3.7 % in 2003, 5.65% in 2005 and 8.12% in 2011 (Abela, 2016). The rate of cohabitation or consensual union is also relatively low – at 2.5% in 2015 (Eurostat, 2016). The number of households registered as same sex consensual union couple with and without resident children is also very low at 0.1 % (NSO, 2014). It is important to point out that the figures regarding same sex couples were compiled before the legislative changes in the Marriage Equality Act 2017. It remains to be seen how such legislative changes will impact same sex couple formation in Malta.

A deeper look at couple relationships in the local context is taken by the quantitative study conducted by the National Centre for Family Research within the President's Foundation for the Wellbeing of Society (National Centre for Family Research, 2016) among 2500 individuals of age range from 18 to 81. This study focused on how couple relationships are experienced and valued. The people interviewed were single, or in a short- or long-term relationships, married, cohabitating, separated, divorced, childless or with children.

It is interesting to note that although differences between age groups were minimal, respondents aged 66 to 80 years reported the highest level of life satisfaction. Life satisfaction levels then start to decline at age 81. One hypothesises that this decline may be understood by the general decline in health.

Being in a relationship was significantly associated with higher life satisfaction, as was satistfaction in one's relationship. However, respondents who had a married or single civil status reported higher levels of satisfaction compared to the separated, widowed or divorced, throwing light on the fact that relationship conflict and/or loss of relationships have a significant impact on the wellbeing of persons. In fact, a decrease in life satisfaction for persons whether single or in a relationship was associated with other problems such as having insufficient financial resources, dealing with conflict in personal and work relationsips, and facing physical and mental health difficulties.

Domestic Violence and Conflict

It is also important to look at conflict and domestic violence in relationships which have a profound impact on the wellbeing of the family members involved.

The definition of domestic violence that we adopt in this chapter is the one used by the Council of Europe (2014) in its Istanbul Convention: "All acts of physical, sexual, psychological or economic violence that occur within the family or domestic unit or between former or current spouses or partners, whether or not the perpetrator shares or has shared the same residence with the victim". This definition recognises all forms of violence including psychological violence and also child to parent violence; it is gender-inclusive; acknowledges relationships in a family context, both in the past and present; and it explicitly recognises issues of power and control in the acts of violence.

The 2014 European Agency for Fundamental Human Rights (F.R.A.) has found that 15% of women in Malta have experienced physical and/or sexual violence by a current or a previous partner (F.R.A., 2014). Based on the current Maltese female population, this amounts to 31,800 women. If we include emotional violence, it is 26.5% of ever partnered women who have experienced one or more acts of violence by a current or a former partner at some point in their lives (Comission on Domestic Violence, 2011). Victims of physical and psychological abuse experience more physical injuries; they have poorer physical functioning and health outcomes; higher rates of psychological symptoms and disorders; and poorer cognitive functioning compared to non victims (Lawrence, Orengo-Aguayo, Langer, & Brock, 2012). We also know that the consequences of abuse are significantly worse for female victims coming from low income and ethnic minority groups and/or unemployed with the most extreme form of violence against women and domestic violence being femicide.

Children's Wellbeing and Domestic Violence

Living in a family where there is intimate partner violence has long been recognised as a public health concern that seriously impacts the physical, and mental health of children (Boxer & Sloane-Power, 2013). Children's exposure to parental or intimate partner violence is associated with a wide range of psychological, emotional, behavioural, social and academic problems (Margolin & Gordis, 2000; Levendosky & Graham-Bermann, 2011), both in the short term but also in the longer term when these children become adults (Sammut-Scerri, 2015). As stated by the adult children themselves, living with irreconcilable contradictions of love and abuse in family relationships and trying to make sense of these experiences is a never-ending process. This impacts the individuals' wellbeing and that of the persons' significant relationships as partners and as parents.

In Malta, we do not have prevalence rates for children exposed to domestic violence in their families. We only know that 23% of women in Malta have experienced physical and/or sexual and/or psychological violence before the age of 15 years (F.R.A., 2014). Evidently, more data are needed. Moreso, when we also know that there is signficant overlap between child abuse and experiencing intimate partner violence in one's family, with rates of occurence in the range of 6% to 18% in community samples and higher rates of 40% for clinical samples (Appel & Holden, 1998; Jouriles, McDonald, Smith Slep, Heyman, & Garrido, 2008). This means that the incidence of children being exposed to or experiencing domestic violence could be significant.

Economic Wellbeing, Including Issues Related to Employment, and Poverty

In a nation-wide study among couples and singles, income adequacy emerged as a major predictor for life satisfaction (National Centre For Family Research, 2016). Looking at the interplay between family life and employment, Malta is currently enjoying a low unemployment rate of 3.3% which reflects greater economic growth in Malta than in most other European countries at the time of writing (Eurostat, 2018). In addition, according to the Labour Force Survey (NSO, 2017) the percentage of employed women has increased quite rapidly in the new millenium – to a figure of 58.1% in July–September, 2017. If one specifically looks at the percentage of employed women in the child-bearing ages of 25–54 years, the figure is even higher, standing at 69.6% in 2017. This indicates a shift from the male bread winner model to a dual career model in families, when compared to previous years when less women were in the labour market.

It is interesting to note that in the abovementioned study by the National Centre for Family Research (2016), when participants were asked what they liked least in their relationship, although respondents mentioned work issues such as "We work too much and have no time for the relationship" (p. 29), nine in ten dual earners where both partners were in full time employment were still more likely to rate their relationship as positive or very positive when compared to respondents where one partner worked full time and the other partner was a home maker (87.4%).

At the same time, in a study that looked at the relationship between adolescents (11 years to 16 years of age) and their parents, the children stated that they wished for more quality time with their parents and they wished that their parents would speak more calmly with them and shout less (Abela, Farrugia, Galea, & Schembri, 2013). Some of the fathers who were interviewed complained about the overtime work that they had to do to cope with expenses and about the fact that when they returned home they were too tired to engage with the children. The mothers struggled to win the children's trust. Future research needs to look into what kind of impact dual earner couplehood has on the well being of Maltese families. Further reseach also needs to be carried out with families with adolescents as local studies indicate that couple relationship satisfaction declines when children are in their teenage years (National Centre for Family Reseach, 2016). On the other hand, couples who were unemployed and receiving benefits were more than twice as likely to perceive their relationship as negative.

If one looks at economically vulnerable families, current statistics on poverty in Malta show that the at-risk-of-poverty rate is at 16.5%, which is 0.2 percentage points higher than that recorded for the previous year (NSO, 2017.) Eurostat statistics (2017) show that amongst households, single parents with dependent children (47.8%), single persons (32.9%) and two adults with three or more dependent children (31.7%) had the highest risk of poverty or social exclusion.

In terms of age groups, Maltese children and the elderly (65 years and over) remain the more vulnerable groups, with children continuing to be our most vulnerable group – 28.2% of children remaning at risk of poverty or social exclusion (Abela, 2017). Children's risk of poverty or social exclusion is related to their parents' level of education and as well as living in low to very low work intensity households. Children with a migrant background were at a greater risk of poverty than children whose parents were native born (Eurostat, 2017).

When focusing on income distribution, such statistics echo previous studies which have highlighted how low income families struggle to cope with financial hardships (Abela, 2016; Abela et al., 2012). The situation is further worsened by the fact that the rental market prices have risen very steeply over the last few years, hitting vulnerable groups the hardest (Martin, 2018). These include amongst others, persons with mental health challenges, young couples. victims of domestic abuse, and more recently migrants from both EU and Sub-Saharan countries (Vella, 2018). A coalition of 17 NGOs have called for the introduction of effective rent regulation to ensure that the rental market would not be driven solely by profit to the detriment of vulnerable groups (Martin, 2018). The views of the recently appointed Housing Authority Chief Executive Officer, Leonid McKay echoes similiar sentiments in concurring with proposals that the State needs to take an active role in addressing market failures to provide social housing units to the most disadvantaged in society (Vella, 2018).

Studies conducted by Caritas in 2012 and 2016 also indicated that the minimum wage is below subsistence minimum standards and does not aid families enough to combat poverty (Centre for Labour Studies, 2017). Migrant families who are often paid below the minimum wage and are part of precariat labour find themselves even in worse circumstances (Pajnik, 2016). The recent increase in minimum wage agreed upon by the Malta Council for Economic and Social Development (MCESD) and the Government (The Malta Independent, 2017), is a first step in the right direction, together with other budgetary measures such as the energy benefit for low income families to mitigate the effect of water and electricity bills, the tapering of unemployment benefits for persons entering employment and in-work benefits for low income families with children (Abela, 2017). It is important to continue evaluating whether these are effective measures to make a tangible difference in the lives of low income families and their dependent children.

The fact that 27.8% of Maltese children were at risk of poverty or social exclusion in 2015 merits a further focus on the topic. There is a higher prevalence of child poverty among those children who are brought up in lone parent families or in families with numerous children. Various studies show that children who live in poverty tend to perform worse in school than children from more higher socio-economic backgrounds (APA, 2004). These differences persist through childhood and children from poor families often complete less schooling, work less, earn less as adults and end up in an intergenerational cycle of poverty (Magnuson, 2013). Emerging research in neuroscience and developmental psychology suggests that children in poverty may be so sensitive to living in poverty because of the rapid development of young children's brains in early childhood which then leaves them more susceptible to difficulties in their home and family life (Clay, 2015). In the context of poverty, parents who are negatively affected by a lack of income and related anxiety, depression and possibly other physical health issues, experience higher level of parenting stress (Steele et al., 2016) and provide their children with less than optimal parenting behaviour. Recent research also shows that parents living in poverty who reported higher levels of anxiety including persistent feelings of worry, and restlessness, also reported significantly higher amount of hassles in the parenting role on average (Finegood, Raver, DeJoseph, & Blair, 2017). This is consistent with other research showing that difficulties with regulating anxiety has an effect on how adults perceive their parenting and parenting behaviours (Moller, Majdandzic, & Bogels, 2015).

Such findings underscore the importance of policy guidelines that support parental employment in ways that are family-friendly, particularly when addressing single parents with young children (Abela, Bezzina, Casha, & Azzopardi, 2015). In this respect, the introduction of the Free Child Care Scheme for women in education or working with children from 0 to 3 years, is consistent with these guidelines (Abela, 2017). In addition, sustained efforts are needed to support adults who are willing to improve their level of education. Such examples include the accreditation of prior learning (University of Malta, admission regulations, 2016) as well as the opportunity for interested learners to complete certificate, diploma, higher diploma or degree at the Malta College of Arts, Science and Technology (MCAST). All these initiatives can increase the employability of adults and would also increase Malta's performance on the EU benchmarks for Higher Education (European Commission/ EACEA/Eurydice, 2013). However, all these policy measures will obviously never reach the most vulnerable for whom it is very difficult to thrive in a neo liberal economy without the protection of the State.

The policy proposals incorporated within the National Strategic Policy on Positive Parenting 2016 – 2024 (Abela & Grech Lanfranco, 2016) seek to mitigate risk and vulnerability in children and families by adopting prevention and early intervention in the lives of these families and children. This Policy calls, among others, for the provision of: routine screening by midwives of pregnant mothers for mental health and for other adverse situations such as domestic violence in the home; services like home-based Family Therapy services for families whose children are at risk of being put into care; evidence-based positive parenting courses in schools and Family Resource Centres; and Community services that offer a timely and specialised service to children and families in need.

The Health of Family Members, the Physical Environment and Its Impact on Family Wellbeing

With a total population of 420,521 persons in 2017, covering a total area of 316 km2, Malta is the smallest EU member state by population but has one of the highest population densities, ranking 7th in population density in the world (Malta Population, 2017). Life expectancy in Malta is slightly higher than the EU average. In 2014, life expectancy for men was 79.8 years (compared to 78.1 years for the EU whilst that for women was 84.3 years (compared to 83.3 years for the EU) (Azzopardi-Muscat, Buttigieg, Calleja, & Merkur, 2017). In addition, on average Maltese people spend close to 90% of their life span in good health.

The main public health concern is obesity with 25% of the adult population being obese and approximately 40% of school-aged children between the ages of 4.6 to 17 years being overweight or obese (Grech et al., 2016). This is a worrying figure given that obesity contributes to a range of health conditions, including circulatory diseases and diabetes. In 2014, circulatory diseases were the leading cause of death in Malta. A current policy document aimed to combat obesity as a preventable factor is the Healthy Weight for life strategy 2012 – 2020 (Superintendence of Public Health. Ministry for Health, the Elderly and Community Care, 2012). This policy includes actions such as, support to schools so that meals and snacks do not contain excessive amounts of fats, trans-fatty acids, salt and sugar, the promotion of physical activity and the improvement of weight management of children and adults through various priority actions, and work with stakeholders on consumer education about healthy eating and the importance of moderation.

Another important public health issue is alcohol consumption. Binge drinking in adults seems to have increased between 2008 and 2014, whilst data from ESPAD shows that patterns of alcohol use among people aged 15 and 16 years involving episodic drinking (drinking more than five drinks in a row) and drunkenness have declined downwardly when looking at trends in 1999 to 2015 (Azzopardi-Muscat et al., 2017). Respiratory conditions such as chest infections and chronic obstructive airways diseases are also of concern to public health policy makers. Although respiratory infections accounted for the 9.5% of deaths in 2014, whilst cancers accounted for 28.5%, having asthma or chronic obstructive pulmonary diseases were one of the three conditions requiring the most hospital admissions in 2013 (Azzopardi-Muscat et al., 2017).

Air pollution also remains a public concern. In 2018, Malta eceived a very poor rating on the European Air Quality index (European Environment Agency, 2017) Major sources of air pollution include inefficient modes of transport, household fuels, waste burning, coal power plants, and industrial activities. Air quality data looks for concentrations of fine particulate matter which includes sulphates, nitrates, mineral dust and black carbon. These penetrate the lungs and the cardiovascular systems and are now known to be great risks for cardiovascular diseases, stroke, chronic obstructive pulmonary diseases, lung cancer and acute respiratory infections (WHO, 2017). In 2014, more than 40% of the population complained about air quality compared to the EU average of 15% and it was in breach of EU pollution limits by exceeding the permittted level of nitrogen oxide which come from persistently high vehicle emissions (Muscat, 2014). In 2016, Malta exceeded the WHO recommended limit in terms of median fine particulate matter, showing a 14 micrograms of particulate matter per cubic metre when the WHO limit is 10 microgram per cubic metre (The Malta Independent, 2016). The air quality is hopefully expected to improve now that the country's energy supply has been converted to natural gas (Sansone, 2017). Still the country's dependence on fossil fuels and green house emissions has not declined in any signficant way and given the implications of climate change and Malta's vulnerability to these changes, it is important that immediate action is taken in terms of preventative measures by everyone, to sustain health and social wellbeing (President of Malta, 2017).

CONCLUSION

In this chapter, we present a brief snapshot of Maltese families' wellbeing by focusing on local literature that has looked at some quality of life indicators related to individuals in couples and families. Despite a growing diversity of couple and family forms, being in a relationship that is warm, safe and supportive is the foundation for wellbeing in families and is also associated with high life satisfaction. Income adequacy is also a major predictor for life satisfaction and it is important for Maltese society to prioritise effective measures that make a difference in the lives of low-income families particularly in the lives of children living in poverty. Urgent priority also needs to be given to improving the health of Maltese children particularly where obesity is concerned. Finally, the general wellbeing of Maltese families is also inextricably tied to the health of the natural environment and more work needs to be done in the area, particularly in addressing air pollution.

REFERENCES

Abela, A. (2016). Family life. In M. Briguglio & M. Brown (Eds.), *Sociology of the Maltese Islands* (pp. 18–46). Malta: Miller.

Abela, A. (2017, March 23–24). *Fighting povety and social exclusion by nipping poverty in the bud. Examples of good practice*. Presentation at the meeting of the Chairpersons of the Committees on Social Affairs, EU2017 Parliamentary Dimension Malta. Retrieved from https://www.academia.edu/32369029/Fighting_Poverty_and_Social_Exclusion_by_Nipping_Poverty_in_the_Bud_Examples_of_Good_Practice

Abela, A., & Casha, C. (2017). *Thinking about welfare-to-work in the context of state and family support systems for lone mothers. Malta's move away from the Southern European model*. Submitted for publication.

Abela, A., & Grech-Lanfranco, I. (2016). *Positive parenting. National strategic policy for Malta 2016–2024*. Retrieved from https://www.academia.edu/30417704/POSITIVE_PARENTING_National_Strategic_Policy_2016-2024

Abela, A., & Walker, J. (Eds.). (2014). *Contemporary issues in family studies. Global perspectives on partnerships, parenting and support in a changing world*. West Sussex: Wiley Blackwell.

Abela, A., Bezzina, F., Casha, C., & Azzopardi, R. M. (2015, January). *Improving the quality of life of lone parents in Malta*. Paper presented at the Conference on Single Parenthood in Malta: Key Findings from Two Research Studies, Malta.

Abela, A., Casha, C., Borg Xuereb, R., Clark, M., Inguanez, J., & Sammut-Scerri, C. (2012). The needs of Maltese families with dependent children: A focus group study among professionals. *Bank of Valletta Review, 45*, 55–86. Retrieved from https://www.bov.com/Content/bov-review

Abela, A., Farrugia, R., Casha, C., Galea, M., & Schembri, D. (2013). *The relationship between Maltese adolescents and their parents* (Department of Family Studies Research Report No.1). Malta: Office of the President of Malta.

Amato, P. R., & Afifi, T. D. (2006). Feeling caught between parents: Adult children's relations with parents and subjective well-being. *Journal of Marriage and Family, 68*(1), 222–235. doi:10.1111/j.1741-3737.2006.00243.x

American Psychological Association. (2004). *Early intervention can improve low-income children's cognitive skills and academic achievement* (APA Monitor). Retrieved from http://www.apa.org/research/action/early.aspx

Appel, A. E., & Holden, G. W. (1998). The co-occurrence of spouse and physical child abuse: A review and appraisal. *Journal of Family Psychology, 12*(4), 578–599. doi:10.1037/0893-3200.12.4.578

Azzopardi-Muscat, N., Buttigieg, S., Calleja, N., & Merkur, S. (2017). Malta: Health systems review *Health Systems in Transition, 2017, 19*(1), 1–137. Retrieved from http://www.euro.who.int/__data/assets/pdf_file/0009/332883/Malta-Hit.pdf?ua=1

Beck, U. (1992). *Risk society*. London: Sage Publications.

Belsky, J., Hsieh, K., & Crnic, K. (1998). Mothering, fathering and infant negativity as antecedents of boys' externalizing problems and inhibition at age 3 years: Differential susceptibility to rearing experience? *Development and Psychopathology, 10*(2), 310–319. doi:10.1017/S095457949800162X

Bowlby, J. (1979). *The making and breaking of affectional bonds*. London: Tavistock Publications.

Boxer, P., & Sloane-Power, E. (2013). Coping with violence. A comprehensive framework and implications for understanding resilience. *Trauma, Violence and Abuse, 14*(3), 209–221. doi:10.1177/1524838013487806

Bronfenbrenner, U. (1979). *The ecology of human development: Experiments by nature and design*. Cambridge, MA: Harvard University Press.

Casanueva, C., Martin, S. L., Runyan, D. K., Barth, R. P., & Bradley, R. H. (2008). Quality of maternal parenting among intimate-partner violence victims involved with the child welfare system. *Journal of Family Violence, 23*(6), 413–427. doi:10.1007/s10896-008-9167-6

Clay, R. (2015). Fighting poverty. *APA Monitor, 46*(7), 1–6. Retrieved from http://www.apa.org/monitor/2015/07-08/cover-poverty.aspx

Commission on Domestic Violence. (2011). *The prevalence of domestic violence against women in Malta and its impact on their employment prospects* (Project No. ESF 3.43). Retrieved from http://mfss.gov.mt/en/DomesticViolence/Documents/Publications/nationwide_research_study__prevalance_impact_employment_prospects.pdf

Council of Europe. (2014). *Convention on preventing and combating violence against women and domestic violence* (Istanbul Convention). Retrieved from http://www.coe.int/t/dghl/standardsetting/convention-violence/about_en.asp

Centre for Liberal Arts & Sciences. (2017). *University of Malta.* Retrieved from http://www.um.edu.mt/clas

Centre for Labour Studies. (2017). *Memorandum to political parties. June 2017 general election. The memorandum: Ten points to ponder.* Malta: University of Malta. Retrieved from https://www.um.edu.mt/__data/assets/pdf_file/0003/316299/Final-Memorandumtopoliticalparties2017Election.pdf

Crossley, S. (2016). Realising the (troubled) family: Crafting the neoliberal state. *Families, Relationships and Societies, 5*(2), 263–279.

Davis, E. F., Schoppe-Sullivan, S. J., Mangelsdorf, S. C., & Brown, G. L. (2009). The role of infant temperament in stability and change in coparenting across the first year of life. *Parenting, Science and Practice, 9*(1–2), 143–159. doi:10.1080/15295190802656836

European Commission/EACEA/Eurydice. (2013). *Education and training in Europe 2020: Responses from the EU Member States. Eurydice Report.* Brussels: Eurydice. Retrieved from http://eacea.ec.europa.eu/education/eurydice/documents/thematic_reports/163EN.pdf

European Environment Agency. (2017). Air quality in Europe – 2017 Report. EEA report, No 13/2017. Retrieved from https://www.eea.europa.eu/publications/air-quality-in-europe-2017

European Union Agency for Fundamental Rights. (2014). *Violence against women: An EU-wide survey: Main results.* Retrieved from http://fra.europa.eu/sites/default/files/fra-2014-vaw-survey-main-results-apr14_en.pdf

Eurostat. (2015a). *Statistics explained. Quality of life indicators – measuring quality of life.* Retrieved from http://ec.europa.eu/eurostat/statistics-explained/index.php/Quality_of_life_indicators

Eurostat. (2015b). *Statistics explained. Marriage and births. New ways of living together in the EU.* Retrieved from http://ec.europa.eu/eurostat/statistics-explained/index.php/Marriage_and_birth_statistics_-_new_ways_of_living_together_in_the_EU

Eurostat. (2017). *Children at risk of poverty or social exclusion – Statistics explained.* Retrieved from http://ec.europa.eu/eurostat/statistics-explained/index.php/Children_at_risk_of_poverty_or_social_exclusion

Eurostat. (2018). *Statistics explained. Unemployment statistics.* Retrieved from http://ec.europa.eu/eurostat/statistics-explained/index.php/Unemployment_statistics

Fahey, T., Keilthy, P., & Polek, E. (2012). *Family relationships and family wellbeing: A study of the families of nine year-olds in Ireland.* Dublin: University College Dublin & Family Support Agency.

Finegood, E. D., Cybele Rayer, C., DeJoseph, M. L., & Blair, C. (2017). Parenting in poverty: Attention bias and anxiety interact to predict parents' perceptions of daily hassles. *Journal of Family Psychology, 31*(1), 51–60. doi:http://dx.doi.org.10.1037/fam0000291

Grech, V., Aquilina, S., Camilleri, E., Camilleri, K., Busuttil, M. L., Farrugia Sant-Angelo, V., & Calleja, N. (2016). The Malta childhood national body mass index – A population study. *Journal of Pediatric Gastroenterology & Nutrition, 65*(3), 327–331. doi:10.1097/MPG. 0000000000001430

Jouriles, E. N., McDonald, R., Smith Slep, A. M., Heyman, R. E., & Garrido, E. (2008). Child abuse in the context of domestic violence: Prevalence, explanations, and practice implications. *Violence and Victims, 23*(2), 221–235. doi:10.1891/0086-6708.23.2.221

Knapp, D. J., Norton, A. M., & Sandberg, J. G. (2015). Family-of-origin, relationship self regulation and attachment in marital relationships. *Contemporary Family Therapy, 37*(2), 130–141.

Kravchenko, Z., Stickley, A., & Koyanagi, A. (2015). Close relationships matter: Family well-being and its effects on health in Russia. *Europe-Asia Studies, 67*(10), 1635–1655. doi:10.1080/09668136.2015.1100370

Lawrence, E., Orengo-Aguayo, R., Langer, A., & Brock, R. L. (2012). The impact and consequences of partner abuse on partners. *Partner Abuse, 3*(4), 406–428.

Lesthaege, R. (2014). *The second demographic transition: A concise overview of its development.* Special series of Inaugural Articles by members of the National Academy of Sciences. Retrieved from http://www.pnas.org/content/111/51/18112.full.pdf

Levendosky, A. A., & Graham-Bermann, S. A. (2001). Parenting in battered women: The effects of domestic violence on women and their children. *Journal of Family Violence, 16*(2), 171–192. doi:10.1023/A:1011111003373

Luthar, S. S., Cicchetti, D., & Becker, B. (2000). The construct of resilience: A criticalevaluation and guidelines for future work. *Child Development, 71*(3), 543–562. doi:10.1111/1467-8624.00164

Magnuson, K. (2013). *Reducing the effects of poverty through early childhood interventions* (Fast Focus, 17-2013). Madison, WI: University of Wisconsin-Madison, Instittue for Research on Poverty. Retrieved from https://www.irp.wisc.edu/publications/fastfocus/pdfs/FF17-2013.pdf

Malta Population. (2017). *2017 world population review*. Retrieved from http://worldpopulationreview.com/countries/malta-population/

Margolin, G., & Gordis, E. B. (2000). The effects of family and community violence on children. *Annual Review of Psychology, 51*(1), 445–479. doi:10.1146/annurev.psych.51.1.445

Martin, I. (2018, February 24). Proposals to regularise spiralling rental market. *Times of Malta*. Retrieved from https://www.timesofmalta.com/articles/view/20180224/local/proposals-to-regularise-spiralling-rental-market.671583

McGregor, J. A. (2006). *Researching wellbeing: From concepts to methodology*. WeD Working paper 20. Economic and Social Research Council: Rsearch Greoup on Wellbeing in Deeveloping Countries, University of Bath, Bath. Retrieved from http://www.welldev.org.uk/research/workingpaperpdf/wed20.pdf

Mikulincer, M., & Shaver, P. R. (2007). *Attachment in adulthood: Structure, dynamics, and change*. New York, NY: The Guilford Press.

Moller, E. L., Majdandzic, M., & Bogels, S. M. (2015). Parental anxiety, parenting behaviour, and infant anxiety. Differential associations for fathers and mothers. *Journal of Child and Family Studies, 24*, 2626–2637. Retrieved from http://dx.doi.org/10/1007/s10826-014-00657

Muscat, C. (2014, March 28). Air pollution is the 'single biggest environmnetal risk'. *Times of Malta*. Retrieved from https://www.timesofmalta.com/articles/view/20140328/local/Air-pollution-is-the-single-biggest-environment-risk-.512482

National Centre for Family Research. (2016). *Sustaining relationships: Couples and singles in a changing society*. Malta: The President's Foundation for the Wellbeing of Society.

National Statistics Office. (2014). *Census of population and housing 2011* (Final report). Retrieved from https://nso.gov.mt/en/publicatons/Publications_by_Unit/Documents/01_Methodology_and_Research/Census2011_FinalReport.pdf

National Statistics Office. (2017, December). *Labour force survey Q3/2017* (News release). Malta: Author.

National Statistics Office. (2017, September). *Silc 201: Salient Indicators* (News release). Malta: Author.

Pajnik, M. (2016). Wasted precariat: Migrant work in European societies. *Progress in Development Studies, 16*(2), 159–172.

Rutter, M. (1999). Resilience concepts and findings: Implications for family therapy. *Journalof Family Therapy, 21*(2), 119–144. doi:10.1111/1467-6427.00108

Sammut-Scerri, C. (2015). *Living with contradictions of love and violence: A grounded theory study of women's understanding of their childhood experiences of domestic violence* (Unpublished doctoral dissertation). University of Surrey, Guildford, United Kingdom.

Sansone, K. (2017, January 11). Watch: First gas delivered to power station – cold snap leads to record demand. *The Times of Malta*. Retrieved from https://www.timesofmalta.com/articles/view/20170111/local/cold-leads-to-record-electricity-demand-gas-tanker-arrives-to-supply.636181

Sennett, R. (1998). *The corrosion of character: The personal consequences of work in the new capitalism*. New York, NY: Norton.

Steele, H., Bate, J., Steele, M., Dube, S. R., Bonuck, K., Meissner, P., & Murphy, A. (2016). Adverse childhood experiences, poverty and parenting stress. *Canadian Journal of Behavioural Sciences, 48*, 32–38.

Stephens, J. (2015). Reconfiguring care and family in the era of the "outsourced self". *Journal of Family Studies, 21*(3), 208–217.

Sugarman, J. (2015). Neoliberalism and psychological ethics. *Journal of Theoretical and Philosophical Psychology, 35*(2), 103–116.

Superintendence of Public Health. Ministry for Health, the Elderly and Community Care. (2012). *A healthy weight for life: A national strategy for Malta 2012–2020.* Malta: Superintendence of Public Health.

The Malta Independent. (2016, October 4). WHO study shows Malta's air pollution still above the recommended limits. *The Malta Independent.* Retrieved from http://www.independent.com.mt/articles/2016-10-01/local-news/WHO-study-shows-Malta-s-air-pollution-still-above-recommended-limits-6736164545

The Malta Independent. (2017, April 28). Malta's minimum wage increase reflects progress and stability – PES. *The Malta Independent.* Retrieved from http://www.independent.com.mt/articles/2017-04-28/local-news/Malta-s-minimum-wage-increase-reflects-progress-and-stability-PES-6736173620

The President of Malta. (2017). *The 2nd national conference on wellbeing. Environmental health and wellbeing. Excerpts from the speech of her excellency, the president of Malta.* Retrieved from https://president.gov.mt/2017/04/05/appeal-diligence-integrity-sectors-including-planning-sector-absolute-recognition-people-must-come-profits/

University of Malta. (2016). *Education act (Cap 327). Admission regulations 2016.* Retrieved from https://www.um.edu.mt/__data/assets/pdf_file/0011/265709/adminregs2016.pdf

Vella, M. (2018, August 28). Housing boss says Sate must assist persons ineligible for social housing. *Maltatoday.* Retrieved from http://uploads.maltatoday.com.mt/news/national/89080/housing_boss_says_state_must_assist_persons_ineligible_for_social_housing#.W5S1kS2B3-Z

Vetere, A. (2013). What supports resilient coping among family members? A systemicpractitioner's perspective. In J. Ribbens McCarthy, C.-A. Hooper, & V. Gillies (Eds.), *Family troubles? Exploring changes and challenges in the family lives of children and young people* (pp. 279–290). Bristol: The Policy Press.

Wacquant, L. (2010). Crafting the neoliberal state: Workfare, prisonfare and social insecurity. *Sociological Forum, 25*(2), 197–220.

Waldfogel, J., Craigie, T. A., & Brooks-Gunn, J. (2010). Fragile families and child well-being. *Future Child, 20*(2), 87–112.

Waldinger, R. J., & Schultz, M. S. (2016). The long reach of nurturing family environments: Links with midlife emotion-regulatory styles and late-life security in intimate relationships. *Psychological Science, 27*(11), 1443–1450. doi:10.1007/s10591-015-9332-z

Weinberg, M. (2016). Critical approaches to ethics in social work: Kaleidoescope not bleach. *Social Alternatives, 35*(4), 85–89.

WHO. (2017). *WHO releases countries' estimates on air pollution exposure and health impact.* Retrieved from http://www.who.int/mediacentre/news/releases/2016/air-pollution-estimates/en/

Wollny, I., Apps, J., & Henricson, C. (2010). *Family wellbeing. Can government measure family wellbeing. A literature review.* London: Family and Parenting Institute.

Wood, M. M. (2018). All in the family? *Journal of Cultural Economy, 11*(1), 83–88, doi:101080/17530350.2017.1407955

RUTH FALZON

6. LITERACY AND WELLBEING

ABSTRACT

Literacy is a 21st century fundamental human right and one of the most effective weapons against poverty.

Those who are illiterate or who struggle to break the code to literacy continue to be challenged in schooling and to experience a poorer quality of life. This chapter challenges the reader to reflect on the meaning of literacy, the prevalence and effect of illiteracy on wellbeing, and compensatory strategies to access literacy. Readers will be challenges to reflect on the definition and parameters of literacy, the importance of literacy and what strategies to implement when literacy is an issue, also in relation to wellbeing, specific effects of illiteracy, and compensatory strategies that can be adopted when literacy is a challenge.

Keywords: literacy, illiteracy, empowerment, quality of life, wellbeing

INTRODUCTION

The word 'literacy' represents several systematic representations of knowledges and skills, including 'computer literacy', 'cultural literacy', 'moral literacy' 'emotional literacy' and 'critical literacy' (Corradetti, 2017; Leu, Kinzer, Coiro, Caste, & Henry, 2017). This chapter focuses on the traditional understanding of literacy – namely reading, traditional writing and extracting messages from printed texts (International Social Science Council (ISSC), Institute of Development Studies (IDS), United Nations Educational, Scientific and Cultural Organization (UNESCO), 2016). Although this chapter deals with access to literacy rather than critical literacy itself, it shares with critical literacy a full commitment to empowerment and social justice. Critical literacy is a theoretical, political and practical concept which promotes an understanding of "the relationship between texts, meaning-making and power to undertake transformative social action that contributes to the achievement of a more equitable social order" (Janks & Vasquez, 2011, p. 1). Critical literacy allow for frameworks that address literacy teaching and learning that can withstand continuously changing realities across time, space, place and situation (Vasquez, 2016). Inspired by the work of the 1920s Frankfurt School (Corradetti, 2017) and later on by Paulo Freire's work (Freire, 1972; Freire & Macedo, 1987), critical literacy embraces multimodalities and new technologies, including the concept

© KONINKLIJKE BRILL NV, LEIDEN, 2019 | DOI:10.1163/9789004394179_007 of multilingual settings. This chapter deems that critical literacy is the best way forward to eradicate poverty and helplessness.

Historically, literacy has only been part of human civilisation for about 10,000 years, compared to 100,000 years of human language (Palmer, 2009). Civilisations who utilised literacy have connected with world leaders and other civilisations who now form part of the United Nations (UN) (Nadin, 1997). Further, literacy became more widely available to all and was given more prominence around 160 years ago, when nations started to focus on education and literacy for all as opposed to the few elite (Collins & Blot, 2003). Literacy now pervades every part of our lives and affects wellbeing (Antonelli et al., 2014; Burden & Burdett, 2005). This chapter builds on four basic premises: (a) Literacy is a fundamental human right (b) literacy is vital for access to education, employment and wellbeing; (c) non-access to literacy leads to poorer quality of life; and (d) for those who find difficulty accessing print, the use of technology must be considered.

DEFINING READING AND WRITING

Reading is gleaning meaning from print (Butler, 1982). This involves reading accurately and fluently to access meaning (Moats, 1999). The ability to decode single words – simultaneously recognising letter/s (graphemes representing phonemes) and blending them into a word accurately – does not automatically lead to the ability to read paragraphs with the fluency and ease to process comprehension (Aro, 2004). An analogy can be made with new and seasoned car drivers. New drivers concentrate on mechanics, whilst seasoned drivers concentrate on destinations. Beginner-drivers can start cars, change gears and manoeuvre steering (the skills of reading); but what about their performance on the road (the message)? If decoding (reading skill) is not an automatic process and if readers do not have the adequate sight-word vocabulary bank, then reading comprehension (the message) is affected. For example, if it takes one ten seconds to read 'indicate' or 'cerebral', can one equate this with the ability to access print fluently and effortlessly?

As you are reading this text, you may want to reflect on how many words you are actually decoding or recognising (Bell, 2001). You are probably an efficient reader, hence beyond the decoding stage due to practice. Practice has led you to amass thousands of sight words in your memory, which words you recognise automatically. You will only slow down when decoding unfamiliar (e.g. machairophyllum latifolium) or made-up (e.g. phlograthompinantation) words. How would you feel if you had to read a paragraph full of unfamiliar words? What would you do in such a situation?

The experience is also comparable for spelling and writing. Spelling is the ability to automatically transform words into their written format. Accomplished and efficient readers and spellers have sight word vocabulary banks which lead them to recognise rather than decode (read) and retrieve rather than encode (spell). This automaticity is vital for accessing meaning from print and transforming thoughts into written language. Writing then involves translating ideas to vocabulary to sentences to word orders to words to sounds in words to letters and to punctuation. If these skills are not automatic than the production suffers. One notes that expected adult reading fluency to easily glean meaning from print is loosely rated at around 200–250 words per minute and average adult handwriting speed at 25 words per minute (Lemov, Driggs, & Woolway, 2016).

LITERACY AND WELLBEING

All that mankind has done, thought, gained, or been; it is lying as in magic preservation in the pages of books. (Carlyle, 1981, p. 160)

A basic difference between animal and human learning is that animals learn mostly from instinct while humans from each other. The need to learn from others and to pass on learning has led us to find ways to record our knowledge for future generations (Ormrod, 2011) Most civilisations have opted for a visual method, namely written messages (Bartlett, López, Vasudevan, & Warriner, 2011).

The post-industrial era witnessed the introduction of literacy on educational, economic, and political agenda (Clinton, 1997). Today literacy is regarded as a human right to access education and employment (Massarelli, Giovannola, & Wozowczyk, 2011), often seen as a means to address poverty (Moretti & Frandell, 2013) and oppression (UNESCO, 2018b) through the skills of "understanding, evaluating, using and engaging with written texts to participate in society, to achieve one's goals, and to develop one's knowledge and potential" (The Organisation for Economic Co-operation and Development [OECD], 2016, p. 19). The OECD 2016 survey reports that "adults with lower skills are far more likely than those with better literacy skills to report poor health, to perceive themselves as objects rather than actors in political processes, and to have less trust in others" (p. 3).

LITERACY, WELLBEING AND QUALITY OF LIFE

Literacy is the key to unlocking the cage of human misery; the key to delivering the potential of every human being; the key to opening up a future of freedom and hope. (Annan, 2003, para. 6)

Literacy empowers livelihoods, enhances community participation, helps gain access to community services and realizes citizens' rights (Bartlett et al., 2011). UN Secretary General Ban Ki-moon's International Literacy Day message (2009) notes that literacy is not "just about reading and writing; it is about independence, respect, human development and opportunities for learning and employment" (para. 8). Ki-moon cautions that, despite enormous global wealth where education and knowledge are passports to a better life, illiteracy is still rampant:

> [g]lobally ... at least 750 million youth and adults still cannot read and write and 250 million children are failing to acquire basic literacy skills. This results in an exclusion of low-literate and low-skilled youth and adults from full participation in their communities and societies. (UNESCO, 2018a, para. 4)

Females account for almost two thirds of this populations (UNESCO, 2018b). On the occasion of the designation of Ms Lauren Child as UNESCO Artist for Peace, UNESCO Director-General Mr Koïchiro Matsuura (2008) explained,

> Since its foundation in 1946, UNESCO has been at the forefront of global efforts to keep literacy high on national, regional and international agendas. However, with some 776 million adults lacking minimum literacy skills, literacy for all remains an elusive target. (p. 2)

Indeed, AlNasser (2012) refers to illiteracy as "a staggering problem" (p. 3). This is even more tragic as it would not take much human or financial resources to change this situation. "[E]ven the simplest acquisition of literacy can have a profoundly empowering effect personally, socially and politically" (Ki-moon, 2009, para. 3). Ki-moon reminds us that literacy is regarded invaluable for social and economic benefits and enables individuals and communities empower themselves (UNESCO, 2018a, 2018b).

The 1997 International Adult Literacy Survey (Kirsch & Jenkins, 1998) reminds that individuals with lower levels of literacy are more likely to be on social welfare, in poverty or involved in crime; and less likely to be working full-time (Noble, 2018). Literate parents are more likely to send their children to school and are better able to access continuing educational opportunities. Furthermore, literate societies are better geared to meet pressing and continuous developments (OECD, 2016). Literacy difficulties cost the global economy 1.1 trillion euros each year and the EU economy over 350 billion euros each year due to lost earnings and limited employability; lost business productivity; lost wealth creation opportunities; lower technology skills capacity; higher spending related to health problems; higher spending on the justice system due to more crime; higher spending on social services and benefits; and higher spending on education due to students falling (European Literacy Policy Network [ELINET], 2015; The World Literacy Foundation [WLF], 2015).

LITERACY – A NECESSITY FOR LIVING?

In a context where globalization is placing new demands on the 'literacies' we need in our work and everyday life, good quality basic education aims to equip one with literacy skills for life and further learning (Freire, 1970). The UN Department of Economic and Social Affairs (DESA, 2007) notes that educational opportunities depend on literacy. The Education for All (EFA) committee (UNESCO, 2005) stresses that eradicating poverty, reducing child mortality, addressing population growth, achieving gender equality and ensuring sustainable development, peace, democracy and empowerment are some of the good reasons why literacy is at EFA's core.

PREVALENCE AND EFFECT OF ILLITERACY ON WELLBEING

The OECD (2003) notes that although it was thought that oral and aural modes of communication used for the telephone and television would replace printed text, the opposite has happened. Literacy enhances coping skills in modern environments, giving individuals possibilities to access society, institutions, available resources and structures within communities such as courts, commerce and entertainment. Literacy also affects how we develop cognitively as it enhances and supports learning processes (OECD, 2016).

Since 2001 The International Association for the Evaluation of Educational Achievement (IEA) has periodically conducted Progress in International Reading Literacy Studies (PIRLS). The latest 2016 PIRLS (Howie et al., 2017; IEA, 2017; Mullis) concludes that, compared to 15 years ago, there are more 'good readers', and that literacy improved in 18 countries between 2011 to 2016. Ten countries, including Malta, registered a decline in literacy during this period. Malta's scores were less than the mean and placed 40th of 50, only scoring better than nine other countries: Bahrain, Qatar, Saudi Arabia, Iran, Oman, Kuwait, Morocco, Egypt, and South Africa. This is of great local concern, even when one takes into consideration that PIRLS does not recognise Malta's bilingual situation (Borg, Mifsud, & Sciriha, 1996), and situations where relatively small student numbers do not allow big data statistical analyses. It would be interesting to compare local results with countries that have a similar reality to Malta such as Estonia and Cyprus, which did not participate. The Pisa 2015 results indicate that the reading average score for Maltese students was significantly lower than the international average, with 41 countries' mean reading score significantly higher, and 28 countries significantly lower, than Malta (Ministry for Education and Employment [MEDE], 2015).

The National Centre for Educational Statistics (NCES, 2017) and the National Association for Educational Progress (NAEP, 2017) quote similar alarming figures in the United States: a third of 10–11 year olds are unable to read simple books fluently with 38% reading below basic levels; and over 50% of adolescents with a history of criminal and substance abuse evidence reading problems. Sulkunen (2013) reports increasing numbers of Europeans with poor literacy skills, with low performance increasing. The Maltese National Statistics Office (NSO, 2010) quotes 11.24% illiteracy in 1995, 7.2% in 2005 and 1.7% illiteracy in 2008 among 11- to 19-year olds. The PISA 2009+ report (Walker, 2011) reveals that 36% of Maltese 15-year olds leave school without baseline functional literacy, compared to 19% mean in OECD counties. Malta is notable among PISA 2009+ participants in that it has a relatively large proportion of advanced readers but also relatively large proportions of poor and very poor readers (Walker, 2011, p. XV).

One in seven Europeans quits education or training without adequate qualifications. Although rates have declined from 54.2% in 2000 to 36.8% in 2009, in 2011 Maltese early school leavers (ESL) remained the highest in the European Union (EU Commission, 2011), with 40% not attaining the School Leaving Certification (NSO, 2010). However, NSO (2013) reports some anomalies regarding these data. Following discussion with Eurostat, "Eurostat provided a number of instructions regarding the extent of the revisions to educational attainment data and consequently to Early School Leaving rates" (p. 3). This allowed NSO to remap the data. By 2014, ESL was down to 20.4% (NSO, 2015). Notwithstanding this decrease and remapping, Eurostat (2017) still evidences Malta with this highest number of school leavers: "[i]n 2016, an average of 10.7 % of young people (aged 18–24) in the EU-28 were early leavers from education and training (para. 3) … [T]he proportion of early leavers in 2016 ranged from 2.8% … to 19.6% in Malta" (para. 4).

The 2010 Confederation of British Industry (CBI) survey concludes that 52 % of employers were dissatisfied with school leavers' basic literacy, with "anger from employers that after 11 years of education, literacy and numeracy skills can often be so bad" (Birdwell, Grist, & Margo, 2011, p. 47). Employers also feel that the burden of upgrading these skills should not fall on them or, if it does, governments should provide compensation. Birdwell et al. (2011) report that for every sterling invested to address poor literacy and numeracy, such as Every Child a Reader (Burroughs-Lange & Douetil, 2006) or Every Child Counts (Torgerson et al., 2011) there can be a return of £11 to £19 per lifetime. A local survey (Jobsplus, Malta Enterprise, National Commission for Further and Higher Education [NCFHE], 2017) presents a similar situation. UNESCO (2017) pledges to advance literacy as an integral part of lifelong learning and the 2030 Agenda for Sustainable Development (para. 5), "[to] achieve this by building strong foundations; quality basic education for all children; scaling-up functional literacy levels for youth and adults who lack basic literacy skills; and developing literate environments" (bullets para. 6).

The EU Council (EC) unequivocally turns to education as crucial in addressing socio-economic statuses and always links literacy and education to labour market increase, such as its ten-year (2010–2020) plan to raise EU employment from 64.2% to 75% (Massarelli, Giovannola, & Wozowczyk, 2011). The EC (2006) refers to difficulties due to low literacy performance, early school leaving, and challenges experienced by learners from migrant families or disadvantaged groups.

The Matthew Effect

If you see inequality and poverty, you're seeing the impact of illiteracy. (Branson, 2015, para. 2)

Access to print paves the way for learning and economic growth, justifying the importance given to ensuring that young learners learn to read as early and as expediently as possible. The path to efficient reading starts (environmental reading) and ends (fluent reading) with sight-word reading. The speed and effectiveness of early literacy learning process affects success in learning and has a Matthew Effect (Stanovich, 1986, 2000).

The "Matthew Effect" (Rigney, 2010) reflects concepts of quality of life and EFA (UNESCO, 2007). Coined by Robert K. Merton in 1968, the term derives its name from "For to him who has shall be given and he shall have abundance; but from him who does not have, even that which he has shall be taken away" (Matthew 25:29, King James Version). Merton describes how in science, eminent and established scientists often get more credit than comparatively unknown researchers, even if their work is similar (Rigney, 2010). Stanovich (1986, 2000) adopts this term to early reading success and school achievement. He describes the phenomenon that early literary success usually leads to later successes in reading and general learning; whilst failing to learn to read by early primary schooling may indicate life-long problems in learning new skills. Since non- or weak readers would read less and have less access to the verbal-visual printed text, the gap between them and their peers would increase and they would fall further and further behind in school. This may also result in higher school drop-out rates (Stanovich, 1986, 2000). "[I]n the words of a tearful nine-year-old, already falling frustratingly behind his peers in reading progress, 'Reading affects everything you do'" (Adams, pp. 59–60).

Catch Them before They Fall (Torgesen, 1998)

In this context, the relevance of early literacy success becomes vital, leading to a need for effective and expedient teaching techniques to address literacy in early years (Falzon, 2012). Early literacy classroom instruction is considered a core contributor to high incidences of literacy challenges (Birsh, 2005). Research findings attribute poor classroom instruction to lack of basic understanding of concepts related to language structure (Moats, 2009). In a context where (a) reading "serves as the major conduit for all learning" (Podhajski, Mather, Nathan, & Sammons, 2009, p. 403); and where (b) the PISA 2009+ report (Walker, 2011) indicates significantly lower percentages of Maltese fifteen year olds (64%) with baseline literacy when compared to other OECD countries (81%), one needs to reflect on initial teacher training (ITT) curricula, policies and politics locally and abroad.

ITT curricula are generally composed of four major areas: (a) foundational knowledge in education-related areas of knowledge; (b) skills in assessing and addressing student learning; (c) content-area, methods, knowledge and skills; and (d) supervised teaching practice (Ashby et al., 2008). ITT is the subject of political discussion and usually reflects governments' values, culture and significant financial resources. Thus, what knowledge, attitudes, behaviours and skills educators should possess is an important debate. Teachers are entrusted with the transmission of government-led purposely selected knowledge, attitudes, behaviours and skills necessary for effective living in societies with sustainable economies (Demaine & Entwistle, 2016).

A critical analysis of the literature points to a need for more links between theories and the classroom experience (Alexander, 2004); more emphasis on hard-core pedagogy (Louden & Rohl, 2006); and a better effort to produce early literacy teachers with a sound theoretical and knowledge background backed by effective teaching techniques for early literacy (Moats, 2009). Falzon (2012) reports that whilst Maltese early educators in her study appreciated reading theories they were exposed to, they perceived a need for more training to be effective literacy teachers, echoing EU's concern that "[m]ember States are often failing to give teachers the training they need" (EC Communication, 2007, p. 1). Hirsch (1996) proposes that failing to teach children literacy in order to cope with further learning is the greatest form of injustice in education which can actually be prevented.

50% of just-graduated engineers' knowledge becomes obsolete within five years; 90% of our present seven-year olds will possibly be in jobs which do not yet exist; and unemployed people are mostly negatively affected by attitudinal barriers, lack of confidence in their ability to learn, increasing lack of training motivation with age and, mostly, lack of literacy (Richmond et al., 2008). Knowledge is growing and changing so fast that education is turning towards development of generic competences, or character strengths (Bezzina, 2016). These are also referred to as 'soft' (Adnan, Daud, Alias, & Razali, 2017) or 'transversal' (Ribeiro, Severo, & Ferreira, 2016) skills and include continuously changing and new competencies, and knowledges (Camilleri, Caruana, Falzon, & Muscat, 2012), wherein literacy remains paramount.

Failure to Learn

Excluding other reasons for failure in learning how to read, a conservative 10% of populations have specific challenges with literacy (Lyon, Schaywitz, & Schaywitz, 2003) whilst capable in and coping with other areas of learning, if literacy were not a barrier (American Psychiatric Association [APA], 2013). These are usually referred to as having a profile of dyslexia (World Health Organisation [WHO], 1992) or specific reading difficulties (APA, 2013). In spite of having access to education, people with dyslexia may experience barriers to learning, qualifications and employment if their literacy challenges are not appropriately addressed (Joshi, Dahlgren, & Boulware-Gooden, 2002). When addressing and supporting literacy challenges, one needs to address intervention from two perspectives: facilitating access to knowledge and improving literacy skills (Falzon, 2012).

COMPENSATORY STRATEGIES TO ACCESS LITERACY

With regard to access to learning, technology has improved so much (Schmar-Dobler, 2003), that schools must consider its use to access print (Lysenko & Abrami, 2014). Technology is regarded as the "fourth revolution in the means of production of knowledge following language, writing and print" (Harnad, 1991, p. 39). Warschauer and Matuchniak (2010) report that there is broad consensus among educators, communication scholars, sociologists and economists that "information and communication technologies (ICT) ... bridge the interactive features of speech and archival characteristics of writing" (p. 179).

Gutenberg's printing press (c.1440) started the third revolution (printing). It took centuries for print to truly infiltrate and affect society with the advent of industrial Revolution (c.1760). The transition between the Print and Technology was faster. We transitioned from an industrial to an informative economy in mere decades (Castells, 2010). We are now experiencing two realities: the fourth revolution (technology) in economy and most strata of life and the third revolution (Print) which still dominates our education systems.

Educational pedagogy, examination systems and implementation and resources have not transformed at the same speed of technology. Our young and future generations still experience very traditional forms of access and opportunity to perform in assessment, namely learning and assessment mostly relying on paper and pen.

Technological Support to Literacy

Since the speed and effectiveness of early literacy learning affects success in learning (Stanovich, 2000), technology to access and present print should be utilised more, especially for those struggling with literacy (Gotesman & Goldfus, 2010). Standard computers already incorporate adaptations to address all aspects of literacy (Abilitynet, 2015). Free downloadable material (e.g. My Computer My Way https://mcmw.abilitynet.org.uk/), are available and allow add-on applications to computers, such as text-to-speech (https://www.naturalreaders.com/online/). The market also has commercial affordable computer programmes (e.g. Nuance Dragon Professional https://www.nuance.com/en-gb/dragon/business-solutions/dragon-professional-individual.html) which not only include speech to text but also organisation features; and tools, such as the Reader Pen (http://www.readerpen.com/pen reader) for general use or the Exam Reader (http://www.examreader.com/) for use during examinations. Falzon and Camilleri (2014) go even further:

> whether candidates should sit for [examinations] orally ... typewritten ... or ... handwritten ... should be as basic as the choice of ... wearing or not wearing ... prescription glasses ... examination objectives are not compromised if aural input and oral output are used, unless reading and spelling themselves are being assessed. (p. 1)

Just as literacy should be given priority in education, for those with neurological challenges to access it, technology should be used as a compensatory strategy. Literature clearly evidences the negative effects challenges with literacy have on wellbeing (Burden, 2008). Educational systems and educators must avoid unnecessary suffering by challenging their definition of learning and performance in examinations and knowledges (Chetcuti, Falzon, & Camilleri, 2016, 2018).

REFLECTION

In America 43% of adults with Level 1 (most basic) literacy skills live in poverty compared to only 4% at Level 5. Three out of four food stamp [American social support provision] recipients perform in the lowest two literacy levels. 90% of welfare recipients are highschool dropouts; 85% of juvenile court systems' populations are functionally illiterate; and more than 60% of all prison inmates are functionally illiterate (Haberman, Gillette, & Hill, 2017). Clinton's 1994 International Literacy Day message implored: "Literacy is not a luxury, it is a right and a responsibility … [T]o meet the challenges of the 21st century we must harness the energy and creativity of all our citizens" (para. 2). EU Directive and Regulation 2017/1563 (Office Journal of the EU, 2017) on access to print was published in September 2017 and decreed that the law shall apply from October 2018. This law "facilitate[s] access to published works for persons who are blind, visually impaired, or otherwise print disabled, and to allow people with print disabilities to access books and other print material in formats that are accessible to them" (European Commission, 2017, para. 1). This supports my argument regarding alternative access to and presentation of literary material.

In this chapter, I endeavoured to present a definition and parameters of literacy, the importance of literacy and what to implement when literacy is an issue. The aim was to help the reader reflect on (a) this skill in relation to wellbeing, (b) specific effects of illiteracy, and (c) compensatory strategies that can be adopted when literacy is a challenge. We need to take an active role to ensure that the fundamental right of literacy is indeed given to all. The negative experiences of children and parents for whom literacy is a difficult skill, and the stories of opportunities lost due to lack of literacy skills locally and world-wide need to be eradicated. Sadness, frustration and opportunities lost due to lack of traditional literacy skills need to be eradicated both by appropriate teaching and alternative routes to accessing and presenting print.

REFERENCES

AbilityNet. (2015). *Factsheet – Dyslexia and computing.* Retrieved from https://www.abilitynet.org.uk/sites/abilitynet
Adams, M. J. (1990). *Beginning to read: Thinking and learning about print.* Cambridge, MA: MIT Press.
Adnan, Y. M., Daud, M. N., Alias, A., & Razali, M. N. (2017). Importance of soft skills for graduates in the real estate programmes in Malaysia. *Journal of Surveying, Construction and Property, 3*(2).
Alexander, R. (2004). Still no pedagogy? Principle, pragmatism and compliance in primary education. *Cambridge Journal of education, 34*(1), 7–33.
Al Nasser, N. A. (2012). *Celebrating international literacy day. Rethinking literacy: How far have we gone in reaching the literacy goal?* Retrieved from http://www.un.org/en/ga/president/66/International-Literacy-Day%20Brochure-Modified.pdf

American Psychiatric Association. (2013). *Diagnostic and Statistical Manual of Mental Disorders (DSM-5)* (5th ed.). Arlington, VA: American Psychiatric Publishing.

Annan, K. (2003). *The secretary-general's remarks to mark the launching of the United Nations literacy decade*. Retrieved from https://www.un.org/press/en/2003/sgsm8606.doc.htm

Antonelli, L., Bilocca, S., Borg, D., Borg, S., Boxall, M., Briffa, L., Debono C., Falzon, R., Farrugia, V., Formosa, M., Gatt, L., Mifsud, D., Mizzi, K., Scurfield, L., Scurfield, M., & Vella, G. L. (2014). Drama, performance ethnography, and self-esteem: Listening to youngsters with dyslexia and their parents. *SAGE Open, 4*(2). doi:10.1177/2158244014534696

Aro, M. (2004). *Learning to read: The effect of orghography*. Jyväskylän yliopisto.

Ashby, P., Hobson, A. J., Tracey, L., Malderez, A., Tomlinson, P. D., Roper, T., Chambers, G. N., & Healy, J. (2008). *Beginner teachers' experiences of initial teacher preparation, induction and early professional development: A review of literature*. London: Department for Children, Schools and Families (DCSF).

Bartlett, L., López, D., Vasudevan, L., & Warriner, D. (2011). The anthropology of literacy. *A Companion to the Anthropology of Education*, 177–196.

Bell, T. (2001). Extensive reading: Speed and comprehension. *The Reading Matrix, 1*(1).

Bezzina, A. (2016). *Personal and social development practice at the University of Malta: Its presence and positive contribution: A reality or a mirage?* (Doctoral dissertation). University of Nottingham, Nottingham.

Birdwell, J., Grist, M., & Margo, J. (2011). *The forgotten half: A DEMOS and private equity foundation report*. London: DEMOS. Retrieved from http://www.demos.co.uk/files/The_Forgotten_Half_-_web.pdf?1300105344

Birsh, J. R. (2005). Research and reading disability. In J. R. Birsh (Ed.), *Multisensory teaching of basic language skills* (2nd ed., pp. 1–21). Baltimore, MD: Paul H. Brookes.

Borg, A., Mifsud, M., & Schiriha, L. (1996). *The position of Maltese in Malta. Meeting for experts on language planning*. Malta: Council of Europe.

Branson, R. (2015). *Branson backs global literacy campaign* (As reported by Pearson). Retrieved from https://www.pearson.com/corporate/news/media/news-announcements/2015/10/richard-branson-backs-global-literacy-campaign.html

Burden, R. (2008). Is dyslexia necessarily associated with negative feelings of self worth? A review and implications for future research. *Dyslexia, 14*(3), 188–196.

Burden, R., & Burdett, J. (2005). Factors associated with successful learning in pupils with dyslexia: A motivational analysis. *British Journal of Special Education, 32*(2), 100–104.

Durroughs-Lange, S., & Douetil, J. (2006). *Evaluation of reading recovery in London schools: Every child a reader, 2005–2006*. London: Institute of Education, University of London.

Butler, D. (1982). Reading begins at home. *Theory into Practice, 21*(4), 308–314.

Camilleri, S., Caruana, A., Falzon, R., & Muscat, M. (2012). The promotion of emotional literacy through PSD – The Maltese experience. *Pastoral Care in Education: An International Journal of Personal, Social and Emotional Development', 30*(1), 19–37.

Carlyle, T. (1981). *All that mankind has done, thought, gained or been*. US: Greenbrae Press.

Castells, M. (2010). *End of millennium* (Vol. 3). New York, NY: John Wiley & Sons.

Chetcuti, D., Falzon, R., & Camilleri, S. (2016). *d pebble in my shoe: Teenagers' experience of dyslexia and examinations*. Malta: Outlook Coop.

Clinton, W. J. (1994, August 24). *Statement on the observance of international literacy day* (Online by G. Peters & J. T. Woolley, The American Presidency Project). Retrieved from http://www.presidency.ucsb.edu/ws/?pid=49016

Clinton, W. J. (1997). *State of the Union address*. Retrieved from http://clinton2.nara.gov/WH/SOU97

Collins, J., & Blot, R. (2003). *Literacy and literacies: Texts, power, and identity* (Vol. 22). Cambridge: Cambridge University Press.

Confederation of British Industry (CBI). (2010). *Ready to grow: Business priorities for education and skills. Education and skills survey 2010*. Retrieved from http://www.britishcouncil.org/zh/education_and_skills_survey_2010.pdf

Corradetti, C. (2017). The multiple identities of critical theory: A Hydra or a Proteus? *Philosophy & Social Criticism, 43*(3), 306–307.

Council of the European Union. (2006). *Presidency conclusions 23/24 March 2006*. Retrieved April 30, 2018, from http://www.consilium.europa.eu/uedocs/cms_data/docs/pressdata/en/ec/89013.pdf

Demaine, J., & Entwistle, H. (Eds.). (2016). *Beyond communitarianism: Citizenship, politics and education*. New York, NY: Springer.

Department of Economic and Social Affairs (DESA), UN. (2007). *The United Nations development agenda: Development for all*. New York, NY: UN.

European Commission. (2017, September 25). *Implementation of the Marrakesh treaty* (News Article). Retrieved from https://ec.europa.eu/digital-single-market/en/news/implementation-marrakesh-treaty-eu-law

European Literacy Policy Network (ELINET). (2015). *Literacy in Europe: Facts and figures*. Retrieved from http://www.eli-net.eu/fileadmin/ELINET/Redaktion/Factsheet-Literacy_in_Europe-A4.pdf

European Union Commission. (2011). *Malta has largest early school leavers rate in EU: The EU in Malta*. Retrieved from http://ec.europa.eu/malta/news/early_school_leavers_en.htm

Eurostat. (2011). *Your key to European statistics*. Retrieved from http://epp.eurostat.ec.europa.eu/portal/page/portal/education/introduction

Eurostat. (2017). *Early leavers from education and training*. Retrieved from http://ec.europa.eu/Eurostat/statistics-explained/index.php/Early_leavers_from_education_and_training

Falzon, R. (2012). *Early educators' awareness and knowledge of structured multisensory literacy techniques* (Doctoral dissertation). Northumbria University, Newcastle. Retrieved from http://nrl.northumbria.ac.uk/10837/1/falzon.ruth_phd.pdf

Falzon, R., & Camilleri, J. (2014). *Request for oral examinations at the SEC and MATSEC levels*. National petition presented to the Maltese Parliament. Retrieved from https://www.change.org/p/ministry-for-education-and-employment-give-the-option-to-students-to-do-their-examinations-in-writing-orally-or-using-a-word-processor

Freire, P. (1970). *The pedagogy of the oppressed*. London: Harper and Harper.

Freire, P., & Macedo, D. (1987). *Literacy: Reading the word and the world*. Westport, CT: Praeger.

Gotesman, E., & Goldfus, C. (2010). The impact of assistive technologies on the reading outcomes of college students with disabilities. *Educational Technology, 50*(3), 21–25.

Haberman, M., Gillette, M. D., & Hill, D. A. (2017). *Star teachers of children in poverty*. London: Routledge.

Harnad, S. (1991). Post-Gutenberg galaxy: The fourth revolution in the means of production of knowledge. *Public-Access Computer Systems Review, 2*(1), 39–53.

Hirsch, E. D. (1996). *The schools we need and why we don't have them* (2nd ed.). New York, NY: Anchor Books, Doubleday.

Howie, S., Combrinck, C., Roux, K., Tshele, M., Mokoena, G., & Palane, N. M. (2017). *PIRLS 2016*. Pretoria, South Africa: Centre for Evaluation and Assessment. Retrieved from http://www.up.ac.za/media/shared/164/ZP_Files/1.-pl-highlights-website_14.12.17.zp137666.pdf

International Association for the Evaluation of Educational Achievement (IEA). (2017). *PIRLS 2016 – International results in Reading*. Boston, MA: TIMMS & PIRLS International Study Centre, Lynch School of Education, Boston College and International Association for the Evaluation of Educational Achievement (IEA).

International Social Science Council (ISSC), Institute of Development Studies (IDS), United Nations Educational, Scientific and Cultural Organization (UNESCO). (2016). *World social science report 2016. Challenging inequalities: Pathways to a just world*. Paris: UNESCO Publishing.

Janks, H., & Vasquez, V. (Eds.). (2011). *Critical literacy revisited. A special issue of teaching practice and critique*. New Zealand: Waikato University Press.

Jobsplus, Malta Enterprise, NCFHE. (2017). *National employee skills survey, Malta*. Retrieved from https://ncfhe.gov.mt/en/research/Documents/Employee%20Skills%20Survey/Employee%20Skills%20Survey%20report.pdf

Joshi, R. M., Dahlgren, M., & Boulware-Gooden, R. (2002). Teaching reading in an inner city school through a multisensory teaching approach. *Annals of Dyslexia, 52*, 229–242.

Ki-moon, B. (2009). *Message for international literacy day*. Retrieved from http://www.un.org/press/en/2009/sgsm 12423.doc.htm

Kirsch, I. S., & Jenkins, L. B. (1998). Introduction. In T. S. Murray, I. S. Kirsch, & L. B. Jenkins (Eds.), *Adult literacy in OECD countries: Technical report on the first international adult literacy survey* (pp. 13–22). Washington, DC: National Centre for Education Statistics Office of Educational Research and Improvement: U.S. Department of Education. Office of Educational Research and Improvement. Retrieved from http://nces.ed.gov/pubs98/98053.pdf

Lemov, D., Driggs, C., & Woolway, E. (2016). *Reading reconsidered: A practical guide to rigorous literacy instruction*. New York, NY: John Wiley & Sons.

Leu, D. J., Kinzer, C. K., Coiro, J., Castek, J., & Henry, L. A. (2017). New literacies: A dual-level theory of the changing nature of literacy, instruction, and assessment. *Journal of Education, 197*(2), 1–18.

Louden, W., & Rohl, M. (2006). Too many theories and not enough instruction: Perception of pre-service teacher preparation for literacy teaching in Australian Schools. *Literacy, 40*(2), 66–78.

Lyon, G. R., Shaywitz, S. E., & Shaywitz, B. A. (2003). A definition of dyslexia. *Annals of Dyslexia, 53*(1), 1–14.

Lysenko, L. V., & Abrami, P. C. (2014). Promoting reading comprehension with the use of technology. *Computers & Education, 75*, 162–172.

Massarelli, N., Giovannola, D., & Wozowczyk, M. (2011). EU-27 employment and unemployment levels stable. *Eurostat Statistics in Focus, 8*, 2011.

Matsuura, K. (2008). *Address on the occasion of the designation of Ms Lauren Child as UNESCO artist for peace*. Paris: UNESCO. Retrieved from http://unesdoc.unesco.org/images/0017/001786/178614E.pdf

Ministry for Education and Employment. (2015). *PISA 2015 Malta National Report*. Retrieved from https://curriculum.gov.mt/en/international_studies/Documents/PISA_2015_Malta%20Report.pdf

Moats, L. C. (1999). *Teaching reading IS rocket science: What expert teachers of reading should know and be able to do*. Washington, DC: American Federation of Teachers.

Moats, L. C. (2009). Still wanted: Teachers with knowledge of language. *Journal of Learning Disabilities, 42*(5), 387–391.

Moretti, G. A. S., & Frandell, T. (2013). Literacy from a right to education perspective. *Report of the director general of UNESCO to the United Nations General Assembly 68th Session*.

Nadin, M. (1997). *The civilization of illiteracy*. Dresden: Dresden University Press.

National Association of Educational Progress (NAEP) (2017). *Mathematics and reading assessment. Highlighted results at Grade 4 and 8 for the nation, state and districts*. Washington, DC: US Department of Education. Retrieved from https://www.nationsreportcard.gov/reading math 2017 highlights/

National Centre for Educational Statistics (NCES). (2017). *The Programme for the International Assessment of Adult Competencies (PIAAC)*.Washington, DC: Institute of Education Sciences of the U.S. Department of Education. Retrieved from https://nces.ed.gov/surveys/piaac/

National Statistics Office (NSO). (2010). *Education statistics 2007*. Valletta: National Statistics Office.

National Statistics Office (NSO). (2013). *Re-mapping of information relating to the rate of early leavers from education and training*. Retrieved from https://nso.gov.mt/en/nso/Sources_and_Methods/Documents/Education/Re-mapping_of_information_relating_to_the_rate_of_Early_Leavers_from_Education_and_Training.pdf

National Statistics Office (NSO). (2015). *Key indicators on the labour market: 2005–2014*. Retrieved from https://nso.gov.mt/en/NewsReleases/View_by_Unit/Unit_C2/Labour_Market_Statistics/Documents/2015/News2015_124.pdf

Noble, C. (2018). Social work, collective action and social movements: Re-thematising the local-global nexus. In L. Dominelli (Ed.), *Revitalising communities in a globalising world* (pp. 109–118). London: Routledge.

Official Journal of the European Union. (2017). *Regulation 2017/1563 of the European parliament and of the council of 13 September 2017 on the cross-border exchange between the Union and third countries of accessible format copies of certain works and other subject matter protected by copyright and related rights for the benefit of persons who are blind, visually impaired or otherwise print-disabled*. Retrieved from https://eur-lex.europa.eu/legal-content/EN/TXT/PDF/?uri=CELEX:32017R1563&from=EN

Organisation for Economic Co-operation and Development (OECD). (2003). *Literacy skills for the world of tomorrow – Further results from PISA 2000*. Retrieved from http://www.oecd.org/dataoecd/43/9/33690591.pdf

Organisation for Economic Co-operation and Development (OECD). (2016). *The survey of adult skills: Reader's companion* (2nd ed.). Paris: OECD Skills Studies, OECD Publishing. Retrieved from http://dx.doi.org/10.1787/9789264258075-en

Organisation for Economic Co-operation and Development (OECD). (2018). *PISA 2015 pisa results in focus*. https://www.oecd.org/pisa/pisa-2015-results-in-focus.pdf

Organisation for Economic Co-operation and Development (OECD), Development. Programme for International Student Assessment, OECD Staff, Development (OECD) Staff, Programa Internacional para el Seguimiento de Adquisiciones de los alumnos (PISA) de la OCDE, Programme for International Student Assessment, … & SourceOECD (Online service). (2004). *PISA learning for tomorrow's world: First results from PISA 2003* (Vol. 659). New York, NY: Simon and Schuster.

Ormrod, J. E. (2011). *Human learning*. London: Pearson Higher Ed.

Palmer, K. A. (2009). Understanding human language: An in-depth exploration of the human facility for language. *Inquiries Journal, 1*(12).

Podhajski, B., Mather, N., Nathan, J., & Sammons, J. (2009). Professional development in scientifically based reading instruction: Teacher knowledge and reading outcomes. *Journal of Learning Disabilities, 42*(5), 403–417.

Ribeiro, L., Severo, M., & Ferreira, M. A. (2016). Performance of a core of transversal skills: Self-perceptions of undergraduate medical students. *BMC Medical Education, 16*(1), 18.

Rigney, D. (2010). *The Matthew effect: How advantage begets further advantage*. New York, NY: Columbia University Press.

Schmar-Dobler, E. (2003). Reading on the internet: The link between literacy and technology. *Journal of Adolescent & Adult Literacy, 47*(1), 80–85.

Stanovich, K. E. (1986). Matthew effects in reading: Some consequences of individual differences in the acquisition of literacy. *Reading Research Quarterly, 21*(4), 360–407.

Stanovich, K. E. (2009). Matthew effects in reading: Some consequences of individual differences in the acquisition of literacy. *Journal of Education, 189*(1–2), 23–55.

Stanovich, K. E. (2000). *Progress in understanding reading: Scientific foundations and New Frontiers*. New York, NY: Guilford Press.

Sulkunen, S. (2013). Adolescent literacy in Europe—An urgent call for action. *European Journal of Education, 48*(4), 528–542.

Torgerson, C. J., Wiggins, A., Torgerson, D. J., Ainsworth, H., Barmby, P., Hewitt, C., Jones, K., Hendry, V., Askew, M., Bland, M., Coe, R., Higgins, S., Hodgen, J., Hulme, C., & Tymms, P. (2011). *Every child counts: The independent evaluation*. London: Department for Education (DfE). Retrieved from http://dera.ioe.ac.uk/2376/1/2376_DFE-RR091A.pdf

Torgesen, J. K. (1998). Catch them before they fall. *American Educator, 22*, 32–41.

United Nations Educational, Scientific and Cultural Organization (UNESCO). (2005). *Education for all global monitoring report – Education for all: 2006 literacy for life*. Paris: UNESCO. Retrieved from http://unesdoc.unesco.org/images/0014/001416/141639e.pdf

United Nations Educational, Scientific and Cultural Organization (UNESCO). (2007). *Education for all by 2015: Will we make it?* Paris: UNESCO Publishing.

United Nations Educational, Scientific and Cultural Organization (UNESCO). (2016). *Global education monitoring report 2016: Education for people and planet – Creating sustainable future for all*. Paris: UNESCO.

United Nations Educational, Scientific and Cultural Organization (UNESCO). (2018a). *Literacy*. Retrieved from https://en.unesco.org/themes/literacy

United Nations Educational, Scientific and Cultural Organization (UNESCO). (2018b). *Literacy*. Retrieved from http://uis.unesco.org/en/topic/literacy

Vasquez, V. M. (2016). *Critical literacy across the K-6 curriculum*. London: Routledge.

Walker, M. (2011). *PISA 2009 plus results. Performance for 15 year-olds in reading mathematics and science in 10 additional participants*. Camberwell: ACER Press (Australian Council for Educational Research).

Warschauer, M., & Matuchniak, T. (2010). New technology and digital worlds: Analyzing evidence of equity in access, use, and outcomes. *Review of Research in Education, 34*(1), 179–225.

World Health Organization. (1992). *The International Classification of Diseases (ICD)-10 classification of mental and behavioural disorders: clinical descriptions and diagnostic guidelines* (Vol. 1). World Health Organization.

World Literacy Foundation. (2015, August 24). *The economic and social costs of illiteracy; A snapshot of illiteracy in a global context.* Final report from the World Literacy Foundation.

ANDREW AZZOPARDI

7. VOICES OF THE YOUNG SO-CALLED VULNERABLE

How Well Is Their Being?

ABSTRACT

Young people remain a highly contested group within our society (Dimitrova, 2017). The positioning of this population within the community is complex and multifarious (Zizek, 2009). Considering that youth has emanated from a social construction (Roche, Tucker, Thomson and Flynn, 2006) there has always been the risk of instrumentalisation as youth have been understood as simply there to engender consumerism and exemplify commodification best illustrated in the notions around Cohen's 'moral panics' (1972). In this chapter, I will be arguing around the ambivalent positioning of a segment of the youth population considered as vulnerable because of the social productions that relegate them, best illustrated in the narratives I will be proposing in this work. Vulnerability suggests discrepancy and insufficiency and needs to be explored within a discourse that is governed by complexity and uncertainty. In other words, it is a term that conveys power volatility and precariousness. To counter act this discourse, the focus of this chapter is the young peoples' narratives.

Keywords: youth, vulnerability, affiliation, intersectionality, wellbeing

INTRODUCTION

Young people are not a homogenous group and youth should be contemplated as "a time of opportunity, or flux and transformation" (Furlong, 2013, p. 25). I maintain in this chapter that it is the current social context enmeshed with their experiences that impacts their identity and not their distinctiveness. This work will also demonstrate that youth exclusion happens on multiple levels, in that age, race, gender, class and lifestyle all affect youth life experiences within a given culture. This intersectionality affects how young persons experience exclusion from their community. Context plays a big role in this discourse on segregation.

BRUISED YOUTH

The influence of socio-demographic characteristics in the portrayal of youth is always a very complex one (Klimke & Scharloth, 2008). In the empirical work that drives this chapter, I attempted to engage with the voices of young people who feel short-changed and who believe that life has dealt them a weak hand. In most of the narratives I documented for this chapter, the informants' stories surfaced issues around victimisation, rejection and dismissal. There is also a common thread that seems to suggest disenchantment with social services, NGOs and a general lack of family understanding. Naturally, the challenges that they face are anything but a choice that they make for themselves. The constituents of wellbeing in a context driven by a debate that preaches 'freedom to all on everything' presents us with an interesting and challenging paradigm (OECD, 2017). If one had to zoom in on the transitions of young people who are placed on the spectrum of vulnerability it would immediately illustrate the complexity when attempting to develop youth policy and strategy (Azzopardi, 2011). Basic notions around social class, social conditions and ethnicity are also informed by the role, or absence thereof, of education as a mechanism for social mobility. The education system and non-formal educational structures should not only contend but also promote social volatility (Furlong, 2013) and help respond to marginalisation of segments of this population.

THE RESEARCH

To enable me to understand what is bruising young people, I engaged with this population through the National Youth Agency who had initially commissioned this study. The objective of this research was to highlight the main challenges faced by young people between 18 and 25 years of age who are positioned at a social disadvantage, as they try to find solace in family and community life and to access welfare and other state and voluntary support systems. These young people would typically be seen as vulnerable in myriad ways, not only economically, socially and culturally but also in terms of gender, ethnicity, religious affiliation, sexual orientation and health and personal wellbeing (OECD, 2017). This chapter has the scope of surfacing the pungent matters, through the voice of young people themselves, with a view to informing policy (Roche, as cited in Roche, Tucker, Thomson, & Flynn, 2006). This chapter addresses vulnerabilities experienced by young people nationally. The categories selected to participate in this study were identified after consultation with the National Youth Agency and a number of workshops with service providers and NGOs. It was at that stage that it was decided that the choice of participants is based on the level of income, the level of risk to their development and their well-being. The participants were young people exposed to potential extreme, life-threatening circumstances and violence that emerge during their key life-transitions (Hardgrove, Pells, Boyden, & Dornan, 2014).

As I went about collating the data, I naturally looked into safeguarding the interests of young people I interviewed by creating a gatekeeping line of approach. In fact, I got access to my informants from a number of NGOs and State run/funded organisations, namely; the National Commission Persons with Disability (now Commission for the Rights of Persons with Disability), Drachma (an LGTQi support group), Caritas (a Church run agency), COURSE, (the Prisons youth section), Integra Foundation (who work with young migrants, ethnic and religious minorities), *Dar Kenn ghal Sahhtek,* (a residential home for young people with eating disorders), the National Youth Agency programme through the Youth.Inc, and Jobsplus (for those registered as NEETs – Not in Education, Employment and Training). Each participant was interviewed and their narrative recorded by the researcher. The effectiveness of this chapter lies in the fact that it is only through listening to young people's actual experiences that we can provide responses that are humane, informed and effective even though they might feel disempowered with these markers (Azzopardi & Grech, 2012).

Each interview lasted for approximately two hours. In all 23 young people participated in the study (not all are quoted in this study due to space restrictions).

YOUNG PEOPLE AND COMMUNITY

To frame young people within the community context is fundamental in this chapter. How community impacts on the lives of young people, especially those mounted within a discourse of 'vulnerability' (Beiner, 1995) helps us to locate the debate and conceptualise the discourses that young people will be 'talking about' (in the narratives). It is only when young people are linked with bonds of citizenship that they can feel part of the community. An absence of this sense of belonging disenfranchises, alienates and subjugates them (Bauman, 2001; Dimitrova, 2017).

> The 'citizen' – the Greek polites or Latin civis – is defined as a member of the Athenian polis or Roman res publica, a form of human association allegedly unique to these ancient Mediterranean peoples and by them transmitted to 'Europe' and 'the West'. (Beiner, 1995, p. 29)

Outlined in this context, young people remain one of the most contested populations to that navigate in our communities. Within all the discourses that engage the notion of inclusion, youth (Batsleer, 2008) present an interesting challenge that merits our academic attention. What we conceptualise as 'youth' differs across theoretical positions, schools of thought and socio-cultural experiences but common to many definitions is a perception of youth as rational, responsible, free, conscious, choosing, autonomous, and self-regulatory population (Coleman & Hendry, 2000).

This chapter debates this matter not from a detached and disengaged standpoint but one that is critical of the 'moral panic' that too often surrounds young people and which is based on a perception of youth as wicked, as Cohen pointed out in 1972:

> The term 'folk devil' was introduced by Stan Cohen in 1972 in his now-famous book Folk Devils and Moral Panics. The case study central to his work was that of the mods and rockers of the 1960s for their pitched battles at seaside resorts .... Media reporting of these fights reached to a point that they became a matter of major public concern. (Hetherington, 1997, p. 247)

Too often, young people are turned into scapegoats and that is why the debate that encapsulates vulnerability is a very complex one. 'Vulnerability' conveys much more than social need – it is a social state. It is the way how communities tamper with the power structures (Cutajar, 2009).

> Words have meanings: some words, however, also have a good 'feel'. The word 'community' is one of them. It feels good: whatever the word 'community' may mean, it is good 'to have a community', 'to be in community'. (Bauman, 2001, p. 1)

We need to understand young people, within their contexts, their frustrations and their vexations. Young people are being short-changed because communities do not always offer them the 'spaces' they promise they would (Hetherington, 1997) and are often perceived as 'the stranger'. They are often defined by boundaries and values, by criteria and measurements, with the tensions that such deliberations generate (Azzopardi, 2011).

While youth certainly do not make a homogenous population, on many fronts we are simply disengaged with the needs of young people and their voices and our discourse is more centred around the inability of young people to carry their life choices and decisions (Roche et al., 2006).

> ... if we have a concern for what current life is like for today's generation of young people, or what may help them in their futures, we cannot use our own experiences of being young or the aspirations we then held as much of a guide. (Rogers, Rogers, Vyrost, & Lovas, 2006, p. 19)

What comes to mind is what German sociologist George Simmel wrote in the 1890s about the "figure of the stranger" (cited in Hetherington, 1997, p. 250) an allegory that can be applied to this segment of the population, namely young people who are vulnerable not by choice but by the social conditions imposed on them. Simmel defines 'the stranger' as unable to find oneself within a specific realm of tensions that go beyond proximity.

The longing for social affiliation is a fundamental human need even though as manifested in the stories I captured, there are individual differences in the need for belongingness. Community adheres unambiguously to the code of social justice. Strong communities are those that hold fast to a code of social justice, yet which is becoming more difficult in a world in which, absurdly, we are faced with mounting crises shaped by social detachments.

> I don't feel vulnerable because I was always able to take tough decisions in my life. At 5 years I already had to take care of my sister and cook for her. It is a

fact that there were moments when I wanted to hide my past, to forget all I went through because of the pain that that created in me but now I feel relaxed and I accept myself. I remember having to bandage my breasts so that I would look like a boy. I obviously couldn't go swimming because I was so embarrassed to do so. I was so confused at the time. At 17 years I started having operations which caused a great deal of physical pain but I was always satisfied and happy that I took that decision. I started taking decisions on the operations I needed to do when I was still young. In fact, I had to do a hysterectomy, remove my breasts and am now preparing for the most difficult and complicated operation which is the change in the genitalia. When still very young I wasn't happy and comfortable with myself. I always felt that I was in the wrong body. But I believe that at the end of the day it's up to 'you' if you want to live a lie. … the parents of my girlfriend (with whom I have been going out with for these last two years) do not accept me at all. I've also had a turbulent relationship with my dad – he was never supportive of what I was going through. On the other hand, my relationship with mum is perfect, it is very good. I feel lucky in that respect because my mum never judged me but provided me with all the necessary support and was close to me. She allowed me to take my own decisions. I feel that my mother not only understood me but provided me with all the support required. … When I asked for some help from the school counsellor at secondary school he had no idea how to help me. The only organisation that tried to get involved and to support me was MGRM. Nowadays I live a normal life, I work, I study, I go out with friends. (Zack, young transsexual)

VULNERABILITIES

In this study it was made increasingly clear that young people are being faced with countless struggles. … struggles and other life challenges. Firstly, this segment of the youth population is being short-changed by the system (de-personalisation and the lack of interface between the individual and the community) itself be it schools, NGOs and other non-formal set-ups and secondly, young people are being victimised by the language of exclusion that is directed at them, leading to a segment of young people being ostracised and cold-shouldered by their peers, their family and community (Barton, 2000).

The nature of vulnerabilities can vary (Craig, Popple, & Shaw, 2008). Susceptibilities are the end result of social constructions and politics of marginalisation (Azzopardi, 2013a), whether it is disability, sexual orientation, addictions, social and economic exclusion or other. The effect of vulnerability remains the same; loneliness, anxiety, distress, pain, fear and, possibly might eventually lead to despair (Barton, 2000; Zizek, 2009). The negative impact of vulnerabilities is multiplied and made worse by the reactions and behaviours of others – indifference, antipathy, bullying, and not knowing how to respond or help (Maynard & Stuart, 2017). In spite of this, vulnerable young people often display a strong desire to deal with the consequences of their helplessness and to rebuild their lives (Azzopardi, 2013a).

So-called 'vulnerable' young people, as we read in their accounts, want solutions to their problems. They recognise the need for personal effort and commitment, but also know that their problems cannot be overcome without the support of others, in particular, their parents, family and friends; professionals; social and education services; the voluntary sector and the wider community (Dewey, 1916).

> I wanted to die, I wanted to end it all then and there. (Janet, young person with an eating disorder)

> However, my biggest pain is that at times I feel so isolated and alone, forgotten by everyone. (Noel, young offender)

> I felt lonely, depressed and ashamed in this transition phase. Bullying at a certain point in my adolescence was rife and it was creating in me a sense of social anxiety. I would be called names and would be made to feel abnormal. (Mark, gay young person)

> I feel so lonely. Day-in day-out it feels as if there is nothing in life for me .... (Simon, low education achiever)

> I feel so ashamed being in prison but the truth is that I know I have an addictive personality and didn't get the necessary support at any stage of my life. The system is responsible for what has happened to me. I admit that I was at fault for what I did and do not in any way try to excuse my behaviour and actions. However, since I was young the immense problems there were at home were for all to see and being so young, if some of those issues were nipped in the bud, I would have done well for myself. I knew that with the right type of support I wouldn't have ended up where I am now. The social work agency left me on my own – I never got any support from them. When I needed them most they turned their gaze away from me. (Gianella, young person with a drug addiction problem and currently incarcerated)

> I am 20 years-old. I suffer from a mental health condition called bi-polar. I've had to struggle with this condition for so many years. At a certain stage in my adolescence I would drink and smoke and hang around with the wrong crowd which wasn't helping me at all. I think I was doing that because I couldn't take the pressure of feeling so bad at certain moments in my life and so high during others. These so called 'friends' were pushing me towards drug use. They used to tell me that taking drugs makes you deal better with your problems – and I used to believe them. ... Schooling when still young was also a very negative experience for me. (Jesmond, young person with mental health problems)

The influence of socio-economic-demographic characteristics in the discourse around 'youth' is a very complex one (Bauman, 2001). The voices of young people have often been not only contested, but pushed to the side (Azzopardi, 2003). Even though access to media, first and foremost social media, and other forms of communication are on the increase, the opportunity for young people to have space and negotiate their positions has often gone unavailed A sense of frustration and a perceived lack of adequate response and support from professional and social/educational services is also apparent among vulnerable young people (Dimitrova, 2017). The responsiveness of voluntary services tends to be seen in a more positive light. There is also a sense that professionals do not always recognise or appreciate the often complex nature and impact of their vulnerabilities as well as an apparent lack of confidence and trust in professionals (Romer, 2003). Vulnerable young people need the support of their parents, families and friends. But, too often, parents and families also need support themselves. Supporting young people should also mean supporting their parents and families.

> I had a difficult time as I was growing up. My parents weren't good role models but I still wanted to have a family. My life was so hard. I know I am a good person deep down. I am so angry at my parents, I lacked so much love. I was brought up in a children's home and the experience was terrible. I had a family history of family members taking drugs; my grandfather was on drugs and so were my mother and father. Eventually even I started taking drugs – it was almost a natural thing to do. I'm not feeling sorry for myself but nothing comes easy for me in life as it is all uphill. ... I try to make the best use of my time whilst I am here but I must say that there are no services. Even YOURS (Young Offenders Unit Rehabilitation Services) lacks services. There are no councillors I can refer to and no Youth Workers or any other professional. However, my biggest pain is that at times I feel so isolated and alone, forgotten by everyone. (Noel, young offender)

> I am a Maltese Muslim girl. My father is Syrian but my mother is Maltese. I have lived in Malta all my life and identify completely with the Maltese culture. I was born and bred in Malta and I deserve to be respected. I wear a hijab which I feel is not only a symbol of the religion I pertain to but also an icon of the struggle for religious inclusion. The scarf is part of the 'ideal I believe in', a cultural symbol. Having said that I admit that wearing the scarf is not necessarily a choice I made completely freely. I would have preferred to have been left to make a choice myself whether to wear the hijab or not. Nevertheless, once you start wearing it you remain with it. I experience discrimination, bullying and oppression continually in my life and even though I have generally got used to it, I still can't understand how come people are so insensitive towards me. I feel exceptionally bad and sad when people discriminate against black people or any other minority. Even student colleagues at University tell me to my face that they hate Muslims! I've had people spit at me and tell me to go back to my country, when my country is here! This hatred is thrown at me happens all the time even on Face Book and as I walk down the street, but I still

believe that my life is a political statement and I need to pursue this struggle. … Schools are not doing enough to educate … that should be the primary way to overcome stereotypes. (Saadah, young Muslim)

My problems started surfacing when I was 11 years old. Nothing was more important than my weight at the time. This spilled over during my time at secondary school and I started binge eating and no one was realising what I was getting into. I used to feel bad with myself but would still eat non-stop. At a certain point I would spend till 6am watching people eat on TV especially when I was at the worse time of my anorexia. (Janet, young person with an eating disorder)

I am 24 years old and consider myself a mental health survivor. When I used to go to school I enjoyed myself a lot. At a certain stage I developed a nervous tick and people would laugh at me including teachers and I didn't want to go to school anymore. Eventually I started collapsing every time I felt stressed – I started passing out. I did not have any friends my only friend was at secondary school. When I went to Junior College I enjoyed it there. However, at a later stage I started developing depression and got suicidal. There was a period in my life when I was constantly sad and depressed, spending all my time in my room. It was the moment when I realised it was time to be admitted to Mater Dei Hospital for treatment. … I am very critical of the teachers in general and the PSD teachers in particular. They never supported me in my life. There was a teacher who even made fun of me. (Irene, mental health survivor)

Cross-sectoral community supports, services and referrals for vulnerable young people and their families are also of fundamental importance (Barton, 2000). That is why we need to keep in contact with the grassroots, to reach out to the community and to take our research back to the community. All of this needs to be governed by a deep-seated commitment towards social justice (Roche et al., 2006). In a society where the shape and make-up of communities is constantly evolving, this study will converge a number of concepts that will help us localise the complex discourses around social movements. The truth is that in many ways a number of groups of disadvantaged youth are suffering the brunt because of their social experiences (Mizen, 2004; Batsleer, 2008). It is imperative that as we develop social policies and ensuing strategies, young people are present in the debate and feature prominently in the way that social planning develops (Maynard & Stuart, 2017).

Youth participation (Mizen, 2004) is a lynchpin in the whole debate on social cohesion and civil society (Roberts, 2009). This research highlights very clearly the fact that young people expect to be part of their community rather than wait submissively for an opportunity to come their way to be able to influence the matters that concern them. Being open to young people's active participation is not enough – what is required, as it emerges in this research is that we have adequate social structures.

It is true that 'society' was always an imagined entity, never given to experience in its totality; not so long ago, however, its image was one of a 'caring-and-sharing' community. Through welfare provisions seen as the birth-right of the citizen rather than a charitable hand-out for the less-capable, invalid or indolent, that image radiated a comforting trust in a collective insurance against individual misfortune. Society was imagined after the pattern of a powerful father, stern and sometimes unforgiving, but a father nevertheless, someone to whom one could confidently turn for helping case of trouble .... No wonder either that the 'good society' is a notion most of us would not bother thinking about, and that many would think such thinking to be a waste of time. (Bauman, 2001, p. 111)

RELATIONSHIPS AND NETWORKS

Relationship with parents, siblings and friends, and sometimes the lack of them, play an important role in the lives of vulnerable young people. While sometimes a source of strength and love, vulnerable young people often lack the understanding and support of their parents (Storrie, 2006). Parents with problems of their own and intergenerational and family challenges have a negative and debilitating effect on young people. Naturally a key notion to debate is how these difficulties seem to be mimicked from one generation to the next (Dimitrova, 2017).

> Nowadays I don't have many regrets, except that because my father was so religious I was afraid to tell him and never had the courage to share who I really was with him as I thought he would be embarrassed. (Greta, young lesbian)

> I do not have any friends who understand me. (Oliver, low education achiever)

> I would have preferred to have been left to make a choice myself whether to wear the hijab or not. (Saadah, young Muslim)

> My mother used to throw me out of the house when she had her boyfriend at home. (Colin, young person with a disability)

While vulnerable young people recognise the need for professional support in their lives and the assistance of social and educational services, their actual experience, while sometimes positive, is in general negative (Azzopardi, 2013b). A sense of frustration and a perceived lack of adequate response and support from professional and social/educational services is also apparent among vulnerable young people.

> Whenever I needed the support of the police I never found it and now I do not trust them because they take our issues lightly. (Nancy, young person with ethnic minority background)

> The worse thing is that there are a lot of family doctors that are not aware of this condition and wouldn't know how to deal with it. (Cindy, young woman with disabling illness)

> I am very critical of the teachers in general and the PSD teachers in particular. They never supported me in my life. (Irene, mental health survivor)
>
> It was only through Youth.inc that I found a true friend whom I could speak with and share my dreams. (Simon, low education achiever)
>
> I know I have an addictive personality, but that doesn't mean I don't get the necessary support. (Grace, drug addict and prisoner)
>
> We clean, we wash our clothes, we cook and we play football – but there are no helpers and social workers. At times I want to kill myself, I feel very sad but some of my friends here help me. (Idris, migrant and young offender)
>
> I am infinitely grateful for the work done by the members of staff at Dar Kenn ghal Sahhtek who were absolutely fantastic. (Denise, young person with an eating disorder)

Vulnerable young people, like all young people feel the need for a sense of belonging and connection with those around them. Being a member of a community is a source of identity, stability and support but one that needs to be reciprocal, inclusive and accepting (Barnett, 2012). Vulnerable young people have a complex relationship with the communities in which they live. Their vulnerabilities can often determine how they react and behave at community level and they display a tendency to see communities only through the lens of their vulnerabilities (Azzopardi & Grech, 2012).

> Maltese people started saying that I'm not Maltese, even though my mum is Maltese (my dad is Nigerian). (Nancy, young person with ethnic minority background)
>
> It is so difficult to 'come out' and be accepted, especially in certain areas of Malta. (Greta, young lesbian)
>
> It is all because I am a Libyan – it is always the same story, Maltese people hate us. (Idris, migrant and young offender)
>
> I used to try to work but in most cases I used to spend hours on the street and if I was given work they would not pay me. (Connor, homeless young man)

CONCLUSION

Vulnerable young people want solutions to their problems (Azzopardi, 2013a). They recognise the need for personal effort and commitment, but also know that their problems cannot be overcome without the support of others. Professional and support services and the voluntary sector need to be more proactive and engaged with vulnerable young people, who often need to be 'sought out' and more actively supported and encouraged (Maynard & Stuart, 2017). Cross-sectoral community supports, services and referrals for vulnerable young people and their families are also of fundamental importance. We need to recall that welfare emerged from the need to negotiate and reinvigorate the social responsibility for collective needs. Benevolence, goodwill and compassion towards all those who are at the fringe of society is not good enough. Social and community operators have developed myriad initiatives to meet the imperative to help the casualties of the economic system but is surely missing the wood for the trees. There are other elements, for example, the need to create a dialectic and a conversation with young people to bring about the conceptual changes. Social inclusion expands our moral currency. It is another path that leads towards full citizenship and societal engagement (Hardgrove et al., 2014).

... consideration of youth vulnerabilities is timely since there is growing political will in the international community and among many national governments and civil society groups to develop more effective policies for the young. (Hardgrove et al., 2014, p. 3)

Nowadays we can speak of symbolic boundaries of a community that relate to community identity and definition, power of community, culture(s) of community, and residents' attachment to and identification with community. Boundaries mark the beginning and instantaneously the end of a community, the notion of 'space' and location come into play. The boundary encapsulates the identity of the community and, like the identity of young people, is called into being by the exigencies of social interaction. Community is a morally charged understanding of human collective life, and its deepest driving force is derived from human beings' essential needs of endurance, enlargement and performance. Do our communities do enough to allow for young people to live a full and complete life (Azzopardi & Grech, 2012)? The life stories we witnessed in this chapter don't seem to indicate this.

REFERENCES

Atkinson, A. (2015). *Inequality*. Cambridge, MA: Harvard University Press.
Austin, A. (2016). On wellbeing and public policy: Are we capable of questioning the hegemony of happiness? *Social Indicators Research, 127*(1), 123–138.
Azzopardi, A. (2003). Inclusive education and the denial of difference: Is this the Cottonera experience? Exploring whether the discourse of inclusive education has been hijacked by concerns over standards. *International Journal of Inclusive Education, 7*(2), 159–174.
Azzopardi, A. (2011). Conceptualising discursive communities: Developing community in contemporary society. *International Journal of Inclusive Education, 15*(1), 179–192.
Azzopardi, A. (2013a). Youth activism: Social movements in the making on in the taking? In A. Azzopardi (Ed.), *Youth: Responding to lives – an international reader* (pp. 45–56). Rotterdam/Boston/Taipei: Sense Publishers.
Azzopardi, A. (Ed.). (2013b). *Youth: Responding to lives – An international reader.* Rotterdam/Boston/Taipei: Sense Publishers.
Azzopardi, A., & Grech, S. (2012). *Inclusive communities: A critical reader*. Rotterdam/Boston/Taipei: Sense Publishers.
Barnett, R. (2012). Learning for an unknown future. *Higher Education Research & Development, 31*(1), 65–77.
Barton, H. (2000). *Sustainable communities*. London: Earthscan Ltd.

Batsleer, J. R. (2008). *Informal learning in youth work*. London: Sage Publications.
Bauman, Z. (2001). *Community – Seeking safety in an insecure world*. Malden: Blackwell Publishing Ltd.
Beiner, R. (1995). *Theorizing citizenship*. New York, NY: State University of New York Press.
Cohen, S. (1972). *Folk devils and moral panics*. London & New York, NY: Routledge.
Cohen, S. (1997). Symbols of trouble. In K. Gelder (Ed.), *The subcultures reader*. London & New York, NY: Routledge.
Coleman, J. C., & Hendry, L. B. (2000). *The nature of adolescence* (3rd ed.). London & New York, NY: Routledge.
Craig, G., Popple, K., & Shaw, M. (2008). *Community development in theory and practice – An international reader*. Nottingham: Spokesman.
Cutajar, J. (2009). Introduction: Citizenship in the Maltese Islands. In J. Cutajar & G. Cassar (Eds.), *Social transitions in Maltese society*. Malta: Agenda.
Dewey, J. (1916). *Democracy and education: An introduction to the philosophy of education*. New York, NY: Palgrave Macmillan.
Dimitrova, R. (Ed.). (2017). *Well-being of youth and emerging adults across cultures – Novel approaches and findings from Europe, Asia, Africa and America*. New York, NY: Springer International Publishing.
Furlong, A. (2013). *Youth studies: An introduction*. New York, NY: Routledge.
Gelder, K. (1997). *The subcultures reader*. London & New York, NY: Routledge.
Hardgrove, A., Pells, K., Boyden, J., & Dornan, P. (2014). *Youth vulnerabilities in life course transitions* (UNDP Human Development Report Office Occasional Paper).
Hetherington, K. (1997). Blank figues in the countryside. In K. Gelder (Ed.), *The subcultures reader*. London & New York, NY: Routledge.
Klimke, M., & Scharloth, J. (Eds.). (2008). *1968 in Europe – A history of protest and activism, 1956–1977*. New York, NY: Palgrave Macmillan.
Maynard, L., & Stuart, K. (2017). *Promoting young people's wellbeing through empowerment and agency*. London & New York, NY: Routledge.
Mizen, P. (2004). *The changing state of youth*. New York, NY: Palgrave Macmillan.
OECD. (2017). *Evidence-based policy making for youth well-being: A toolkit, OECD development policy tools*. Paris: OECD Publishing. Retrieved from http://dx.doi.org/10.1787/9789264283923-en
Roberts, K. (2009). *Youth in transition – Eastern Europe and the West*. New York, NY: Palgrave Macmillan.
Roche, J. (2006). Children's rights: Participation and dialogue. In J. Roche, S. Tucker, R. Thomson, & R. Flynn (Eds.), *Youth in society* (2nd ed.). London: Sage Publications.
Roche, J., Tucker, S., Thomson, R., & And Flynn, R. (Eds.). (2006). *Youth in society* (2nd ed.). London: Sage Publications.
Rogers, W. S., Rogers, R., S., Vyrost, J., & Lovas, L. (2006). Worlds apart: Young people's aspirations in a changing Europe. In J. Roche, S. Tucker, R. Thomson, & R. Flynn (Eds.), *Youth in society* (2nd ed.). London: Sage Publications.
Romer, D. (Ed.). (2003). *Reducing adolescent risk – Towards an integrated approach*. London: Sage Publications.
Storrie, T. (2006). Citizens or what? In J. Roche, S. Tucker, R. Thomson, & R. Flynn (Eds.), *Youth in society* (2nd ed.). London: Sage Publications.
Zizek S. (2009). *Violence*. London: Profile Books Ltd.

JOANNE CASSAR AND MARILYN CLARK

8. THE CONCEPTUALISATION OF LEISURE AS AN INDICATOR AND COMPONENT OF SOCIAL WELLBEING

ABSTRACT

Leisure is a multidimensional construct, encompassing both personal and social factors. Subjective and social wellbeing are mutually dependent and are intertwined in ways that affect one another through dynamic processes. Participation in leisure has repeatedly been linked to a reduction of stress, which in turn leads to an increase in overall health and life satisfaction. This chapter discusses why leisure is one of the most important components of social wellbeing that contributes to a sense of social belonging. Leisure could however also work to constrain leisure opportunities in the face of unequal social relations and risk-taking behaviours that compromise community wellbeing. We argue that leisure practices are often embedded in relational, social contexts, which go beyond individual differences and preferences and are affected by economic, political, racial, cultural and social factors. The chapter also argues that leisure relations are always political. Firstly, leisure is located in the symbolic space between freedom and control. Secondly leisure provides the possibility for contestation of mainstream norms and the accommodation of alternative lifestyles.

Keywords: leisure, belonging, alternative lifestyles, body modification, wellbeing

LEISURE AND SOCIAL WELLBEING

Leisure revolves around a wide variety of indoor and outdoor activities, such as sports, socialising, watching television and reading. Leisure activities are generally self-selected and are associated with behavioural pursuits that are considered rewarding. Leisure experiences take place in both private and public spaces on both an individual and social level. Individual interests, personality type and peer influence determine leisure choices. Social background, socio-economic status and cultural forms in which leisure is embedded might also influence access to leisure. Yet distinctions in leisure practices based on class are fluid. For instance digitalised technologies in the Western world offer diverse networks within which entertainment can occur across race, gender and class. The popularity of social networking as a form of leisure is attributed to its relative low cost and easy access (Clark & Cassar, 2013).

Engagement in leisure has been found to generate positive feelings in individuals (Murphy, 2003). Active participation in leisure provides ways of detaching oneself from work and associated stress. There is a strong relationship between satisfaction with leisure activities and satisfaction with life generally (Neal & Sirgy, 2004; Sirgy & Comwell, 2001). Earlier research also confirms that leisure participation is positively linked to happiness and psychological wellbeing (Caldwell, 2005). Numerous studies conducted with respondents of different age groups constantly show the advantages of leisure across the lifespan. For example, leisure involving social interaction has been found to positively affect adolescents' identity development, self-esteem and life satisfaction (Trainor, Delfabbro, Anderson, & Winefield, 2010). Structured activities, which combine education and leisure, provide contexts which contribute towards positive youth development (Mahoney, Lord, & Carol, 2005). Iwasaki's study of Canadian youths and adults highlights the importance of leisure activities as a means of increasing wellbeing and coping with stress (2006). Leisure contributes towards young people's physical, cognitive, emotional and social development (Wilson, Gottfredson, Rorie, & Cornell, 2010). Leisure activities may be beneficial for improved health outcomes in older adults (Chang, Wray, & Lin, 2014).

Participation in organized leisure activities generally leads to broader benefits for society (Ellaway & Macintyre, 2000) as a result of social connections and positive emotions it often generates. Leisure activities are an expression of social habits and play an important role in establishing a sense of belonging to particular cultures. Leisure is one of the components of social wellbeing together with other factors, such as sustainable environment, health, community care, education, democratic participation and culture. Social wellbeing is associated with high quality of life, living standards and life satisfaction (Wiseman & Brasher, 2008, p. 358). Leisure creates and maintains social wellbeing through its contribution towards lifestyles characterised by a healthy work-life balance among citizens. Flexibility in work patterns contributes to more leisure participation. The positive effects of leisure activities on social wellbeing have been highlighted in a number of studies (e.g. Hertting & Kostenius, 2012; Han & Patterson, 2007). Psychosocial wellbeing entails being able to relate to other human beings by following similar cultural and social codes (Ahonen, 2010). Leisure activities carried out in groups, such as team sports have been linked with increased quality of life (Brajsa-Zganec, Merkas, & Sverko, 2011). There is also a correlation between positive social relationships and health, mediated through leisure activities (Chang, Wray, & Lin, 2014). Shared leisure practices provide possibilities for constructing 'community' through shared meanings and networks. Community wellbeing involves "the combination of social, economic, environmental, cultural, and political conditions identified by individuals and their communities as essential for them to flourish and fulfil their potential" (Wiseman & Brasher, 2008, p. 358).

Leisure occurs in social contexts that attach meanings to it. These shape how it is perceived and practiced and determine whether, when, what type and with whom leisure experiences occur. Notions of power, culture, ideologies and discourses which constitute the politics of leisure underpin the understanding of the implications of leisure practices on social wellbeing. The understanding of leisure as an aspect of life that "correlates with everything" (Chick & Shen, 2011, p. 59), encompasses our acknowledgment of the complexities involved in understanding the implications surrounding people's leisure choices. Individual and collective wellbeing are related to each other and boundaries demarcating the two could be blurred, as they can easily overlap each other. There is an intricate network of indicators of social wellbeing, which encompasses social, cultural, political, traditional and economic factors. There is no single indicator or set of fixed indicators related to social wellbeing. Markers for social wellbeing in relation to leisure are based on factors which lead to the fulfilment of leisure aspirations that increase self-confidence and secure personal wellbeing. Other indicators are related to positive relationships with leisure companions that develop greater consideration for others.

Leisure practices are impacted by gendered human relations that often dictate how men and women spend their leisure time. Cultural distinctions based on gender identities may constrain or enable leisure opportunities for women and men. Much of the literature on gendered leisure patterns shows that men have more time and choice to engage in leisure, while women remain inhibited in this regard, due to restrictions attributed to beauty regimes (Zones, 2000), 'female frailty' (Theberge, 2000) and their orientation towards an 'ethics of care'" towards others (Gilligan, 1982). Through their care-giving role as traditional primary caregivers in the household, they tend to place the needs of others ahead of their own. This might lead women to feel a lack of entitlement to leisure time (Maume, 2008). Leisure restrictions in a number of cultures also arise from the separation of genders aimed at maintaining a "code of honour", which limit women to the family network whilst men occupy public spaces (Borg & Clark, 2007, pp. 77–78). The use of public leisure spaces by women might differ from that of men in certain environments (Wearing, 1998). For example gay women and men who go to gay bars make use of this leisure space in different ways than straight women do (Skeggs, 1999). Leisure places enact gender relations and identities through meanings assigned to space. In spite of factors, which locate females in disadvantageous positions in terms of leisure time and space, however "a completely different picture has started emerging with the changing gender roles in society. It is now being seen that females are less dominated, disadvantaged or oppressed" (Khan, 2011, p. 110). Leisure practices built on traditional gender stereotypes are reproduced but gender inequities are also contested and transformed in everyday interactions at various levels. Leisure functions as means of social support and coping strategy for women and also acts as a form of resistance to existing unequal power relations in society (Du, 2008).

Discourses of domination and oppression play out in leisure arenas and intersect with discourses that are associated with sexism, racism and heteronormativity. Opportunities for leisure are embedded in complex relations that are intertwined with economic and political opportunism stemming from oppressive, neoliberal consumer capitalism (Spracklen, 2015). The entertainment industry through its subtle marketing strategies might put pressure on citizens to engage in commercial leisure emphasising that they would be missing out if they don't. Consumers of leisure do not have to be passive victims of commercial leisure service providers. Confronted with different choices, they are capable of subverting patterns of consumption by deciding for themselves what their leisure needs are without being driven by consumeristic discourses. Marginalised people living in socially and economically deprived areas could benefit from leisure and use it as a tool to reduce their subordination, draw social support and resist social inequality. These factors cultivate social wellbeing and could reinforce responsible citizenship. From this perspective, leisure could create spaces for people to engage in social dialogue, which could foster more respect for cultural diversity. Leisure experiences can potentially "challenge the way in which power is exercised, making leisure a form of political practice" (Shaw, 2001, p. 186).

DEVIANT LEISURE

While the mainstream literature on leisure highlights its potential to 'recreate', there is a growing evidence base that documents another 'darker' side to leisure. Two issues emerge and will be discussed here. The first concerns the possibly deleterious aspects of normative leisure pursuits; two main examples being: violence in sports and substance use in entertainment, most notably amongst the young. The second concerns leisure as a form of social contestation, potentially redrawing the boundaries between acceptable and unacceptable practices in our society. While above we highlighted that one should be suspect of leisure that could be linked to systems of capitalist exploitation, we also ask why some kinds of leisure behaviours are deemed 'deviant' and 'inappropriate' and whose interest this judgment serves. To explore this further this chapter will also discuss extensive body modification as a leisure pursuit.

The world of sports is infused with violence. Since the time of the gladiators, the culture of violence has been deeply embedded in sporting events. From bullfighting in Latin cultures, to dog fights in the United States, blood sports continue to be found in many parts of the world. Contact sports like rugby, hockey and water polo condone a degree of aggression as 'part of the game', as long as the intent is not to injure. The unconcealed physical actions that take place in some sports can be explained as aggressive (Kerr, 2002, p. 68). Actions like blocking in American football, tackling in rugby and defending in water polo can be classified as aggressive acts yet are within the regulations of the games. In addition, violent incidents often erupt, both among the players and the fans. In Europe violent outburst are fairly common at football matches (Marsh, Fox, Carnibella, McCann, & Marsh, 1996).

Leisure time provides a unique context where social norms are loosened, choice predominates and individuals feel free to engage in behaviours they might otherwise not pursue. Leisure provides 'time out' from the ordinary controls that characterize time otherwise spent (Blanco, 2016). Perhaps nowhere is this more obvious than in young people's entertainment. Parker's normalisation hypothesis, which emerged out of the realization that many conventional young people use drugs, has allowed for the conceptualization that drug taking may simply be a form of 'time out' from the stresses of being young in late modernity and the cultural accommodation of the illicit (Parker, Aldridge, & Measham, 1998). A number of empirical studies document how recreational drug users are not necessarily part of a deviant subcultural network nor are they always marginalized (Parker et al., 1998; Riley, James, Gregory, Dingle, & Codger, 2001). On the contrary, the research shows that most often recreational drug users in the 21st century may be high achievers in their educational and professional careers. Their experimentation and casual use of drugs may be conceptualized as a way of counterbalancing the harsh demands on youth in late modern society. Nonetheless, it is also recognized that such use poses a risk of transitioning to problem use (Jarvinen & Ravn, 2011). Clark and Bonavia (2014) in a study on the career patterns of socially integrated marijuana users in Malta, document how recreational marijuana users are able to negotiate long standing drug using careers with conventional lifestyles and fail to experience the many deleterious consequences often associated with drug addiction. In their narratives, marijuana use is conceptualised primarily as a leisure activity.

Leisure activities are often a site of social contestation. Other than providing social wellbeing leisure functions as a "site of excess, escape, transgression, resistance and change" (Bramham & Wagg, 2011, p. 5). Some kinds of leisure are labeled dangerous and a threat to wellbeing, because they contest agreed-upon norms of what is considered the general good of the individual and the community. The complex nature of what has been termed 'dark' leisure requires a broadening of what we consider to be legitimate and healthy in this regard. According to Elkington and Gammon (2014) the leisure literature remains "faithful to a moralising construction of what is good and what is bad that renders imperceptible leisure activities that might be deemed 'deviant'" (p. 57). The mainstream leisure literature assumes that only 'normal' or conventional leisure pursuits contribute to personal and social wellbeing, thus failing to allow for an understanding of the personal meanings people attribute to recreational activities. Behaviour that is considered deviant in particular social spaces will be deemed as perfectly acceptable in others. Deviant leisure has been given increasing attention by researchers and there has been an interest in examining how both formal and informal sanctions imposed on leisure may stigmatise those who engage in it (Rojek, 1997).

A discussion of extreme body modification throws further light on the issue. A number of double standards exist around body modification. Many commercial enterprises require their employees to cover their tattoos and piercings or will not employ people with visible and extensive modifications. Yet plastic surgeons routinely perform a number of cosmetic surgeries such as facelifts, fat removal and sculpting and breast reductions and augmentations. Stebbins (2006) identified hobbies as a form of leisure and extensive body modification gives significance, a sense of identity, pleasure, excitement, and freedom and may thus be viewed as project-based leisure. Committed body modifiers often plan in advance how they will be modifying their bodies to mirror their identities. Serious body modification has been referred to as 'body projects' or 'reflexive body projects' (Crossley, 2005; Shilling, 1993). Williams (2009) invites the academic community to consider body modification as a new form of leisure producing novel understanding of people's understanding of leisure, wellbeing and pathology. Williams (2009) writes how "radical body modification informs the significance of personal experience as it connects with bodies and identities" (p. 211). While psychiatric discourse frames extensive body modification as self-mutilation and evidencing an underlying psychopathology (Williams, 2009), body modification may be seen as connecting unique embodied persons, to significant life turning points and meaningful biographical trajectories. The medicalization of deviance fails to consider cultural differences, personal narratives and meanings, and subjective and interpersonal motivations.

CONCLUSION

This chapter has emphasised that leisure does not constitute a uniform social entity. There is a myriad of opportunities for citizens to support their development through leisure. We have argued that leisure is an indicator and component of social wellbeing that has important implications for social cohesion and solidarity. The role of leisure in people's everyday lives is being given more attention, due to discourses which emphasise the importance of work-life balance and quality of life. Despite the possibilities that expose people to harm, disadvantage, disempowerment and exploitation through deviant acts operating in the leisure sphere, there is also great potential for personal and social wellbeing generated through the enjoyment of leisure and meaningful social relationships that could emerge from it.

We also propose an extension of the understanding of leisure to include the unconventional and unusual, fostering more inclusive communities. Collective identities are shared through leisure practices, which bring people together in ways that foster a sense of community. We posit that even 'deviant' leisure activities could provide possibilities for meaning making. Despite barriers emanating from social imbalances related to race, gender and class, leisure "may be viewed as a field in which dominant and subordinate cultures meet" (Du, 2008, p. 180). The notion of 'wellbeing' denotes an emphasis on 'being' rather than on 'doing' and this concept might render it static. Healthy social functioning "is itself a way of being active, not just a passive state of satisfaction" (Nussbaum, 2000, p. 14). We therefore propose an 'active' social wellbeing based on leisure practices that provide satisfaction, enjoyment and fun in the context of meaningful relationships that are socially just.

THE CONCEPTUALISATION OF LEISURE AS AN INDICATOR AND COMPONENT

REFERENCES

Ahonen, A. (2010). *Psychosocial well-being of schoolchildren in the Barents region. A comparison from the northern parts of Norway, Sweden and Finland and northwest Russia* (Unpublished doctoral thesis). University of Lapland, Rovaniemi, Finland.

Blanco, J. A. (2016). *Deviant leisure in the collegiate undergraduate population: Predicting participation and affect using self-discrepancy theory* (Unpublished PhD thesis). University of Illinois, Urbana-Champaign, IL.

Borg, S., & Clark, M. (2007). Leisure & young married women in Malta. *Journal of World Anthropology, 3*(1), 74–96.

Brajsa-Zganec, A., Merkas, M., & Sverko, I. (2011). Quality of life and leisure activities: How do leisure activities contribute to subjective well-being? *Social Indicator Research, 102*, 81–91.

Bramham, P., & Wagg, S. (2011). Introduction: Unforbidden fruit: From leisure to pleasure. In P. Bramham & S. Wagg (Eds.), *The new politics of leisure and pleasure* (pp. 1–10). New York, NY: Palgrave Macmillan.

Caldwell, L. L. (2005). Leisure and health: Why is leisure therapeutic? *British Journal of Guidance and Counselling, 33*(1), 7–26.

Clark, M., & Bonavia, M. (2014). *A study among emerging adults in Malta, Papers: International symposium on drug policy and public health* (pp. 167–186). Istanbul: Turkish Green Crescent Society. (ISBN 978-605-9090-15-5)

Clark, M., & Cassar, J. (2013). *Leisure trends among young people in Malta*. Malta: Office of the Commissioner for Children & Aġenżija Żgħażagħ. Retrieved from http://www.agenzijazghazagh.gov.mt/Downloads/60/Leisure_Trends_Amongst_Young_People_in_Malta/

Chang, P. J., Wray, L., & Lin, Y. (2014). Social relationships, leisure activity, and health in older adults. *Health Psychology, 33*(6), 516–523.

Chick, G., & Shen, X. S. (2011). Leisure and cultural complexity. *Cross-Cultural Research, 45*(1), 59–81.

Crossley, N. (2005). Mapping reflexive body techniques: On body modification and maintenance. *Body and Society, 11*, 1–35.

Du, J. (2008). Women's leisure as reproduction and resistance. *Affilia: Journal of Women and Social Work, 23*(2), 179–189.

Elkington, S., & Gammon, S. (Eds.). (2014). *Contemporary perspectives in leisure: Meanings, motives and lifelong learning*. London: Routledge.

Ellaway, A., & Macintyre, A. (2000). Social capital and self-rated health: Support for a contextual mechanism. *American Journal of Public Health, 90*(6), 988–998.

Gilligan, C. (1982). *In a different voice*. Cambridge, MA: Harvard University Press.

Han, J. S., & Patterson, I. (2007). An analysis of the influence that leisure experiences have on a person's mood state, health and well-being. *Annals of Leisure Research, 9*, 328–351.

Hertting, K., & Kostenius, C. (2012). Organized leisure activities and well-being: Children getting it just right! *Larnet: Cyber Journal of Applied Leisure and Recreation Research, 15*(2), 13–28.

Iwasaki, Y. (2006). Counteracting stress through leisure coping: A prospective health study. *Psychology, Health & Medicine, 11*(2), 209–220.

Jarvinen, M., & Ravn, S. (2011). From recreational to regular drug use: Qualitative interviews with young clubbers. *Sociology of health & Illness, 33*(4), 554–569.

Kerr, J. H. (2002). Issues in aggression and violence in sport: The ISSP position stand revisited. *The Sport Psychologist, 16*, 68–78.

Mahoney, J. L., Lord, H., & Carryl, E. (2005). An ecological analysis of after-school program participation and the development of academic performance and motivational attributes for disadvantaged children. *Child Development, 76*(4), 811–825.

Marsh, P., Fox, K., Carnibella, G., McCann, J., & Marsh, J. (1996). *Football violence in Europe*. Washington, DC: The Amsterdam Group.

Maume, D. (2008). Gender differences in providing urgent childcare among dual-earner parents. *Social Forces, 87*, 273–297.

Murphy, H. (2003). Exploring leisure and psychological health and well-being: Some problematic issues in the case of Northern Ireland. *Leisure Studies, 22*(1), 37–50.

Neal, J. D., & Sirgy, M. J. (2004). Measuring the effect of tourism services on travellers' quality of life: Further validation. *Social Indicators Research, 69*(3), 243–277.

Nussbaum, M. (2000). *Women and human development: The capabilities approach*. Cambridge: Cambridge University Press.

Parker, H., Aldridge, J., & Measham, F. (1998). *Illegal leisure: The normalization of adolescent recreational drug use*. London: Routledge.

Riley, S., James, C., Gregory, D., Dingle, H., & Cadger, M. (2001). Patterns of recreational drug use at dance events in Edinburgh, Scotland. *Addiction, 96*(7), 1035–1047.

Rojek, C. (1997). Leisure theory: Retrospect and prospect. *Society and Leisure, 20*, 383–400.

Shaw, S. M. (2001). Conceptualizing resistance: Women's leisure as political practice. *Journal of Leisure Research, 33*, 186–202.

Shilling, C. (1993). *The body and social theory*. London: Sage Publications.

Sirgy, M. J., & Cornwell, T. (2001). Further validation of the Sirgy et al.'s measure of community quality of life. *Social Indicators Research, 56*(2), 125–143.

Skeggs, B. (1999). Matter of place: Visibility and sexualities in leisure spaces. *Leisure Studies, 18*, 213–232.

Spracklen, K. (2015). *Digital leisure, the internet and popular culture*. London: Palgrave Macmillan.

Stebbins, R. A. (2006). Serious leisure. In C. Rojek, S. M. Shaw, & A. J. Veal (Eds.), *A handbook of leisure studies* (pp. 448–456). London: Palgrave Macmillan.

Theberge, N. (2000). Gender, sport, and the construction of difference. In N. Theberge (Ed.), *Higher goals: Women's ice hockey and the politics of gender*. Albany, NY: State University of New York Press.

Trainor, S., Delfabbro, P., Anderson, S., & Winefield, A. (2010). Leisure activities and adolescent psychological wellbeing. *Journal of Adolescence, 33*, 173–186.

Wearing, B. (1998). *Leisure and feminist theory*. Thousand Oaks, CA: Sage Publications.

Williams, D. J. (2009). Deviant leisure: Rethinking "the good, the bad, and the ugly". *Leisure Sciences: An Interdisciplinary Journal, 31*(2), 207–213.

Wilson, D., Gottfredson, D., Rorie, M., & Cornell, N. (2010). Youth development in after school leisure activities. *Journal of Early Adolescence, 30*(5), 688–690.

Wiseman, J., & Brasher, K. (2008). Community wellbeing in an unwell world: Trends, challenges, and possibilities. *Journal of Public Health Policy, 29*, 353–366.

Zones, J. S. (2000). Beauty myths and realities and their impact on women's health. In M. B. Zinn, P. Hondagneu-Sotelo, & M. A. Messner (Eds.), *Gender through the prism of difference*. Boston, MA: Allyn and Bacon.

MARCELINE NAUDI AND BARBARA STELMASZEK

9. DIS/EMPOWERMENT UNDER PATRIARCHY

Intimate Partner Violence against Women

ABSTRACT

This chapter presents the concept of dis/empowerment in the context of women victims of intimate partner violence, identifying the act of violence against women as a product of a patriarchal society. The chapter suggests the idea that empowerment is a stepping stone into power, an ability to act or control one's life, that exists within people and communities, that is shared and transferred among members of society, all the while moving between layers of the individual and the collective. The chapter includes a description of the project Stronger Together as an example of the individual impact on the collective. The collective, or community, however does not exist in a vacuum, but is located within patriarchy itself, and therefore the circle of disempowerment and empowerment happen all in one place, raising the question as to whether cultivating individual power based on one's subjective needs is truly possible from the place where we stand.

Keywords: empowerment, disempowerment, patriarchy, violence against women, wellbeing

INTRODUCTION

Women's experience of male violence, including intimate partner violence (IPV), can lead to their disempowerment. For many women who are survivors of IPV, empowerment is often an important part of the journey towards living free from violence and reclaiming their lives. IPV is a form of violence against women (VAW) and is understood to be a "violation of human rights and a form of discrimination against women … [resulting in] physical, sexual, psychological or economic harm or suffering to women, including threats of such acts, coercion or arbitrary deprivation of liberty …" (Istanbul Convention, 2011, Article 3, para. a).

No society is free of IPV and over the last two decades, researchers have quantified the phenomenon and expressed its magnitude in numbers (European Institute for Gender Equality [EIGE], 2012). Quantifying the resulting harm, however, presents a challenge. The consequences are vast and include health complications, injuries, psychological trauma, inability to work (United Nations Statistics Division, 2015), financial instability, insecurity and fear, low self-esteem, and homelessness, among others. The consequences that include emotional trauma can lead women to rely on alcohol or drugs in an attempt to cope, or even commit suicide (Busch & Valentine, 2000). These painful experiences create a variety of burdens for society, including high medical expenditure due to the diverse disorders that body and mind may succumb to when a person is violated (Chang et al., 2010). All of this represents or leads to a state of disempowerment.

Experiencing IPV can be unsettling and uprooting, because it contradicts the ingrained understanding of intimate love as being a source of safety and comfort. The violence is often not a single act, but several connected acts over a period of time, a course of conduct that is a pattern of behaviour showing continuous intent (Kelly & Westmarland, 2016). Stark (2007) best describes the intent as the "deprivation of rights and resources that are critical to personhood ... [with the] key dynamic [being] ... subordination and the resistance women mount to free themselves from domination" (p. 5). VAW is a particularly unique phenomenon because it is about exercising control and maintaining power, and victims of violence are "involved in a power dynamic" where one person has more power socially than the other (Busch & Valentine, 2000, p. 84). VAW has come to be defined as resulting from unequal power, more specifically a historical power imbalance between women and men (Istanbul Convention, 2011).

Across the globe, VAW has been recognised as a manifestation of the dominant patriarchal system, and through its targeting of women, serves to actively disempower them. This chapter explores the concept of *empowerment* and what it means for women, both individually and collectively. It considers the meaning of the concept of empowerment for women who are experiencing violence (especially IPV), as a historically disempowered group on both the individual and collective levels, and addresses the concept of participation in one's own empowerment, having control over the choices which lead to empowerment and influencing collective empowerment in the process. The fact that this occurs within an existing patriarchal tradition, and the resultant difficulties, are also considered, including by asking whether collective empowerment can meet individual needs. Examples from different countries, such as Germany, United Kingdom and Malta, are used to illustrate the arguments put forward.

DISEMPOWERMENT AND EMPOWERMENT IN A PATRIARCHAL SOCIETY

VAW stems from historically unequal power sharing between women and men. Unequal power sharing between women and men is also known as patriarchy. The London Feminist Network (n.d.) defines patriarchy as follows:

> Patriarchy is the term used to describe the society in which we live today, characterised by current and historic unequal power relations between women

and men whereby women are systematically disadvantaged and oppressed. This takes place across almost every sphere of life but is particularly noticeable in women's under-representation in key state institutions, in decision-making positions and employment and industry.

Male violence against women is also a key feature of patriarchy. Women in minority groups face multiple oppressions in this society, as race, class and sexuality intersect with sexism. (para. 1)

Patriarchy as a Source of Disempowerment

Patriarchy is a system, a culture that influences different aspects of life and is long-standing. VAW continues *because* of this entrenched culture, and at the same time it acts to *sustain* it. Living in a patriarchal society is tiring, because feeling oppressed is tiring, and experiencing violence can lead to fatigue. Violence can wear a person out (Chang et al., 2010). A woman's journey to end violence in an intimate relationship is long and trying, and leaves an impression that lasts a lifetime. On a collective level, ending VAW is almost (and probably) impossible to achieve in a single lifetime.

Depending on women's background and the way in which non-dominant or minority backgrounds are constructed to construe a lesser worth, certain groups are placed in a further position of vulnerability in relation to disempowerment. These groups could include people with disabilities, the gay and lesbian community, the elderly, youths and homeless people among others (Busch & Valentine, 2000). In the field of social work women are deemed to be a disempowered group due to the barriers they encounter in accessing resources and positions of power. These barriers prohibit women from acting in their own self-interest and in becoming sufficiently empowered to find ways to end IPV (Busch & Valentine, 2000, p. 84).

Disempowerment as a Starting Point of Empowerment

Eventually, women victims of violence can reach the threshold beyond which they will not handle any more violence and disempowerment. According to the European Union survey on VAW, the majority of cases of the most serious IPV incidents are not reported to the police or services, and when women do report the violence, it comes "only after [the woman has already faced] a series of violent incidents" (European Union Agency for Fundamental Rights [FRA], 2014, p. 60). At this point, the woman has given enough, or enough has been taken from her and her own concerns matter above all. Stark (2007), recounting the courage of women who fought to overcome subordination, oppression, and power, stated an inspirational point about women who have been abused by men, in that "the spirit that continually resurfaces in these [women's] lives indicates that each of us is capable of remaking the world we are given, even against impossible odds" (p. 17).

Turning Points for Survivors of Intimate Partner Violence

Whilst having one's self constantly eroded, resulting in feeling completely worn out, can seem like a barrier to action, it can equally serve as an impetus for that eventual step towards empowerment. Women describe such a state as being worn out mentally and no longer being able to 'take it', as hitting the lowest possible point, or realising that the blame does not sit with them and that the fault or responsibility for the abuse belongs to the abuser. Fatigue creates a desire for change and lends itself to a permanent shift in perspective, where the woman can and will no longer tolerate the situation. "Fatigue [is] an accumulation of disappointments in various attempts to change the abuser's behaviour" (Chang et al., 2010, p. 255) and leads a woman to recognise that if the abuser does not change, she must find another way to change the situation, which otherwise will continue to be "physically, emotionally, and psychologically draining" (Chang et al., 2010, p. 255).

Most often, women have turning points which result in the decision to change their situation. These may include: protecting others from abuse, especially children or others for whom the women care; increase in frequency and severity of abuse, as well as when the abuser's acts are seen to be threatening the woman's life (Chang et al., 2010). Recognising that a way out exists through support services can be one such turning point[1] (FRA, 2014, p. 69).

Support Services as a Turning Point

Support services can be seen not only as places for long-term empowerment, but also sources of initial turning points for women, serving as catalysts for them to want to seek further empowerment. For this reason, professionals in a position to empower others must become aware of the power that this position brings (Hafford-Letchfield, 2014). IPV already disempowers through the woman being subjected to control, and so the helping professionals should always respect, if not also promote and cultivate, their clients' autonomy as one of the core principles of working with women survivors of violence (EIGE, 2012).

DEFINING THE CONCEPT OF EMPOWERMENT

Violence disempowers, closing off "opportunit[ies] to exit" (Stark, 2007, p. 115) and strips women of the "volitional space [needed] to exercise decisional autonomy" (Stark, 2007, p. 115). Empowerment is the antidote. The word *em-power-ment* is impressive in that it implies an entrance into the state of power. Empowerment is often communicated by social movements that exist to speak for and with the disadvantaged, marginalised, discriminated against, and under-served. Research reports, policy documents, and training manuals are populated with talk of empowerment. Social media postings, including twitter hashtags cannot seem to get enough of it. Already in 1999, Page & Czuba proclaimed the term to be an overused 'buzz word'. Following a literature review, the same authors were unable to develop a clear definition for empowerment, due partly to the fact that the understanding of empowerment differs so much across disciplines. Another possible reason for the challenge stems from the meaning being also personal and subjective (Peled, Eisikovits, Enosh, & Winstok, 2000).

Capturing empowerment as it happens and defining it is difficult because "it takes on different forms in different people and contexts" (Page & Czuba, 1999, 'Understanding Empowerment', para. 1). In the end however, without defining empowerment, practicing it can be a challenge. At the same time, defining empowerment can be disserving since anything that is "formulaic or prescription-like [can be seen to contradict] the very concept of empowerment" (Page & Czuba, 1999, 'Understanding Empowerment' para. 1).

Empowerment takes place on both individual and collective levels. Power can be shared in a collective sense and move between the individual and the collective. Since power is mobile, it cannot be seen as something fixed, stagnant, inherent, or unwavering, instead it is transferable and most of all within reach. When one person or community within a greater marginalised group (e.g. women, grassroots organisations) gain power, the entire group gains power (Page & Czuba, 1999). This idea of individual and collective is especially relevant to preventing VAW and empowering of survivors, because the violence is individually impactful but also originating from a collective system that generates it.

Individual Empowerment

The personal, subjective and context-dependent aspects of empowerment open the door to a variety of ways that women survivors of violence can step into a state of power. As previously mentioned, service provision for women survivors of violence presents one such opportunity. Just like disempowerment, empowerment itself takes place in relationships (Page & Czuba, 1999) and "implies the existence of an empowering agent and an empowered actor involved in a growth process within a social power structure" (Peled et al., 2000, para. 4). Most importantly power is not inherently possessed or owned by any person, instead one steps into power when provided with "opportunities, resources and support that [one needs] to become involved [herself]" (Page & Czuba, 1999, "Empowerment and PEP", para. 2). A European project entitled Cultural Encounters in Interventions against Violence that resulted in the anthology of women's stories entitled *Experiences of Intervention against Violence* (Hagemann-White & Grafe, 2016) shows that empowerment through intervention comes in many forms. The stories come from women from a "minority or migration background [who] travelled through a history of violence and intervention" (Preface).

Examples of Dis/Empowerment through Service Provision

Learning that change is possible. "The support workers noticed what I needed before I even said anything, because I had never imagined a solution would be possible .... They showed me the way, and I did it myself" (Hagemann-White & Grafe, 2016, pp. 33–35). This piece of a woman's story echoes Page & Czuba's (1999) discussion on shifts that take place in life which can set us on a new and hopefully more fulfilling path: "Empowerment ... challenges our assumptions about the way things are and how they can be" (para. 2). The process opens us up to the possibility of change. Once we see the possibility of change, then there is something to work towards, something which gives us the courage to try, to do, to act, to gain or regain control of our lives. "[Empowerment] challenges our basic assumptions [about ourselves and our lives,] about power, helping, achieving, and succeeding" (para. 2).

Guidance towards independence. Busch and Valentine (2000) reflect on the historical developments in social work practice as moving away from controlling the marginalised groups to enabling their "self-determination" (p. 82). "[T]his organisation has helped me with everything. Because then I was scared all the time, I was scared to go out, to get on a bus, but here, first we got my visa sorted .... I am better now because of all the help .... At the beginning they did so much because I could not" (Hagemann-White & Grafe, 2016, p. 20). The woman goes on to say that she eventually became active in improving her situation: "... I had no confidence but they teach you how to become more confident and to learn how to do things on your own and slowly, slowly, I have been learning (Hagemann-White & Grafe, 2016, p. 20).

Acquiring skills. Empowerment is also about "enabling people to master their environments and achieve self-determination (Simon & Parsons, 1983) ... [it is about acquiring] skills, knowledge, and emotional as well as material resources by which personally meaningful social roles are fulfilled (Solomon, 1976)" (Peled et al., 2000, para. 4). One woman felt that her lack of education contributed to her entrapment: "because I am an uneducated woman I don't know what to do, and I was like a servant in front of him and he could do anything to me" (Hagemann-White & Grafe, 2016, p. 17).

Knowing one's rights. The possession of rights is also empowering since it allows women to make undeniable claims to their own benefit that fulfil arising needs. "We have the rights. We've got rights to say, when I need help, you can help us. We've got rights. That's why our confidence is built" (Hagemann-White & Grafe, 2016, p. 28).

Community support. One of the stories describes the step-by-step process of leaving a violent partner. The woman disclosed the violence to her children, then a friend, who in turn referred her to a lawyer. There she received advice and became aware of her legal rights, and eventually through a support service received her own accommodation (Hagemann-White & Grafe, 2016, pp. 14–15). The process was multi-dimensional, where different actors became involved to support a survivor in a way that enabled her to gain control over her own life (Page & Czuba, 1999). This is a process through which power becomes cultivated and available for personal benefit, allowing personal needs and interests to be addressed (Page & Czuba, 1999).

Being listened to. The same anthology also exposes the opposite – moments of disempowerment. Sometimes understanding empowerment is done best through the perspective of its absence (Page & Czuba, 1999). One woman who was a survivor of violence described different professionals as unable or unwilling to acknowledge that she was experiencing abuse. In addition, her child's school staff expressed concern for the child only and threateningly placed on her the responsibility to report the abuse. The moment of change came when a friend listened to her story and recognised her husband's behaviour as abuse. Despite ongoing challenges with support services, what followed were a series of encounters with professionals who listened and provided advice on personal and legal steps (Hagemann-White & Grafe, 2016).

Supportive friends are known to be empowering when women look for ways to end the violence. Klein (2012) shows that informal networks in the form of family, friends, or co-workers who become knowledgeable about the violence "[open] windows of opportunity because [they] are a potential, and largely untapped, resource for intervention, prevention, and social change" (p. 2). In some cases, women simply want to express their feelings of pain and share their story with someone, or detect a hint of empathy and understanding on another person's face. Negative, dismissive, or blaming attitudes cause harm. Citing Symonds (1980, 2010), Klein (2012) states that "distant and passive demeanour increased victims' shame and self-hate, making trauma worse and constituting what [is] termed a "'second injury'" (p. 77).

Overcoming shame. According to Brené Brown (2012), shame is a lethal emotion because it isolates and makes a person feel alone. Where shame grows through silence and judgment, showing empathy for one's situation alleviates shame. Watt Smith (2015) reflects on Plutarch's and Jean-Paul Sartre's respective recounting of shame as "'one of the greatest shaking cracks that our soul can receive'" (p. 234) and a sort of internal flooding. "[Shame] is more often linked to a feeling of social condemnation and the horror of being *seen*" (pp. 234–235). If feeling shame makes one wish to disappear from view (p. 235), and silence and isolation keep violence alive, overcoming shame is part of the empowerment process for women survivors of violence.

According to Baker (2013), since shame impacts how power is felt throughout the body as a self-regulatory mechanism, empowerment must involve addressing shame. Since IPV relies on shame for control, responding to a woman's disclosure with shaming only extends the violent partner's reach. Furthermore, since empowerment happens within relationships and through social outreach, shamed women end up being isolated from these opportunities (pp. 145–146, 150).

Validating one's experiences. Returning to the woman's story above, when third parties recognise a woman's experience as abuse, it can serve as the turning point that changes the woman's situation and future outcome. In some cases, the recognition itself can provide the woman with the knowledge that confirms her feelings and beliefs, or changes her awareness. One woman stated: "… I didn't realise that my husband had raped me. I thought rape was being dragged down the back of an alley, you know. I needed someone from the NGO there to explain to me what rape was" (Hagemann-White & Grafe, 2016, p. 22).

Steering clear of judgment and discrimination. For another woman, the moment of disempowerment came when a support worker deemed her unworthy of being helped because she was not a mother: "… when she first of all asked me if I had children, and when I said that I had none, that woman did not want to talk any further with me" (Hagemann-White & Grafe, 2016, p. 41). Gendered expectations of survivors can be disempowering and therefore, avowing diversity is key to the process of empowerment in order to allow the women to find themselves in the image of those who are worthy of support. Citing Loseke (1992), Peled et al. (2000) see the inadvertent harm that comes with vying for the recognition of a social issue such as VAW. "In the process of giving … visibility …, dramatization, simplification, and homogenization are inevitable … [yet these successful tactics] have created new myths and injustices" (para. 2).

Respect for individual integrity. Referring to the definition adapted by other authors, Busch and Valentine (2000) see empowerment as the "'ability to speak one's own truths in one's own voice and participate in the decisions that affect one's life'" (p. 83). One woman describes this as having a say: "And she always asked me what I wanted, she did not tell me do this or do that …" (Hagemann-White & Grafe, 2016, p. 26). At times, those who serve as change agents may have a different understanding of empowerment and project it onto the women. Peled et al. (2000) discuss this in the context of women who seek help but also choose to stay with violent partners. While one may question whether here *choice* is even possible, women do stay for a variety of reasons, including to stay alive. The goal of support then would be to provide measures of safety and to "attempt to understand women's subjective perceptions and choices without regard for the values and stereotypes of others; these values may be benign, but are of little practical use and often in contradiction to women's sense of autonomy and self-determination" ("Empowerment-Based Approaches", para. 8).

According to Gutierrez et al. (1995) as referred to in Busch and Valentine (2000), those who wish to empower others should do so in a way that is collaborative and builds trust. They should accept the survivor's definition of the problem as well as support the woman in building herself up based on her existing strengths. They should share their own power as well as activate resources for the benefit of the woman, stand on her side, and promote her well-being, as well as utilise their joint relationship as a space for the woman to sense her personal power (pp. 83–84).

The above discussion however shows that support workers must be equally empowered in order to share their power with those they help. Empowerment is also about the interconnectedness of the individual and the collective. "To create change we must change individually to enable us to become partners in solving the complex issues facing us" (Page & Czuba, 1999, 'Interconnection of Individuals', para. 14).

Collective Empowerment

Page and Czuba (1999) discuss empowerment as a process that moves between the individual and the community, from a personal to a collective level, and vice versa. When a group is deemed disadvantaged, either the people in the group or others who identify with their disadvantage form a movement to strengthen the position of the group members. Equally, when the movement strengthens, the strengthening empowers the individuals belonging to that particular movement and those it represents. Individual empowerment feeds collective empowerment and vice versa.

Feminist anti-violence movement making change possible. The VAW movement has been around for five decades (UN Women, n.d.b), having sprung its roots a few centuries ago, with the seed likely to have been born many years in the distant past at a moment when a woman felt that she was treated unfairly. Since then, women have: impacted the development of laws to prevent violence and protect women from it; established support services for survivors; run anti-violence awareness raising campaigns, written books, articles, websites, and blogs about VAW; created state and interstate institutions to monitor progress for women; demonstrated; resisted; persisted; and succeeded in taking one more step toward placing women's freedom from violence closer to reality. Research into three decades of women's global activism shows how women specific interest groups created spaces within society for violence as an important women's issue (Htun & Weldon, 2012).

Collective rights. Today, VAW is globally recognised as a human rights violation and many forms of VAW have been criminalised or otherwise addressed in international, regional, and national laws and conventions. In 2011, the women's anti-violence movement welcomed an ambitious and progressive treaty, the Istanbul Convention.[2] The treaty represents a collective empowerment, where women's needs are turned into claimable rights (Council of Europe, n.d., About Monitoring, GREVIO).

Before the Istanbul Convention, the treaty of relevance to women's rights and VAW was the United Nations Convention on the Elimination of All Forms of Discrimination against Women (CEDAW) (UN Women, n.d.a).[3] Until 2017, VAW was addressed within the scope of the Convention by General Recommendation No. 19, which has now been replaced with General Recommendation No. 35 on gender-based violence (General Recommendation No. 35, 2017).

Validating women's experiences. Prior to the work and accomplishments of the women's anti-violence movement, VAW was relegated to the private sphere and the world's governments refused public accountability for what constituted oppression based on gender. Recognizing VAW as a human rights violation, and hence, placing the responsibility for due diligence into the hands of the state was, at the time, refused on various grounds, from sex discrimination being too trivial in comparison to "larger issues of survival" (Bunch, 1990, p. 488) to women's rights essentially not being related to the constitution of human rights. The gloomiest and most infuriating response was the idea that when "the abuse of women is recognized, it is considered inevitable or so pervasive that any consideration of it is futile or will overwhelm other human rights questions" (Bunch, 1990, p. 488).

Eventually however, the recognition of women's rights as human rights came about. This was a collective stepping into power, when women's reality became recognised as a human experience. Governments were now required to step up their efforts to improve access to rights which were impeded by the historical denial of equality and existing imbalance of power, such as those related to education or the economy, as well as rights specific to women such as reproductive rights, and the right to a life free from violence (Beijing Declaration and Platform for Action, 1995). Recognizing VAW as a human rights violation was inevitable in consideration of the inalienable nature of human rights (Universal Declaration of Human Rights, 1948, Preamble, para. 1), and the logical argument that violence targeted towards women strips them of enjoying rights otherwise made accessible to men, including the right to liberty, and other political and civil, and socioeconomic rights (Bunch, 1990).

This implied due diligence and state accountability. In effect then, "by making the State accountable for violence perpetrated by non-State actors, public international law recognize[d] that [VAW], regardless of who commits it, constitutes human rights violations" (Aziz & Moussa, 2016, p. 1). The states could no longer escape their responsibility, since condoning "private" violence through inaction, or sanctioning violence, was now recognized as on par with committing it (Bunch, 1990, p. 488).

The recognition of rights specific to women as human rights was the result of the collective work of women on local, regional and global levels and included the bringing together of the knowledge of feminist theory and human rights as well as forming alliances on various levels, including those with greatest power such as governments and the United Nations (Aziz & Moussa, 2016). The power to make this happen came from the feminist movement's access to various resources and through forming relationships with agents who could share or transfer their own power to enable the movement to focus on issues most important to those it represented.

Connecting Individual Empowerment to Collective Empowerment

On perceiving the individual and collective empowerment as symbiotic and reciprocal, it becomes evident that power gains by individual women can create empowerment for the community of women, and vice versa. One woman's stepping into power can be an achievement for all women. The above pieces of women's stories show empowerment through women's service provision, which historically in many countries were safe places created by feminists, where women came to be empowered, where feminism grew, and from where demands for universal recognition and codification of women's rights started. In effect now, the universal recognition and codification obliges European governments to ensure such safe places exist and are supported by governments (Istanbul Convention, 2011, Article 22).

Participation is part of empowerment. The institutional/organisational as well as the collective aspect of empowerment is necessary for individual empowerment but its position inevitably places it at a distance from the very people it is aimed at. As a result, practitioners and others claiming to speak for survivors should involve them in the decision making processes that impact the policies that impact them. Essential to becoming empowered is choosing how one wishes to be empowered. There are many policies and programmes that deal with empowering women and some may even do so based on research or discussions, but still they may not actually involve the women who are supposed to be served by those same policies and programmes. When women struggle to leave violence behind, they should not also have to struggle against the organisations that are supposed to help them (Peled et al., 2000).

Stronger Together – Example of Individual Impact on the Collective

In 2016, the Jesuit Refugee Services in Malta in partnership with the Women's Rights Foundation in Malta (and funded by the Commonwealth Foundation) began a project entitled Stronger Together with the collaborative aim of empowering women living in institutional settings such as the migrant open centres and the domestic violence shelters (Gafa, Naudi, & Rossi, 2017).

The project is an example of women choosing how to become empowered. Involving women from the residences in training, conducting research and subsequent advocacy, it empowered them to establish control and influence over their futures, by enabling them to influence national policies that impact their lives, and to improve the quality of life for those women living in the institutions (Gafa et al., 2017).

The work produced insights into necessary improvements such as women needing to better overcome the financial insecurity of being unemployed, easing delays in the courts, fixing structural issues in one of the centres, and addressing the shortage of support staff in one of the centres. The findings were communicated to policy makers (Gafa et al., 2017). The title Stronger Together emphasises that empowerment does not happen alone, but rather when two or more people are together and are involved in a sharing or transfer of power.

Can collective empowerment meet individual needs? In the 1990s, the feminists who actively sought the recognition of VAW as a human rights violation argued that a state apparatus that ignores VAW perpetrates VAW and should be held accountable. Han (2003) refers to the work of Coker (2001) to state that "[w]ithout the cooperation and activism of police officers, prosecutors, and judges, the state sends a message to would-be perpetrators and victims that [violence] is condoned by the state and that it will be permitted without repercussion" (p. 161).

Yet, as states take responsibility for ensuring service provision for survivors of violence or addressing different forms of violence in criminal law, feminist activists equally question the disempowerment that can emerge if, for example, service provision is removed from grassroots women's organisations and placed in the hands of large bureaucracies.

Similarly, seeking help against female genital mutilation or forced marriage can become synonymous with asking a girl to make the choice between her wellbeing and bodily integrity or sending her parents to prison. A balance between too little and too much state intervention is key (Han, 2003).

Some police involvement in IPV has been noted to result in dual arrests (i.e., survivors also being arrested), showing that the placing of responsibility and accountability in the hands of patriarchal institutions leaves women and girls at the mercy of individuals who may have neither the training nor the will to protect them from violence. In some cases, police may arrest women simply as a result of stereotypes the officers hold about women's behaviour, but nonetheless, the damage is done, when a survivor who seeks protection is instead placed in handcuffs (Advocates for Human Rights, Autonomous Women's House Zagreb & Bulgarian Gender Research Foundation, 2012). This is not the type of collective empowerment women sought when pursuing the recognition of intimate violence as a crime to be dealt with by the state.

Other institutional mechanisms are at times nothing short of a replica of power and control, with which the survivor is all too familiar. Violence is impactful in that it leaves a trail of complex needs, and so it is important to keep in mind that:

> ... disentangling a victim from her situation is not as simple as picking her up and carrying her to safety .... When a state or advocate forces a woman to [take a certain action], rather than empowering her to make these decisions on her own, the state has simply succeeded in transferring power from one controlling entity to another. (Han, 2003, p. 166)

The question therefore is how far can women become empowered and stay empowered, when the empowerment takes place within a patriarchal society?

DISCUSSION

This chapter presented the concept of empowerment in the context of women survivors of IPV, noting that the act of VAW is a product of a patriarchal society. Disempowerment however is also a birthplace of empowerment since oppression brings with it a longing for the freedom from oppression. The chapter suggests the idea that empowerment is a stepping stone into power, an ability to control one's life, that exists within people and communities, that is shared and transferred among members of society, all the while moving between layers of the individual and the collective. The collective, or community, however does not exist in a vacuum, but, rather, is located within patriarchy itself, and therefore the circle of disempowerment and empowerment happen all in one place, raising the question as to whether cultivating individual power based on one's subjective needs is truly possible from the place where we stand.

Determining the meaning of empowerment requires a certain level of comfort with the idea that an all-encompassing definition is neither possible nor suitable. Some aspects relevant to empowerment include its potential for being shared and transferred between people, groups of people, and also between individuals and communities. Empowerment involves having a supportive network, becoming aware of the possibility of change, self-determination, new skills and other resources. Lastly and of equal importance is the idea that empowerment is a practice that takes account of and celebrates diversity, recognizing the uniqueness of individual journeys.

Sharing of power is key (passing on power from one body to the next). Is the empowered therefore responsible for empowering others? Is giving it forward an unspoken rule? The idea behind collective power is that individual members of a community benefit when the community does and vice versa – when one woman gains, all women gain. However, this may only occur if she shares her power with others, otherwise, she is doing nothing more than reproducing the patriarchal blueprint of one-sided power accumulation. Power in the patriarchal sense is no power at all, instead it is an *overpower*.

With power comes responsibility, not only to share, but to do so thoughtfully. This is most evident when looking at empowerment in the collective sense. When individual women create movements that open windows for other women to claim their rights, or when social agents share their own power with survivors, it must be ascertained that the empowerment shared is indeed that which is wished. On some level, this requires the collective to respect the subjective. Peled et al. (2000) ask a curious question about providing safety and supporting survivors of IPV who come from cultures where divorce is not a desirable or even a viable option: When we share power, should we also share our dominant beliefs about empowerment? When we create spaces for women to claim their rights, we should also ask the women if what they got is actually what they had wished for.

The question remains how to empower women within the context of a patriarchal society, where the opportunities and options available to survivors of violence can still reflect the very power imbalance responsible for VAW. Firstly, individual and collective empowerment (even if it involves or exists within patriarchal structures), impacts society in the way that all actions big and small diminish the influence of the unjust system. Furthermore, the concept of 'priming' is relevant here. According to Lum (1996), as cited in Busch and Valentine (2000), priming is an indirect practice of empowerment where agents act as educators of the society at large and its systems in order to inform others about the hardships and oppressions faced by the women so that this awareness creates systems that are more receptive to the survivors they encounter (p. 86). Through education of the society at large, women living in abusive relationships within that society may also be reached, and this may act as their turning point towards empowerment. Simply put, awareness raising is the best we can do to ensure that survivors of violence are empowered within a patriarchal society.

Indeed, progress is already visible, indicating that change is possible. This in itself suggests that some empowerment is taking place. However, we have to acknowledge that overall, this is taking its time, and may well continue to do so. Therefore, for those of us who continue to 'act', collectively and individually, a good supply of patience (and anger?) may be needed!

NOTES

[1] The European Union Agency for Fundamental Rights points out that women who were victims of sexual assault did not contact general services like the police or other organisations because of "shame and embarrassment" and therefore recommends that states extend specialist support services for victims of violence that will make it easier for women to reach out for support due to the specialised nature of the services and the understanding they can offer women in comparison to other non-specialised institutions and organisations.

[2] The Istanbul Convention is known by its full name as the Council of Europe Convention on preventing and combatting violence against women and domestic violence.

[3] The Convention was adopted in 1979 and addresses education, employment, political and public life, as well as marriage and family life, among other areas of relevance to women's rights.

REFERENCES

Advocates for Human Rights, Autonomous Women's House Zagreb, & Bulgarian Gender Research Foundation. (2012). *Implementation of Croatia's domestic violence legislation: A human rights report*. Minneapolis, MN: The Advocates for Human Rights.

Aziz, Z. A., & Moussa, J. (2016). *Due diligence project's due diligence framework: State accountability framework for eliminating violence against women*. Malaysia: International Human Rights Initiative, Inc (IHRI).

Baker, H. (2013). The significance of shame in the lives of women who experience male violence. *Liverpool Law Review, 34*, 145–171. doi:10.1007/s10991-013-9134-z

Beijing Declaration and Platform for Action. (1995). Retrieved from http://www.un.org/womenwatch/daw/beijing/pdf/BDPfA%20E.pdf

Brown, B. (2012). *Daring greatly: How the courage to be vulnerable transforms the way we live, love, parent, and lead*. New York, NY: Penguin Random House.

Bunch, C. (1990). Women's rights as human rights: Toward a re-vision of human rights. *Human Rights Quarterly, 12*(4), 486–498.

Busch, N. B., & Valentine, D. (2000). Empowerment practice: A focus on battered women. *AFFILIA, 15*(1), 82–95.

Chang, J. C., Dado, D., Hawker, L., Cluss, P. A., Buranosky, R., Slagel, L., McNeil, M., & Hudson Scholle, S. (2010). Understanding turning points in intimate partner violence: Factors and circumstances leading women victims toward change. *Journal of Women's Health, 19*, 251–259. doi:10.1089=jwh.2009.1568

Council of Europe. (n.d.). *About monitoring*. Retrieved from https://www.coe.int/en/web/istanbul-convention/grevio

European Institute for Gender Equality (EIGE). (2012). *Review of the implementation of the Beijing platform for action in the EU member states: Violence against women – Victim support*. doi:10.2839/612

European Union Agency for Fundamental Rights. (2014). *Violence against women: An EU-wide survey. Main results*. doi:10.2811/981927

Gafa, S., Naudi, M., & Rossi, A. (2017). Stronger together. *Fempower*, 16–17. Retrieved from http://fileserver.wave-network.org/fempowermagazine/Fempower_Magazine_28.pdf

General Recommendation No. 35. General recommendation No. 35 on gender-based violence against women, updating general recommendation No. 19. (2017). Retrieved from from http://tbinternet.ohchr.org/Treaties/CEDAW/Shared%20Documents/1_Global/CEDAW_C_GC_35_8267_E.pdf

Hafford-Letchfield, T. (2014). Chapter six: Power. In L. Bell & T. Hafford-Letchfield (Eds.), *Ethics and values in social work practice*. New York, NY: McGraw-Hill.

Hagemann-White, C., & Grafe, B. (Eds.). (2016). *Experiences of intervention against violence: An anthology of stories*. Opladen: Barbara Budrich Publishers.

Han, E. L. (2003). Mandatory arrest and no-drop policies: Victim empowerment in domestic violence cases. *Boston College Third World Law Journal, 23*(1), 158. Retrieved from http://lawdigitalcommons.bc.edu/twlj/vol23/iss1/5

Htun, M., & Weldon, S. L. (2012). The civic origins of progressive policy change: Combating violence against women in global perspective. *The American Political Science Review, 106*(3), 548–569.

Istanbul Convention. (2011). *The Council of Europe Convention on preventing and combatting violence against women and domestic violence*.

Kelly, L., & Westmarland, N. (2016). Naming and defining 'domestic violence': Lessons from research with violent men. *Feminist Review, 112*(1), 113–127. Retrieved from https://link.springer.com/article/10.1057%2Ffr.2015.52

Klein, R. (2012). *Responding to intimate violence against women*. New York, NY: Cambridge University Press.

London Feminist Network. (n.d.). *What is patriarchy?* Retrieved from http://londonfeministnetwork.org.uk/home/patriarchy

Page, N., & Czuba, C. E. (1999). Empowerment: What is it? *Journal of Extension, 37*(5), 24–32. Retrieved from https://www.joe.org/joe/1999october/comm1.php

Peled, E., Eisikovits, Z., Enosh, G., & Winstok, Z. (2000). Choice and empowerment for battered women who stay: Toward a constructivist model. *Social Work, 45*(1), 9–25.

Stark, E. (2007). *Coercive control: How men entrap women in personal life*. New York, NY: Oxford University Press.

United Nations Statistics Division. (2015). Violence against women. In *The world's women 2015: Trends and statistics* (pp. 139–161). Retrieved https://unstats.un.org/unsd/gender/worldswomen.html

UN Women. (n.d.a). *Convention on the elimination of all forms of discrimination against women*. Available from http://www.un.org/womenwatch/daw/cedaw/text/econvention.htm

UN Women. (n.d.b). *The history and origin of women's sheltering*. Retrieved from http://www.endvawnow.org/en/articles/1368-the-history-and-origin-of-womens-sheltering.html

Watt Smith, T. (2015). *The book of human emotions: An encyclopaedia of feeling from anger to wanderlust*. London: Profile Books Ltd.

VAL WILLIAMS, AMY CAMILLERI ZAHRA AND VICKIE GAUCI

10. DISABLED PEOPLE AND SOCIAL WELLBEING

What's Good for Us Is Good for Everyone

ABSTRACT

Speaking about social wellbeing means focusing on an individual's wellbeing not only on a personal level, but also on a social level. It involves considering the individual's opportunities to be with others, to form healthy relationships, and to engage in various activities with others in the mainstream of society. The concerns of the disabled people's movement, and of the discipline of Disability Studies which developed from that movement, are very similar, dealing as they do with the *social* aspects of disability. This is because the concept of wellbeing has been colonized and suffused with a non-disabled, often overly therapeutic discourse. This chapter will focus on how the concept of social wellbeing has been used (directly and indirectly) in disabled people's struggle for recognition of their right to be an integral part of society and in the discipline of Disability Studies itself.

Keywords: disabled people, agency, social care, relational autonomy, wellbeing

INTRODUCTION

Wellbeing is a concept that is hard to argue with. Particularly when coupled with the term 'social', it would seem self-evident that human beings would seek wellbeing, and that it should therefore also be considered central to the lives of disabled people. This chapter however will complicate matters by questioning the fit of 'social wellbeing' with the core goals of disabled people. We will particularly be concerned with some key values and models which have influenced Disability Studies and the rights for which disabled people have fought hard across the world, namely autonomy and control over their own lives. Disabled people position themselves as citizens, people who have active roles to play in society, and this discourse of 'agency' is at the heart of their own campaign for change. In that context, social wellbeing takes on a new shape, and can be seen maybe not as a goal in itself, but as an outcome of the search for a meaningful role in life.

MODELS OF DISABILITY

In this section we will start by discussing some of the models which over the years have influenced professional and activist thinking about disability. This overview will help in the understanding of the rest of the chapter. A model of disability is simply a framework to help us understand things in a particular way, and no one model can be practised exclusively. Life is more complex. However, we have chosen these models because we feel that they have a great impact on the notion of wellbeing in the lives of disabled people. Before proceeding with an overview of the different models, it is also worth noting that disabled people are not a homogenous group but that disability occurs to men, women, people with different sexual orientations, people of different ages and people of different ethnicity as well as class.

The Medical Model

For a number of years, governments and large organisations such as the World Health Organisation (WHO) have relied on the prevalence of medical diagnoses and causes of death in order to describe the population's overall health (Peterson, 2005). WHO's (1980) International Classification of Impairments, Disabilities and Handicap (ICIDH) and later the revised version known as the International Classification of Functioning, Disability and Health (ICF) (2001) were created to provide an objective measure for a population's health. One of the greatest impacts of these classifications has been the medical model of disability in which disability is seen as extreme ill health. Of course, it is true that disabled people, even more than others, need good quality health services for their "improved care, survival, and quality of life" (Peterson & Elliott, 2008, p. 214). The concept of 'wellbeing' has traditionally arisen in connection with matters of good health. However, a number of disabled activists have criticised the medical model as one which only views disability as a problem of the individual which needs to be solved or cured (Marks, 1999; Traustadóttir, 2009). In turn, disabled people have felt that this view of disability has led to the interpretation of disabled people as individuals who are helpless, dependent, and incapable of making their own decisions and thus a burden on society (Duane, 2014; Shearer, 1981).

The Social Model

As a way of challenging this "disability orthodoxy" (Barnes & Mercer, 2010, p. 1), the 1970s and 1980s saw disabled activists in Europe and North America coming together and organizing themselves to become a vocal lobby for a different model of disability, the Social Model of Disability. Disabled people came to see that society was not inclusive of their needs, and that their human rights to equality were violated (Driedger, 1989). The social model is important for us in this chapter because it switches the view of 'wellbeing' from the individual onto the social context in which they live.

In its UK form, the 'social model' stemmed from the Union of the Physically Impaired Against Segregation (UPIAS), who in the 1970s published a paper titled, 'Fundamental Principles of Disability' (as cited in Oliver, 1996, p. 22). The social model of disability makes a very clear distinction between the definitions of 'impairment' and 'disability'. According to this model, 'impairment' is taken to mean, 'the functional limitation within the individual caused by physical, mental or sensory impairment' (Disabled People's International, 1982, p. 105), whilst 'disability' is taken to mean, 'the loss or limitation of opportunities to take part in the normal life of the community on an equal level with others due to physical and social barriers' (Disabled People's International, 1982, p. 105). This model of disability has been instrumental in bringing about meaningful changes in the lives of disabled people because it "reverses the causal chain to explore how socially constructed barriers have disabled people with perceived impairment" (Barnes & Mercer, 1997, p. 1). Harris and Roulstone (2011) assert that more importantly the social model of disability has been a great influence for the passing of new laws and policies, including the United Nations Convention on the Rights of Persons with Disabilities (United Nations, 2006).

The Relational Model

From the start, there were debates and critiques of the simple 'social'/'medical' model divide (see Thomas, 2004, for a good summary). Thomas (2007), for example, extends the original UPIAS definitions and proposes that, apart from physical and social (public) barriers, disablism also includes what she called "psycho-emotional" (private) factors which undermine disabled people's well-being (p. 73) and their relationships with those around them. In the Nordic countries it is the relational model of disability which has dominated the conceptualisation of disability (Gustavsson, Sandvin, Traustadóttir, & Tossebrø, 2005). One of the reasons that the relational model has been influential in Nordic countries is because Nordic languages do not lend themselves well to the distinction between 'impairment' and 'disability', as put forward by the British social model of disability (Traustadóttir, 2004, 2006). According to Goodley (2011) and Tossebrø (2002), the Nordic relational model is based on three assumptions: disability stems from a discrepancy between the person and the environment; disability depends on the particular situation or context; and disability is relative. Thus the focus on 'relational' or social wellbeing fits well with a perspective in which we look at the individual as connected with others. These ideas have had influence beyond Nordic countries, and are very relevant to the increasing emphasis on the disabling (or enabling) effects of interactions with disabled people.

The Affirmative Model

Finally, social wellbeing can never be just a 'bolt-on' extra. It is about the way people think about themselves, their identity and their achievements in life. The affirmative model of disability is considered to be a development of the social model (Goodley, 2011). It was originally formulated by French and Swain in 2000 and comes in direct opposition to the tragic view of disability. The development of this model is based on the premise that, "[t]he writings and experiences of disabled people demonstrate that, far from being tragic, being impaired and disabled can have benefits" (Swain & French, 2000, p. 574). Similarly to gay pride, the affirmative model promotes disability as a positive aspect of one's identity (Brueggemann, 2013; Swain & French, 2008). Disabled people for instance can have a strong role, not only as advocates, but also as artists (Hargrave, 2015). It is this type of strength of identity which lies at the heart of how disabled people see their 'social wellbeing'.

WELLBEING AS A CORE VALUE IN POLICY

Wellbeing is a notion that traditionally has been allied with health concerns. 'Being well' is the opposite of sickness, and thus medical practitioners are urged not just to cure the body, but also to create 'happiness' or a sense of wellbeing. However, in a 2016 special edition of the prestigious medical journal, *The Lancet,* the editor acknowledges some of the looseness of the term:

> Indices of overall wellbeing must not obscure the need for ongoing progress in reducing disease, mental illness, and premature death. Without life, there is no happiness to be realized. (The Lancet, 2016, p. 1251)

In the context of visual impairment, for instance, wellbeing can be a slippery concept: 'the term 'wellbeing' may at once mean everything and nothing' (Marques-Broksopp, 2011). Particularly when it is conflated with the term happiness, 'wellbeing' can become a subjective notion, something residing in emotions and feelings, and of course also in belief systems. The 2016 edition of the 'World Happiness Report' acknowledges some of these dangers, and urges us to consider the inequalities between and within countries in the actual distribution of happiness, turning back to the social determinants of health, such as poverty, hunger, housing or gender. For instance, when the term 'wellbeing' is used to refer to economic wellbeing, disabled women tend to always be more disadvantaged than disabled men and non-disabled women (Emmett & Alant, 2007).

Some of these debates about subjective or objective measures of health are particularly prominent currently, in debates about the value of life itself. As genetic technology increases the ability of medical practitioners to predict genetic conditions before birth, parents are increasingly given the choice to terminate pregnancies of babies with conditions such as Downs Syndrome (Philips & Richards, 2016) or even less life-threatening ones such as a cleft palate (Day, 2003). Their choice is driven by objectively measured, medical facts. However, that choice is a profoundly ethical, subjective one. It raises the question of whether a child with Downs Syndrome or a cleft palate is actually valued at all as a human being, whether it is likely that their 'quality of life' would be sufficient to constitute wellbeing, whether also they might affect the wellbeing of others in their lives. Those who have and love children with Downs Syndrome or cleft palate think positively of course about their right to life, as Sally Phillips (Philips & Richards, 2016) demonstrates in her TV documentary and as Jepson has demonstrated through her court case (Day, 2003). That is also true of course for many people with Downs Syndrome and other conditions who speak up for themselves and argue for a more comprehensive understanding of the diversity of human beings. In order to achieve wellbeing, in this sense, we need to recognise not only that all human beings are different, but that we are interconnected. Kittay's (2002) 'ethics of care' re-directs our thinking towards the values in being interconnected, the ways in which both carer and cared-for can experience wellbeing together. For instance, Phillips puts over movingly how deeply she and all her family benefit from the very existence of her son with Downs Syndrome.

Thus the arguments about subjective wellbeing lead us directly to the 'social', the core values in what we mean by humanity. In the following section, therefore, we will add the word 'social' and consider what social wellbeing might consist of.

SOCIAL WELLBEING AND DISCOURSES OF SOCIAL CARE

Moving beyond the field of medicine, social care has also recruited the term 'wellbeing' in recent years, and the current 2014 Care Act in the UK for instance frames 'wellbeing' as a primary principle in delivering social care:

> local authorities must promote wellbeing when carrying out any of their care and support functions in respect of a person. (para. 1.2)

In Malta, so far, none of the acts related to disability have incorporated or defined the term 'wellbeing'. However, 'wellbeing' is mentioned in five instances in the National Policy on the Rights of Persons with Disability which was published in 2014. Contrastingly, 'wellbeing' is not mentioned at all in the draft of the National Disability Strategy which was published for consultation in May 2015.

The practice guidance accompanying the 2014 Care Act in the UK specifies carefully that wellbeing has to be defined by the individual client, recognising again the subjective nature of the term. One disabled person might define their own wellbeing as including access to leisure and night life, for instance; another might want wellbeing through their own family, living independently, or employment. However, as Slasberg and Beresford (2014) point out, the delivery of 'wellbeing' is still in the hands of social care practitioners, who themselves will decide whether a person's outcomes are going to be funded through the public purse. As one of the current authors (Symonds, Williams, Miles, Steel, & Porter, 2018) discusses, research that is just completed about assessments of social care under the Care Act in England has also shown that disabled people are not always trusted to judge accurately their own wellbeing. Social workers and other practitioners have to assess needs, and to decide what needs will ultimately be funded. In theory, they tend to adhere to the ideas of choice contained in the latest legislation:

> If it's an area that the customer has no concern about for their well-being, or it doesn't bother them, then it won't bother us. (Social care practitioner)

However, another social worker describes the range of clients she sees for assessments, and the dilemma for social care in determining how to distribute resources:

> sometimes they need help but don't want it, and sometimes they want help and don't need it. (Social care practitioner)

The fundamental problem in social care is the tension between protection and autonomy, and this is thrown into sharp relief when money is involved. A limited, cash-strapped social care system will always tend to revert to the former principle, of protection. Individual choice and control can arguably lead to chaos, with some people shouting louder than others, and with resources being distributed according to the arbitrary whim of individuals. However, the principle of protection allows the welfare state to operate within safe boundaries, ensuring that people are protected in some instances from their own unwise decisions, and taking on itself the decision of what is best for each disabled person.

How does this argument relate to social wellbeing? The definition of wellbeing within social care is not necessarily that of 'social wellbeing', but the two are often conflated. For instance, a person with intellectual disabilities and autism might wish to live a life which is perceived to be very anti-social. However, his social care funding depends on him becoming more 'sociable', taking part in social life, and maybe even living with other people. Cynically, then, we can see how social wellbeing can be used as a way of ensuring that goals are met communally, that disabled people are grouped together for the purpose of service provision, and that ultimately the delivery of social care can be manageable within a restricted budget.

In the UK, we have seen how the welfare state is being retrenched, with a call to communities and the 'Big Society' to be active in supporting disabled people. Like so many of these themes, this move towards community 'assets' is both welcomed and feared by disabled people. Social wellbeing within the wider community is of course a prized goal for all, within a society that is truly adapted to ensure inclusion. However, there are also worries that without funding for personal care, for social support or for personal development, disabled people will be prey to a hostile, uncaring community. It is difficult to find statistics regarding bullying and harassment of disabled people in Malta, but, for instance, the Equal Opportunities Compliance Unit Annual Report 2015, notes 7 reported cases of bullying and ill-treatment at the place of work, day centres or residential homes/institutions between 2014 and 2015 (Commission for the Rights of Persons with Disability, 2016). Hate crime might be considered the polar opposite to social wellbeing, but may be seen as a possible outcome of the withdrawal of the right to social care itself. Indeed, the withdrawal or retrenchment of social care support can result in 'social wellbeing' equating with family care, placing both the disabled person and their family in increasingly difficult positions.

In order to consider what 'social wellbeing' might look like in an ideal world, then, there are some complex issues to consider. The next section of this chapter will therefore look at what disabled people themselves feel about social wellbeing, and in doing so, we will turn towards ideas about relational autonomy. Being together with other people is not enough; it is also about people genuinely working together to produce solutions for and with disabled people.

SOCIAL WELLBEING AND RELATIONAL AUTONOMY

We started this chapter with one of the core values in disabled people's own theories relating to disability, that of autonomy. The right to decide what is best for oneself, the right to speak up and to have a voice in matters that concern you, all of these have been core to the development of the disabled people's movement. However, there have always been some groups of disabled people who have found it hard to gain a foothold in the disability movement, particularly those with cognitive or intellectual impairments. In this section, we will take examples from research carried out with people with intellectual disabilities which included them in speaking up for themselves and in research (Williams, 2011). Despite their supposed lack of voice and lack of self-determination, people with cognitive disabilities can nevertheless think for themselves, and can tell us about what really matters to them.

First of all, what do people with intellectual disabilities want from their own support workers? Williams, Ponting, Ford, and Rudge (2010) worked with Kerrie Ford and Lisa Ponting, two researchers who themselves have learning disabilities, to discuss this question with people with intellectual disabilities in different parts of England. From the analysis, Kerrie and Lisa felt that the following five themes were central to 'good support': (1) Respect; (2) Supporting choices; (3) Being friendly; (4) Giving good advice; (5) Supporting people to speak up. Central to this was the idea of relationships. None of the people with intellectual disabilities in this study wanted to make their decisions completely alone. They wanted to be listened to, but they also wanted good advice to come to a joint decision.

Since that study, there has been further discussion about 'choice and control' as experienced by people using personal budgets (Williams & Porter, 2017). When asked about how they managed their support plans, people with intellectual disabilities in this study said that they think it is most important for them to grow more confident in managing their relationships with others, and that increased self-confidence will mean a better chance of being in control of their lives.

The notion of individual autonomy, so precious to disabled people, can be seen to shift here towards ideas about 'relational autonomy'. For example, in an ongoing study (Gauci, 2018) about the use/role of technology at the place of work with employees with physical and/or sensory impairments, the majority of the participants claimed that it made them "more independent". But when asked to explain further what this meant to them, comments like "it makes me feel good", "it is liberating", "it increases your self-esteem" and "I'm at an equal level with my colleagues", all indicated that for the participants it was not only important that technology helped them do tasks without other people's help but that it also increased their well-being. Independence here is seen to increase people's well-being not only for the individual but also for the individual in relation to others, in this case to colleagues at work.

Turning back to people with intellectual disabilities, the significant people in their lives may be family members and they in turn nurture and support other social relationships with people outside the family (Forrester-Jones et al., 2006), such as close personal relationships related to love and marriage (Lafferty, McConkey, & Taggart, 2013). Finally, disabled people who have support from professionals will have a wide array of 'others' in their lives. Much will depend of course on the various systems for social welfare and support across the world, but where people have access to paid support services (for instance, in a day centre, in education, or at home), then the paid support staff can become key people in the lives and can contribute importantly to people's 'social wellbeing'. Williams and Porter (2017) also found that friendships and relationships with peers, on a basis of equality, were vital in building valued goals in one's own life, a sense that one can contribute to society and support others. Disabled people generally are not just 'takers'; they are active citizens and gain strength, as we all do, from knowing and helping others who are in similar positions.

Personalised social care and independent living therefore do not mean social isolation. People with disabilities have indicated clearly that they want both 'choice and control', that they want to be listened to, but they also want to build up a stronger identity together. This does not in any way mean that the individual and any impairment-related consequences are removed from the picture when discussing 'social wellbeing'.

CONCLUSION

This chapter has discussed how the concept of 'social wellbeing' could be linked with the ideas of the Disability movement, and would be an important factor for any disabled person in gaining or maintaining a sense of control in their life. This does not mean being 'independent' and isolated, but it can involve meaningful interactions and interrelationships with others in the community. Disabled people have rights. However, there are many different rights, which are interconnected, and which might appear to conflict at times. For instance, the right to be protected and the right to be safe have to be balanced against the right to take risks. What this chapter argues is that these rights are acted out in the sphere of the 'social', when other people respect and value what disabled people themselves have to offer.

Disability is not a simple, unitary concept. For most of us, disability may be associated with chronic conditions, pain and unpleasant or very negative experiences. Thus when it is coupled with 'wellbeing' it would be naïve to claim that good social feelings can wipe out the effects of pain (Freedman, Stafford, Schwarz, Conrad, & Cornman, 2011), and McCabe and O'Connor (2009) point out rightly that economic pressures, loss of earning potential and other negative social effects can further compound the experience of impairment.

Nevertheless, a sense of wellbeing and happiness is not just to do with the number of people you know and say 'hello' to each day. It is to do with having a purpose in life, something which you yourself value and wish to achieve. Thus social wellbeing is not something which can be conferred on disabled people by those who 'care for them'. It is a common goal for all of us, and with the agency and actions of disabled people in our midst, a common wellbeing might be achieved by non-disabled and disabled people becoming part of the same society.

REFERENCES

Barnes, C., & Mercer, G. (1997). *Doing disability research*. Leeds: The Disability Press.
Barnes, C., & Mercer, G. (2010). *Exploring disability* (2nd ed.). Cambridge: Polity Press.
Brueggemann, B. J. (2013). Disability studies/disability culture. In M. L. Wehmeyer (Ed.), *The Oxford handbook of positive psychology and disability* (pp. 279–299). Oxford: Oxford University Press.
Commission for the Rights of Persons with Disability (CRPD). (2016). *Equal opportunities compliance unit annual report 2015*. Malta: CRPD.
Day, E. (2003, November 23). The law is saying there are reasons why I shouldn't be alive. I look at my life and think: That's rubbish. *The Sunday Telegraph*. Retrieved from http://www.telegraph.co.uk/news/uknews/1447486/The-law-is-saying-there-are-reasons-why-I-shouldnt-be-alive.-I-look-at-my-life-and-think-Thats-rubbish.html
Disabled People's International (DPI). (1982). *Disabled Peoples' International. Proceedings of the first world congress, Singapore*. Singapore: DPI.
Driedger, D. (1989). *The last civil rights movement: Disabled people's international*. London: Hurst & Company.
Duane, A. M. (2014). Volunteering as tribute: Disability, globalization and the hunger games. In M. Gill & C. J. Schlund-Vials (Eds.), *Disability, human rights and the limits of humanitarianism* (pp. 63–82). Surrey: Ashgate Publishing Limited.
Emmett, T., & Alant, E. (2007). Women and disability: Exploring the interface of multiple disadvantage. *Development Southern Africa, 23*(4), 445–460.
Forrester-Jones, R., Carpenter, J., Coolen-Schrijner, P., Cambridge, P., Tate, A., Beecham, J., Hallam A., Knapp, M., & Wooff, D. (2006). The social networks of people with intellectual disability living in the community 12 years after resettlement from long-stay hospitals. *Journal of Applied Research in Intellectual Disability, 19*(4), 285–295.
Freedman, V., Stafford, F., Schwarz, N., Conrad, F., & Cornman, J. (2011). Disability, participation and subjective wellbeing among older couples. *Social Science & Medicine, 74*(4), 588–596.
Gauci, V. (2018). *Enabling technology in the workplace: Exploring the dis/ability-assemblage* (Unpublished doctoral manuscript). University of Leeds, Leeds, UK.
Goodley, D. (2011). *Disability studies: An interdisciplinary introduction*. London: Sage Publications.
Goodley, D., & Runswick-Cole, K. (2015). Big society? Disabled people with the label of learning disabilities and the queer(y)ing of civil society. *Scandinavian Journal of Disability Research, 17*(1), 1–13.
Gustavsson, A., Sandvin, J., Traustadóttir, R., & Tøssebrø, J. (2005). *Resistance, reflection and change: Nordic disability research*. Lund: Studentlitteratur.
Hargrave, M. (2015). *Theatres of learning disability: Good, bad, or plain ugly?* Hampshire: Palgrave Macmillan.
Harris, J., & Roulstone, A. (2011). *Disability, policy and professional practice*. London: Sage Publications.
Helliwell, J., Layard, R., & Sachs, J. (2016). *World happiness report 2016 update*. Retrieved from http://worldhappiness.report/ed/2016/
Kittay, E. (2002). The ethics of care, dependence, and disability. *Ratio Juris, 24*(1), 49–58.

Lafferty, A., McConkey, R., & Taggart, L. (2013). Beyond friendship: The nature and meaning of close personal relationships as perceived by people with learning disabilities. *Disability & Society, 28*(8), 1074–1088.

Marks, D. (1999). *Disability: Controversial debates and psychosocial perspectives.* London: Routledge.

Marques-Broksopp, L. (2011). The broad reach of the wellbeing debate: Emotional wellbeing and vision loss. *British Journal of Visual Impairment, 30*(1), 50–55.

McCabe, M., & O'Connor, E. (2009). A longitudinal study of economic pressure among people living with a progressive neurological illness. *Chronic Illness, 5*(3), 177–183.

Oliver, M. (1996). *Understanding disability: From theory to practice.* Basingstoke: Macmillan.

Parliamentary Secretariat for Rights of Persons with Disability and Active Ageing. (2014). *National policy on the rights of persons with disability.* Malta: Government of Malta.

Parliamentary Secretariat for Rights of Persons with Disability and Active Ageing. (2016). *Consultation document: The Malta national disability strategy.* Malta: Government of Malta.

Peterson, D. B. (2005). International Classification of Functioning, disability and health (ICF): An introduction for rehabilitation psychologists. *Rehabilitation Psychology, 50,* 105–112.

Peterson, D. B., & Elliott, T. R. (2008). Advances in conceptualizing and studying disability. In S. D. Brown & R. W. Lent (Eds.), *Handbook of counselling psychology* (4th ed.). Hoboken, NJ: John Wiley and Son, Ltd.

Philips, S. (Presenter), & Richards, C. (Director). (2016). *A world without down's syndrome?* (Dragonfly Film and Television (Producer)). United Kingdom: BBC2.

Shearer, A. (1981). *Disability – whose handicap?* London: Blackwell.

Slasberg, C., & Beresford, P. (2014). Government guidance for the care act: Undermining ambitions for change? *Disability & Society, 29*(10), 1677–1682.

Swain, J., & French, S. (2000). Towards an affirmation model of disability. *Disability & Society, 15*(4), 569–582.

Swain, J., & French, S. (2008). Affirming identity. In J. Swain & S. French (Eds.), *Disability on equal terms* (Chapter 6). London: Sage Publications.

Symonds, J., Williams, V., Miles, C., Steel, M., & Porter, S. (2018). The social care practitioner as assessor: People, relationships and professional judgement. *British Journal of Social Work, 48*(7), 1910–1928. Retrieved from https://doi.org/10.1093/bjsw/bcx154

The Care Act 2014 c.23. Retrieved from http://www.legislation.gov.uk/ukpga/2014/23/contents/enacted

The Lancet. (2016). Editorial: Health and happiness. *The Lancet, 387,* 1251.

Thomas, C. (2004). How is disability understood? An examination of sociological approaches. *Disability and Society, 19*(6), 569–583.

Thomas, C. (2007). *Sociologies of disability and illness: Contested ideas in disability studies and medical sociology.* Basingstoke: Palgrave Macmillan.

Tossebrø, J. (2002, August). *Leaving the individual out: Practical and logical problems. In Understanding disability: The UK social model and the nordic relational approach.* Symposium conducted at the 6th NNDR Conference, Disability Research, Theory and Practice, Reykjavik, Iceland.

Traustadóttir, R. (2004, July). *Disability studies: A Nordic perspective.* British Disability Studies Association Conference, Lancaster, United Kingdom.

Traustadottir, R. (2006, May). *Disability studies: A Nordic perspective.* Applying Disability Studies Seminar Series, Centre of Applied Disability Studies, University of Sheffield, Sheffield, United Kingdom.

Traustadóttir, R. (2009). Disability studies, the social model and legal developments. In O. M. Arnardóttir & G. Quinn (Eds.), *The UN convention on the rights of persons with disabilities: European and scandinavian perspectives* (pp. 3–16). Leiden: Martinus Nijhoff Publishers.

United Nations. (2006). *United Nations Convention on the Rights of Persons with Disabilities (UNCRPD).* Retrieved from https://www.un.org/development/desa/disabilities/convention-on-the-rights-of-persons-with-disabilities.html

Williams, V. (2011). *Disability and discourse: Analysing inclusive conversation with people with intellectual disabilities.* Chichester: Wiley-Blackwell.

Williams, V., Ponting, L., Ford, K., & Rudge, P. (2010). Skills for support: Personal assistants and people with learning disabilities. *British Journal of Learning Disabilities, 38*(1), 59–67.

Williams, V., & Porter, S. (2017). The meaning of 'choice and control' for people with intellectual disabilities who are planning their social care and support. *Journal of Applied Research in Intellectual Disabilities, 30*(1), 97–108.

World Health Organisation (WHO). (1980). *ICIDH: International Classification of Impairments, Disabilities and Handicaps. A manual of classification relating to the consequence of disease.* Geneva: WHO.

World Health Organisation (WHO). (2001). *International Classification of Functioning, disability and health (ICF).* Geneva: WHO.

MARIE BRIGUGLIO

11. WELLBEING: AN ECONOMICS PERSPECTIVE

ABSTRACT

This chapter examines the study of wellbeing within the discipline of Economics, arguing that the ultimate purpose of economic enquiry is precisely the question of how to maximise societal welfare given scarce resources. The chapter focuses on some of the methods typically employed in Economics to measure wellbeing and to investigate the factors that determine it. It makes reference to some data sources that may be useful for research projects, as well as to data-collection methods that may be employed when secondary data is not readily available. The chapter also highlights some of the main findings from research in the field, together with policy recommendations that have emerged. Juxtaposing this research against some of the trends and evidence emerging from a European Union country (Malta), the chapter then carves out an agenda for economic research on social wellbeing, while also discussing some of the limitations of research in the field.

Keywords: economics, wellbeing, life satisfaction, quantitative, self-assessed, Malta

INTRODUCTION

While some people may find it surprising that economists are concerned with subjects like social wellbeing, the truth is that wellbeing is at the very heart of the subject of Economics. Economics is the study of choice under conditions of scarce resources. More specifically, the subject is concerned with how to allocate scarce (natural, human, capital) resources in society, *in order to maximise the welfare* of society as a whole and of different groups within it. In fact, a core question asked in both microeconomics (the study of individual markets) and macroeconomics (the study of the economy as a whole) is whether market forces are capable of achieving the so-called "Efficient" allocation of resources – that is the allocation that maximises wellbeing (Pareto, 1896). Most economists now agree that if markets are left to operate freely, they fail to reach that objective, and that some level of government intervention is necessary to regulate what Adam Smith had referred to as an 'Invisible Hand' of the market as early as the eighteenth century (Smith, 1776).

In turn, several studies in the many of the subfields of Economics (for example Environmental Economics, Industrial Economics, Public Sector Economics, Health

Economics, Agricultural Economics) focus on the *nature and extent* of government intervention, necessary to correct market forces and improve social outcomes in different contexts. Such intervention can take the shape of regulation, the provision of information, public spending, and market-based incentives (like subsidies and taxation). But Economics has also been criticised for counter-productively over-relying on market incentives and information to regulate social interactions (Jordan, 2008). In recent years, an important field of economic enquiry has emerged, examining not only the (complex) response to incentives and information, but also the fundamental assumptions in Economics, namely that people make decisions in a rational and self-interested way.

In what is now a burgeoning literature (Behavioural Economics), bringing together Economics and Psychology, new insights have emerged on human decision-making in both market and social contexts, and on the kind of intervention that may be suitable (Thaler, 2015). This subfield has also brought considerable attention to the study of wellbeing *itself,* asking the pertinent question as to whether day-to-day decision-making by individuals aligns with the quest for wellbeing, how to measure wellbeing, and what its key correlates and determinants are. Interestingly, this echoes questions asked by the very pioneers of economic theory, centuries earlier. In his 1759 writings, Adam Smith himself was concerned with the importance of moral sentiments and affective interactions, arguing that social value is created in non-productive work (Smith, 2009).

Be it directly or indirectly, what brings the various subfields of Economics together is the ultimate purpose of their enquiry, namely that of examining how to maximise societal wellbeing (even if diversely defined), given scarce resources. The next section focuses on some of the methods typically employed in Economics in both the measurement of wellbeing and in the investigation of what determines it. It also makes reference to some key data sources that may be useful for research projects, as well as to data-collection methods that may be employed when secondary data are not readily available. The chapter also highlights some of the main findings from research in the field, as well as some of the key policy recommendations that have emerged. Juxtaposing this research against some of the trends and evidence emerging from Malta, the chapter then carves out an agenda for economic research on social wellbeing in this context. The chapter concludes by discussing some of the limitations of research in the field.

THE ECONOMICS APPROACH

Economics has developed several means to measure how society and, in particular, its economy is doing. While there are many tensions at play (including how to define and measure the economic phenomena of interest, what influences these phenomena and what policy solutions may best be deployed to change them), the possibility to measure outcomes allows for evidence-based policy, and also serves to hold governments to account in relation to policy goals. Many such measures are collated in countries' national statistics. Perhaps the most popular measure is the Gross Domestic Product (GDP), which gives a very good indication of the extent of economic activity in a society by measuring how much people in a given country spend, how much they produce, and how much they earn every year. However the welfare generated from economic activity does not necessarily reflect social wellbeing, for a number of reasons.

Firstly, total activity may not be distributed equitably, such that while total or per capita GDP may be strong (on average), some members of society may achieve very low levels and others very high levels of income. Secondly, market activity captured in GDP, neither captures the full extent of activity in an economy (for example leaving out voluntary work), nor does it capture the harmful side effects of activity (like pollution and resource depletion). Thirdly, while income improvements may translate into self-reported improvements in wellbeing at the early stages of a country's development, this does not appear to be the case beyond a certain level of income. This so-called "Easterlin Paradox" describes the experience of Europe from the 1970s to date, as well as that of several other economies (Easterlin, 1974). It is by now, generally accepted that while GDP is a useful measure of the size of the economy, it fails to capture socio-economic wellbeing (Kahneman & Kruger, 2006).

Several other indicators are used to try to get a better understanding of wellbeing. These include the Human Development Indices (HDI) which sees human wellbeing as a function of GDP but also of other indices such as literacy and life expectancy (UNDP, 2017). Another broad approach is the OECD better-life index, which captures both traditional economic measures, as well as other measures like quality of health services, the quality of environmental services and other dimensions (OECD, 2017). The Canadian Index of Wellbeing is a multidimensional index that looks at wellbeing across a number of different facets in society such as education, the health of the population, the quality of social participation, how active people are, how much they socialise, democratic engagement, the quality of employment (Michalos et al., 2011). This too enables comparisons of how the various dimensions are doing and how they contrast with GDP fluctuations.

Increasingly, however, economists have started to focus on measuring wellbeing more directly, typically referring to the notion of 'life-satisfaction'". To measure this, economists employ survey data, conducted among a population of a given country or countries (or a representative sample thereof). One such data set is the Eurobarometer, which asks "On the whole, are you very satisfied, fairly satisfied, not very satisfied or not at all satisfied with the life you lead?" (European Commission, 2017). Spanning a larger range of countries, the World Values Survey, asks "All things considered, how satisfied are you with your life as a whole these days? Please use this scale where 1 means ''dissatisfied'' and 10 means ''satisfied'', to help with your answer" (WVS, 2014). In general, when using this type of question, the data shows a bell-shaped distribution, typically with a slight skew towards the higher end of the spectrum. The process of answering this kind of question would have involved respondents in a cognitive exercise, going beyond their present moment, to come up with the total effect of all the domains that constitute their wellbeing.

In some surveys, respondents are asked to indicate their agreement with five statements: (1) In most ways my life is close to my ideal; (2) The conditions of my life are excellent; (3) I am satisfied with my life; (4) So far I have gotten the important things I want in life; (5) If I could live my life over, I would change almost nothing, using a 7-point (highly agree to highly disagree) scale (Diener et al., 1985). The researcher then constructs an index of Life Satisfaction is derived by summing up the individual measures responses. Sometimes economists use employ more than one scale to measure wellbeing, for instance to test whether results vary or not. This is possible when using the World Values Survey data for instance, which also includes the question: "Taking all things together, would you say you are: 1 'Very happy' 2 'Quite happy' 3 'Not very happy' 4 'Not at all happy'" (WVS, 2014). Several alternatives exist to measure wellbeing, including methods like the Day Reconstruction Method, which seek to measure wellbeing at different parts of the day (Kahneman et al., 2004).

One interesting debate in the research is the extent to which different measures yield reliable and valid insights that can be compared across countries. Cross-sectoral studies reveal that the statistical structure of wellbeing measures is indeed shared, at least among European nations and the United States (Blanchflower & Oswald, 2001), and that they tend to be stable when measured by different scales administered by different organisations (Diener, Inglehart, & Tay, 2013).

But measuring wellbeing is only the starting point in the economic analysis of wellbeing. While it is interesting to understand how wellbeing fluctuates in different contexts and in time, it is also useful to decipher what causes these fluctuations so that policy can be designed and economic resources can be allocated accordingly. To this end, economic analysis involves collecting data not just on the variable of interest (wellbeing), but also on all the factors that could possibly effect it. Such factors include health (physical and mental), social interactions, jobs and income, as well as environmental quality, religion and political situation of respondents. Wellbeing may also depend on the age, the gender, the education levels and marital status, which is why exercises in data collection typically capture such statistics too. Cross-country surveys, such as those organised GALLOP, The European Social Survey, and the World Value survey, in fact, typically include wellbeing statistics in a suite of comparable statistics – which allow such analysis to take place. Statistical agencies in several countries have now started to measure the wellbeing of their population in large samples, together with several other variables, as part of their National Accounts.

When secondary data are not available, economic studies may require the gathering of primary data. This normally involves carefully surveying a sample of the population of interest (Tourangeau et al., 2000). Surveys will typically start with a question or a construct to capture self-assessed wellbeing. Here an 11-point scale is preferable to a 5 or 3 point scale so as to allow for better statistical analysis. The survey may then proceed with questions that capture the demographic characteristics of the respondents, employing similar wording to those used in National Accounts, so as to allow for comparisons between the study's sample and the actual population of interest. With a view to capturing data on the other characteristics which determine wellbeing, interviews normally include questions that ask respondents to report on aspects of their life, such as their current mental and physical health, the environmental situation of their locality, the extent of their social activity, political sentiment and trust. Responses are then coded and collapsed into indices as may be necessary, so as to allow for analysis.

Once data on wellbeing, as well as on each of its possible determinants are available, then it is possible to test relationships. Simple cross-tabulations can first be examined. These allow the researcher to test the strength of negative or positive linear association between respondents' wellbeing and the various other characteristics that respondents describe about their life. Finding significant correlation between wellbeing and the characteristics of the respondents' life is by no means trivial for it helps understand which members of society experience higher or lower wellbeing. However, economic analysis normally proceeds to the next step. This involves creating a model (or equation) of wellbeing that actually synthesises what *causes* wellbeing to fluctuate. Such an equation may take the following format

$$W = a_0 + a_1 X_i + u \tag{1}$$

Here W is self-assessed wellbeing, X_i is a vector of socio-economic variables that can cause wellbeing (such as marital status, income, environmental quality, social life, and so on) and u is the error term which accounts for the other, uncaptured causes of wellbeing. When data on the W and the various X variables exists, then the model can be estimated using statistical techniques, for instance, Ordinary Least Squares. This method involves finding the equation which best fits the data available. It allows the researcher to isolate what actually explains the fluctuations in wellbeing while avoiding confounding effects that may arise in simple cross tabulations (Powdthavee, 2010). As a result of statistical analysis, the coefficients a_0, a_1 can be found on each of the X variables. These represent the extent to which the variables influence wellbeing, as well as the direction (positive or negative) of that influence. When data are also available over time for a given sample (panel data) then it becomes possible to identify causal effects with more certainty.

Studies employing some variant of the techniques described above generally find that the factors that are positive and significantly affect wellbeing, are education, health, marriage, environment, religious participation, socialisation, politics and cultural participation. Happy people in a given country tend to disproportionately be the young and old (not middle-aged), well-off, educated, married, in work, healthy, exercise-takers (Blanchflower & Oswald, 2008a). It is possible to look at these in some detail.

ECONOMICS RESEARCH FINDINGS

Economic studies and policies generally implicitly assume that increasing income will increase life-satisfaction. However as mentioned earlier, beyond a decent level of income, income growth within a country rarely results in higher self-assessed wellbeing among citizens (Kahneman & Deaton, 2010). People tend to habituate to extra levels of income and they compare themselves to other people such that relative income matters more than absolute income. Increased income also tends to come at a cost – of less time. This said, becoming unemployed creates a clear, causal significant and negative impact on wellbeing – with lasting effects (Frey, 2008). The impact of joblessness is not just one of income but also affects one's social identity. Its effect can be as large as becoming chronically ill (Delaney, 2017). For policy-makers this suggests that it may be wise to shift attention away from GDP growth generally, to addressing unemployment (and unemployed people) specifically.

Beyond income and employment, most economic studies also examine education and health. Economic studies mainly find a positive relationship between education and wellbeing, although the impact is often low (Eurofound, 2013). Education in disadvantaged early childhood tends to give the highest return on investment (Heckman, 2008). Better educated individuals also tend to exercise more and to obtain more preventive health care. Health too (both physical and psychological) is in fact one of the strongest observed determinants of wellbeing (Blanchflower, 2009). Cross-country data shows that happiness is negatively related to high blood pressure, strain, inability to sleep, tiredness, stress, and pain (Blanchflower, 2009). Happy countries have lower levels of hypertension than others (Blanchflower & Oswald, 2008b). Life dissatisfaction is also related to obesity (Strine et al., 2008). Mental health is one of the areas that is increasingly receiving attention in Economics (Layard, 2003).

Economic studies also typically control for the effects of age, gender and status. Middle-aged people tend to report lower wellbeing. The U-shaped relationship between age and wellbeing is found in 72 developed and developing nations' in separate wellbeing regressions after adjusting for controls (Blanchflower & Oswald, 2008a). In terms of gender, findings are more complex: women may return higher levels of wellbeing, but with higher variance (Blanchflower & Oswald 2004; Stevenson & Wolfers, 2008). All other factors held constant, wellbeing also tends to be lower among single, widowed, divorced and separated individuals. (Stutzer & Frey, 2006; Waite et al., 2009). Some authors focus on the influence of marital disruption on psychological wellbeing, finding that persons who divorced or separated had a lower wellbeing than those who remained married (Waite, Luo, & Lewin, 2009).

Moving beyond perhaps the more obvious determinants, contextual factors have also been found to cause a significant impact on wellbeing. Environmental variables such as high air pollution, noise, smell and other negative externalities tend to adversely affect wellbeing (Di Tella & MacCulloch, 2008; Brereton et al.,

2008). Linked with this, reported life-satisfaction also responds to community attributes, such as crime and events that threaten societies or communities (Wills-Herrera et al., 2011). Wellness and happiness of individuals are also influenced by the social support of others. Reported wellbeing also seems to be positively related to religiosity (Aghili & Kumar, 2008) though the effect seems to be more based on attendance than belief (Stark & Maier, 2008). Religious organisations offer the opportunity of social interaction with people that have the same beliefs and therefore show mutual support especially in times of need (Pesta et al., 2010). Engaging in cultural activities similarly shows positive correlation with life-satisfaction (Frey, 2009; Grossi et al., 2012). Other correlates studied in the literature include trust in others and in political institutions (Hudson, 2006; Helliwell, 2003). Happy countries tend to have higher levels of democracy and democratic participation (Frey & Stutzer, 2000; Helliwell & Huang, 2008).

An emerging area in the literature is that which questions what this wellbeing literature means for personal decisions and policy. The New Economics Foundation's project synthesised the results of about 400 scientists (New Economics Foundation, 2008). Their results show that what governments ought to be promoting (if wellbeing is the goal) is more exercise, continued adult learning, improved emotional awareness, more social activity including being outdoors and volunteering. Another area receiving increased interest in Economics is the role of personality in wellbeing. While this may not be something that is clearly amenable to policy intervention, the manner in which policy decisions interact with different personality types merits consideration. Unemployment, for instance, is found to have diverse impacts on people depending on their personality type (Boyce & Wood, 2011).

CASE STUDY AND RESEARCH QUESTIONS

With the above sections as background, consider the prospect of an economist embarking on analysis of wellbeing in a given country. Let us take the case of Malta, the smallest member state in the European Union (EU), where wellbeing research is still in its infancy. By many accounts, Malta's economy has been doing well in recent years. GDP per capita compares well with the EU average, growing at a rate of some 6 per cent per annum even after adjusting for inflation (NSO, 2017). The services sector is the mainstay of the Maltese economy, which includes financial services and tourism, employing over 75 per cent of the Maltese population. For over a decade, unemployment rates in Malta have been among the lowest in the EU. Malta's GINI ratio (measuring the degree of inequality in the distribution of family income) also places it among the countries where distribution of income is not particularly problematic (NSO, 2016). Tax rates are in the range of 0 per cent to 35 per cent and yet government gross debt as a percentage of Gross Domestic Product was lower than that of the EU average (Eurostat, 2017).

A basic question to ask is whether wellbeing data tells a different story than that told by such popular economic statistics. In the latest survey data from Malta,

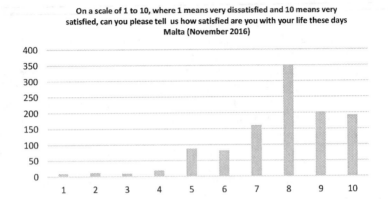

Figure 11.1. Life-satisfaction histogram (Source: NSO, 2016b)

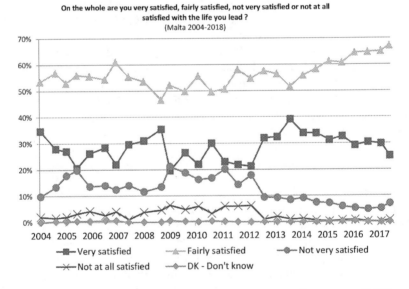

Figure 11.2. Life-satisfaction over time (Source: European Commission, 2017b)

the majority of people in Malta return a self-assessed wellbeing of 8 or more on a 10-point scale (Figure 11.1). But it is certainly useful to assess the socio-economic distinctions of those who return lower levels of wellbeing. A time-trend of wellbeing over recent years (Figure 11.2) using Eurobarometer data (European Commission, 2017b) highlights the periods when large fluctuations in self-assessed wellbeing occurred. It is possible to assess the events, shocks or cyclical patterns which are associated with such fluctuations. Testing the relationship between key events and wellbeing, while controlling for the other factors that influence wellbeing, may yield interesting findings on how intervention may impact wellbeing.

Using composite measures of wellbeing, it is also possible to compare wellbeing in one country with that of other countries. The Gallup survey yields very useful data in this regard (Gallup-Healthways, 2015). It poses a range of questions to respondents, besides those on economic wellbeing, including questions on relationships, the environment, the sense of purpose of physical wellbeing and vitality. Such data also makes it possible to conduct cross-sectoral studies or even panel studies which examine a group of countries over time. It is possible to examine whether different domains of wellbeing are complimentary or substitutes. For instance: does financial wellbeing stimulate or suppress other domains (e.g. environmental wellbeing, mental health)? Returning to our case study, the data reveals that Malta ranks somewhere in the middle of a range, and that while it ranks very highly on the economic front, its score is diluted by the very low score that its citizens return on physical wellbeing.

In countries like Malta wellbeing data is not captured regularly in the National Accounts. In such cases the interested researcher may require a dedicated survey instrument to examine the phenomenon (e.g. Briguglio & Sultana, 2015, 2017). Collecting data on wellbeing and on its associates allows the researcher to examine patterns between the former and the latter. Findings from Malta support those from other countries and indicate that wellbeing is significantly and positively related to physical and mental health, to the propensity to socialise and to be involved in cultural activities, to environmental quality, to government trust, and to holding a (Catholic) religion. As in other countries, wellbeing is lower towards middle age and for single people.

Contextual issues, such as external shocks or changing phenomena, also provide important cues for research. In the case of Malta, several such changes have taken place in recent years, in turn offering a rich agenda for wellbeing research (Briguglio, 2015, 2017). Rapidly increasing incidences of traffic congestion, air pollution and noise (Briguglio & Moncada, 2015) would contribute to the literature on the impact of environmental quality and pollution on wellbeing. Similarly, with the decline in public open space, it is possible to examine the direct and indirect impact of urbanisation on wellbeing. As populations become increasingly diverse with the arrival of migrants from various countries, this makes it possible to assess questions like the role of trust, social connectedness and religion on wellbeing. Changes in policy and legislation also create the kind of scenario where it is possible to assess evidence of impact. Joining (or indeed leaving) a bloc like the European Union, the introduction of divorce legislation, the hosting of mega-events, even national elections can be phenomena whose impact can offer insights to the literature and to policy.

Researchers may also be interested in focusing on methodological questions. Research projects employing quantitative methods will ask questions about data representativeness, investigating whether the sample investigated was sufficiently large and representative to capture the demographic variation in the population. Certain segments of the population may have been left out in sampling – segments which may be particularly important to the question of wellbeing. These include people living in institutions, and people who were sufficiently unhappy to have left the country, for instance. Research which focuses on this question itself may offer important new insights to the literature. Similarly, while research projects often discuss the reliability/validity of the construct/s by which wellbeing is measured, a useful area of research is that which sets out to compare these constructs.

A related and fascinating area of investigation relates to how to deal with cross-cultural comparisons of wellbeing. Wellbeing may well vary among countries, but to what extent is this due to language differences, cultural norms (that can influence whether respondents are happy to admit to un/happiness), or the effect of expectations, as opposed to the expected determinants of wellbeing? The statistical techniques in use typically also form part of the discussion in a research project – if not a research question in their own right. In estimating a statistical model, researchers may also examine whether relationships are linear or whether they take a more complex shape. Relatedly, while research on wellbeing typically focuses on the effect of other phenomena on wellbeing, it is important to examine the prospect of reverse causality, namely that people with higher levels of wellbeing do better in other domains (like income and health).

Of course, one key question which economists may pursue at this juncture in the discipline relates to the collection of wellbeing statistics on a national level. Supra-national organisations which have produced statistics and guidelines on how to collect national statistics include the European Commission's Beyond GDP initiative (European Commission, 2017), the United Nations – World Happiness Report, (Helliwell et al., 2017), and several countries including France's Sarkozy Commission, the UK (Stiglitz et al., 2009) and Canada (Michalos et al., 2011). Different techniques are in use, from objective composite measures to self-assessed survey-based data. The extent to which these differ, and the implications on policy of using wellbeing measures as opposed to (or in conjunction with) GDP is still a very pertinent question.

CONCLUSION

This chapter has outlined some of the considerations in the approach to wellbeing in Economics. In synthesis, the following three key points emerge: Firstly, Economics is indeed intimately concerned with wellbeing. The fundamental question in Economics is how to allocate scarce resources in society, with the ultimate purpose of investigation being to guide the allocation of resources in order to maximise welfare of society as a whole, and of different groups within it. Secondly, more recent work focusing specifically on the topic of wellbeing, generally involve measurement of both wellbeing and of its correlates. Statistical techniques employed to identify causality generally find that wellbeing is positively and significantly affected by, *inter alia,* education, health, marriage, environment, religion participation, socialisation, politics and cultural attendance. Thirdly Economics lends itself to several lines of investigation on wellbeing. Economics is concerned not only with measuring wellbeing (given the general consensus that GPD is a poor proxy), but also with deciphering what causes fluctuations in wellbeing in different countries across time and in response to different stimuli. In turn, Economics offers the possibility of evidence-based recommendations for policy.

REFERENCES

Aghili, M., & Kumar, G. V. (2008). Relationship between religious attitude and happiness among professional employees. *Journal of the Indian Academy of Applied Psychology, 34,* 66–69.

Blanchflower, D. G., & Oswald, A. J. (2008a, April). Is well-being U-shaped over the life cycle? *Social Science & Medicine, 66*(8), 1733–1749.

Blanchflower, D. G. (2009). *International evidence on well-being in measuring the subjective well-being of nations: National accounts of time use and well-being.* Chicago, IL: The University of Chicago Press.

Blanchflower, D. G., & Oswald, A. J. (2001). *Well-being over time in Britain and the USA. The Warwick Economics Research Paper Series (TWERPS).* Warwick: University of Warwick, Department of Economics.

Blanchflower, D. G., & Oswald, A. J. (2004). Well-being over time in Britain and the USA. *Journal of Public Economics, 88,* 1359–1386.

Blanchflower, D. G., & Oswald, A. J. (2008b). Hypertension and happiness across nations. *Journal of Health Economics, 27,* 218–233.

Boyce, C. J., & Wood, A. M. (2011). Personality prior to disability determines adaptation agreeable individuals recover lost life satisfaction faster and more completely. *Psychological Science, 22,* 1397–1402.

Brereton, F., Clinch, J. P., & Ferreira, S. (2008). Happiness, geography and the environment. *Ecological Economics, 65,* 386–396.

Briguglio, M. (2015). A finger on the pulse of happiness in an urbanised island context. In J. Condle & A. M. Cooper (Eds.), *Dialogues of sustainable urbanisation: Social science research and transitions to urban contexts* (pp. 195–199). Penrith: University of Western Sydney. (ISBN 978-1-74108-360-6)

Briguglio, M. (2017). Towards research on wellbeing in Malta. In The President's Foundation for the wellbeing of Society (Eds.), *The determinants of wellbeing, insight from research and implications for Malta* (pp. 52–63).

Briguglio, M., & Moncada, S. (2015). Environmental challenges in Malta. In M. S. Gale de Oliveira, M. Kennet, S. Amaral, E. Tezza, M. Briguglio, & D. Salman (Eds.), *The greening of the Mediterranean* (pp. 52–27). Oxford: The Green Economics Institute.

Briguglio, M., & Sultana, A. (2015). The effect of the Maltese festa on well-being: An Economic Analysis, with a focus on youth participation. In A. Azzopardi (Ed.), *Young people and the "festa" in Malta* (pp. 51–73). Malta: Best Print Co. Ltd.

Briguglio, M., & Sultana, A. (2017). Man cannot live by bread alone: Cultural participation and life satisfaction in Malta. In V. A. Cremona (Ed.), *Capitalising on culture? Malta and the European capital of culture* (pp. 15–36). Malta: Malta University Publishing.

Delaney, L. (2017). Wellbeing economics and public policy. In The President's Foundation for the wellbeing of Society (Eds.), *The determinants of wellbeing, insight from research and implications for Malta* (pp. 16–37).

Diener, E. (1984). Subjective well-being. *Psychological Bulletin,* 95(3), 542.

Diener, E., Inglehart, R., & Tay, L. (2013). Theory and validity of life satisfaction measures. *Social Indicators Research, 112,* 497–527.

Di Tella, R., & MacCulloch, R. J. (2008). Gross national happiness as an answer to the Easterlin Paradox? *Journal of Development Economics, 86*, 22–42.

Easterlin, R. (1974). Does economic growth improve the human lot? Some empirical evidence. In R. David & R. Reder (Eds.), *Nations and households in economic growth: Essays in honor of Moses Abramovitz*. New York, NY: Academic Press.

Eurofound. (2013). *Third European quality of life survey – Quality of life in Europe: Subjective well-being*. Luxembourg: Publications Office of the European Union.

European Commission. (2017). *Standard Eurobarometer*. Retrieved from http://ec.europa.eu/commfrontoffice/publicopinion/index.cfm/Survey/getSurveyDetail/instruments/STANDARD/surveyKy/2143

European Commission. (2017a). *Beyond GDP*. Retrieved from http://ec.europa.eu/environment/beyond_gdp/index_en.html

European Commission. (2017b) *Eurobarometer interactive*. Retrieved from http://ec.europa.eu/commfrontoffice/publicopinion/index.cfm/General/index

Eurostat. (2017). *New release – Euro indicators: Third quarter of 2016 compared with second quarter of 2016*. Eurostat Press Office.

Frey, B. S. (2008). *Happiness: A revolution in economics*. Cambridge, MA & London: The MIT Press.

Frey, B.S. (2009). Cultural Ecomomics. *CESifo DICE Report, 7*, 20–25.

Frey, B. S., & Stutzer, A. (2000). Happiness, economy and institutions. *Economic Journal, 110*(466), 918–938.

Gallup-Healthways. (2015). *State of global well-being: 2014 country well-being rankings*. Retrieved from http://info.healthways.com/hubfs/Well-Being_Index/2014_Data/Gallup-Healthways_State_of_Global_Well-Being_2014_Country_Rankings.pdf

Grossi, E., Blessi G., P. L., & Buscema, M. (2012). The interaction between culture, health and psychological well-being: Data mining from the Italian culture and well-being project. *Journal of Happiness Studies, 13*, 129–148.

Heckman, J. J. (2008). Schools, skills, and synapses. *Economic Inquiry, Western Economic Association International, 46*(3), 289–324.

Helliwell, J. F. (2003). How's life? Combining individual and national variables to explain subjective well-being. *Economic Modelling, 20*, 331–360.

Helliwell, J. F., & Huang, H. (2008). How's your government? International evidence linking good government and well-being. *British Journal of Political Science, 38*(4), 595–619.

Helliwell, J. F., Layard, R., & Sachs, J. (2017). *World happiness report 2017*. New York, NY: Sustainable Development Solutions Network.

Hudson, J. (2006). Institutional trust and subjective well-being across the EU. *Kyklos, 59*, 43–62.

Jordan, B. (2008). *Social value in public policy*. Bristol: Policy Press.

Kahneman, D., & Deaton, A. (2010). High income improves evaluation of life but not emotional well-being. *Proceedings of the National Academy of Sciences of the United States of America, 107*, 16489–16493.

Kahneman, D., & Krueger, A. B. (2006). Developments in the measurement of subjective well-being. *Journal of Economic Perspectives, 20*(1), 3–24.

Kahneman, D., Krueger, A. B., Schkade, D. A., Schwarz, N., & Stone, A. A. (2004). A survey method for characterizing daily life experience: The day reconstruction method. *Science, 306*(5702), 1776–1780.

Layard, R. (2003). *Happiness: Has social science a clue?* London: Lionel Robbins Memorial Lectures, London School of Economics.

Michalos, A. C., Smale, B., Labonté, R., Muharjarine, N., Scott, K., Moore, K., Swystun, L., Holden, B., Bernardin, H., Dunning, B., Graham, P., Guhn, M., Gadermann, A. M., Zumbo, B. D., Morgan, A., Brooker, A.-S., & Hyman, I. (2011). *The Canadian index of wellbeing. Technical report 1.0*. Waterloo: Canadian Index of Wellbeing and University of Waterloo.

National Statistics Office (NSO). (2016a). *News release – Statistics on income and living conditions 2015: Salient Indicators*. Malta: National Statistics Office.

National Statistics Office (NSO). (2016b). *Culture participation survey 2016*. Malta: National Statistics Office.

National Statistics Office (NSO). (2017). *News release – Gross domestic product: 2016*. Malta: National Statistics Office. Retrieved from https://nso.gov.mt/en/News_Releases/View_by_Unit/Unit_A1/National_Accounts/Documents/2017/News2017_041.pdf

New Economics Foundation. (2008). *Five ways to wellbeing: The evidence*. London: NED. Retrieved from http://www.neweconomics.org/publications/entry/five-ways-to-wellbeing-the-evidence

OECD. (2017). *Measuring wellbeing and progress wellbeing research*. Retreived from http://www.oecd.org/statistics/measuring-well-being-and-progress.htm

Pareto, V. (1896). *Cours D'Economie Politique* (vol. II). Lausanne: F. Roguge.

Pesta, B. J., McDaniel, M. A., & Bertsch, S. (2010). Toward an index of well-being for the fifty U.S. states. *Intelligence, 38*, 160–168.

Powdthavee, N. (2010). *The happiness equation: The surprising economics of our most valuable asset*. London: Icon Books Ltd.

Smith, A. (1776). *An inquiry into the nature and causes of wealth of nations* (Reprint). Oxford: Oxford Clarendon Press.

Smith, A. (2009). *The theory of moral sentiments*. New York, NY: Penguin Books.

Stark, R., & Maier, J. (2008). Faith and happiness. *Review of Religious Research, 50*, 120–125.

Stevenson, B., & Wolfers, J. (2008). Economic growth and subjective well-being: Reassessing the Easterlin Paradox. *Brookings Papers on Economic Activity, 39*, 1–102.

Stiglitz, J. E., Sen, A., & Fitoussi, J.-P. (2009). *Report by the commission on the measurement of economic performance and social progress*. Paris.

Strine, T. W., Mokdad, A. H., Balluz, L. S., Berry, J. T., & Gonzalez, O. (2008). Impact of depression and anxiety on quality of life, health behaviours, and asthma control among adults in the United States with asthma, 2006. *Journal of Asthma, 45*, 123–133.

Stutzer, A., & Frey, B. S. (2006). Does marriage make people happy, or do happy people get married? *The Journal of Socio-Economics, 35*, 326–347.

Thaler, R. H. (2015). *Misbehaving: The making of behavioral economics*. London: Allen Lane.

Tourangeau, R., Rips, L. J., & Rasinski, K. (2000). *The psychology of survey response*. New York, NY: Cambridge University Press.

United Nations Development Programme (UNDP). (2017). *Human development report 2016: Human development for everyone*. United Nations Development Programme.

Waite, L. J., Luo, Y., & Lewin, A. C. (2009). Marital happiness and marital stability: Consequences for psychological well-being. *Social Science Research, 38*, 201–212.

Wills Herrera, E., Orozco, L. E., Forero-Pineda, C., Pardo, O., & Andonova, V. (2011). The relationship between perceptions of insecurity, social capital and subjective well-being: Empirical evidences from areas of rural conflict in Colombia. *The Journal of Socio-Economics, 40*, 88–96.

World Values Survey. (2014). *World values survey*. Retrieved from: http://www.worldvaluessurvey.org/WVSDocumentationWV6.jsp

SUE VELLA

12. WELLBEING: A WELFARE PERSPECTIVE

Welfare and wellbeing are terms that are sometimes used interchangeably, though they differ in focus. Welfare typically refers to public services and benefits in various social domains such as health and housing, education and employment, social security and social services, while wellbeing is often understood in more individual, subjective terms. The objective dimensions of wellbeing still matter to people's subjective quality of life. The chapter illustrates how the birth and growth of the welfare state helped raise universal living standards in ways possibly unimaginable before the Second World War. Solidarity became institutionalised as welfare mechanisms allowed people to pool resources to face life's risks collectively. However, the welfare state cannot be taken for granted. This chapter outlines the main challenges to welfare states today and some of the critical debates that have arisen in the face of these challenges. Sustaining the welfare state requires clear values and robust evidence, careful policy design and political choices that support the wellbeing of those most in need of support.

Keywords: welfare state, social citizenship, social investment, care policy, divisions of welfare

INTRODUCTION

The welfare state has made an immeasurable difference to individual and collective wellbeing since the mid-twentieth century. It is hard to imagine how our quality of life might have been different without access to the services and benefits we often take for granted, for instance universal healthcare and education, social work and social security at particular points in one's life. Although the welfare state as we know it is relatively new, its sustainability is challenged by growing fiscal pressures, public expectations and difficult political choices. The aim of this chapter is to provide a background to welfare state development, followed by a brief account of key challenges and of selected critical debates in welfare today.

WELFARE STATE DEVELOPMENT

Although the Welfare State is typically associated with the social and political developments of the twentieth century, evidence of public generosity dates back to the dawn of time. Boswell (1988) for instance, speaks of the 'kindness of strangers' who cared for abandoned children in antiquity. In Europe, Christianity has for centuries both inspired and organised widespread charitable activity (Woods & Canizares, 2005) and continues to do so. However, it was not until the late 1800s that the modern origins of the Welfare State are found, when nation states were established and the French and Industrial Revolutions spurred the growth and spread of democracy and capitalism (Flora & Heidenheimer, 1996).

At the end of the 19th century, working conditions were harsh, and the prospect of socialism was thought to threaten social order in a number of European states. Welfare measures were introduced to prevent class conflict and "to integrate the working classes without fundamental challenge to the institution and distribution of private property" (Flora & Heidenheimer, 1996, p. 23). The introduction of social insurance by Imperial Decree in the German Empire in 1881 is often taken to be the first milestone of the modern Welfare State. The broadest set of social legislation after the Second World War was introduced in the UK, based on Beveridge's 1942 report that argued for government's role in fighting the 'five giants [of] Want, Disease, Ignorance, Squalor and Idleness'.

As new nation states developed their bureaucracies, they strengthened their capacity to take on economic and social roles alongside their traditional ones of law, order and defence. Systems of social insurance (based on workers' contributions) and social assistance (based on needs tests) soon developed and spread across Europe and beyond. The notion of wellbeing went beyond mere survival, and citizens would now be helped to cope with universal risks of the life course, such as unemployment, illness or injury, retirement and bereavement.

While both democracy and capitalism were central to the birth of welfare as we know it today, the design and generosity of different welfare states were shaped by historical struggles between groups to benefit from political decisions over redistribution of resources. The needs of the working class received political support from socialism, but also from social Catholicism through centrist Christian Democratic parties (Manow & van Kersbergen, 2014). However, it was not only the working class that influenced, or benefited from, the growth of welfare. Baldwin (1990) describes how the middle class came to realise that it too stood to benefit from the welfare state, and from a shared logic of solidarity – that all are vulnerable to arbitrary misfortunes and all are safer where risks are tackled collectively. This recognition of our interdependence made solidarity an important dimension of people's sense of wellbeing.

It is typically argued that most mature welfare states have developed through three main phases (see, for instance, Pierson, 2006). The first was a period of growth, which accelerated after World War II in what is commonly known as the Golden Age of the 1950s and 1960s. Garland (2014) speaks of a 'new government rationality', where problems such as poverty and unemployment were no longer seen as simply individual problems but ones which merited action by the State for the benefit of all. The Golden Age was marked by sustained economic growth and rising social expenditure, and by consensus on social welfare across the political spectrum and between labour and capital. Benefits and services were gradually extended to cover not only the poor but also the middle classes, further strengthening their support for the welfare state, not least because of the rapidly increasing number of jobs in welfare from which they benefited.

The second phase started around the middle of the 1970s. As economic difficulties were exacerbated by the 1973 oil crisis, economic growth slowed while unemployment and inflation rose. These developments gave rise to a recession which in turn led to increased welfare expenditure and increased public debt. For Offe (1982), this phase made clear the core contradiction of the welfare state, that "while capitalism cannot coexist with the welfare state, neither can it exist without the welfare state" (p. 11). Welfare benefits and services had provided the economy with healthy and educated workers, and mitigated the inequalities of capitalism, yet at the same time, welfare expenditure came to be seen as a public burden and as crowding out more 'productive' investment.

The Thatcher-Reagan alliance from the late 1970s is often taken to mark the rise of neoliberalism, with its emphasis on 'retrenchment' or smaller government, through privatisation, deregulation and public management reform, including in the area of welfare. Measures were taken in many countries to increase competitiveness by making the regulatory environment – including labour markets – more flexible and more responsive to business, while also seeking to reduce the public debt and deficit. Christopher Pierson (2006) points out that even if welfare in the UK and US was most affected by neoliberalism, other European states also sought to 'recalibrate' their welfare states by containing social expenditure after the 1970s.

The third phase from the early 1990s has seen the continued recalibration of welfare rather than major cutbacks. Path dependence theory illustrates that historical legacy matters, as past decisions become institutionalised and difficult to change. Besides, as Paul Pierson (1996) points out, while welfare expansion is a popular option for politicians, welfare cuts are deeply unpopular; their political consequences can be devastating and are avoided wherever possible. Reforms are thus constrained by the anticipated reactions of voters and interest groups, and often occur by stealth or in piecemeal fashion. The most common and widespread welfare reforms since the 1990s have been pension reform (with longer working lives and contributory periods), stricter benefit conditions (intended to 'activate' beneficiaries), and the introduction of market mechanisms in social services (intended to increase efficiency).

The 2008 financial crisis, and the recession and sovereign debt crisis which followed, were expected by many to result in wide and severe welfare cuts. The impact of the crisis, and governments' responses, have differed across countries. As Heins and de la Porte (2015) point out, the European Union, the European Central Bank and the International Monetary Fund provided rescue packages to the worst-hit countries, and these packages imposed structural reform conditions upon the receiving countries, especially the control of public debt. These conditions gave rise to austerity measures in various countries, which tend to disproportionately affect the poor. Southern Europe was hardest hit, where unemployment and poverty rose steeply, at a time when benefits were cut, labour protection was reduced, and care policies were stalled or reversed. However, since the EU started its recovery in 2014, unemployment has gone down and the policy focus has shifted away from rescue and back to social investment (see for instance Hemerijck 2013) in people's capacities to learn and work along the life course.

Social policy remains a major component of government activity in Europe. Welfare expenditure rose from its negligible initial levels to constitute, by 2016, the equivalent of one fifth of the EU's gross domestic product, or 40% of total government expenditure (Eurostat, 2018a). These aggregate figures hide variations between countries, due to differences in economic conditions, demographic profiles and political and cultural legacies. That said, there has been a degree of social policy convergence between countries in recent decades, due in part to the effect of the European Union. The EU's social agenda, initially limited to matters concerning the free movement of workers, has grown to incorporate a wider range of social areas (see for instance European Commission, 2013a; Hantrais, 2007). While primary responsibility for social policy remains with the member states, the EU legislates on key social issues, allocates significant funding to social inclusion and regional cohesion, and coordinates and monitors national policies. EU principles of solidarity and subsidiarity, and goals such as activation (of persons into the labour market) and social investment (throughout the lifecourse) are now central to a European vision of social wellbeing.

WELFARE CHALLENGES

Welfare has made an immeasurable difference to the lives of millions, particularly in terms of access to education, healthcare and housing, to income smoothing across the lifespan and to support in times of particular need. The impact of welfare has not only been on individual wellbeing but also on social cohesion and economic productivity. However, since the late 20th century, a number of trends have emerged to challenge the sustainability of welfare, the solidarity that underpins the welfare state, and the wellbeing of those who need it. Seven major and interlinked challenges are outlined below.

Demographic change, particularly low fertility and greater longevity, has resulted in population ageing in many European countries. Overall the labour supply will shrink by around 0.2% per year from 2030 onwards (even if the proportion of working age people in work is expected to rise). The old-age dependency ratio in the EU28 (that is, those aged 65 and over divided by those aged 15 to 64) will continue to rise steadily from 25% in 2010 to a projected 51.2% by 2070 (European Union, 2017a). This means that while in 2010, there were four persons of working age to every person of pensionable age, by 2070 two people will be working for every pensioner. The fiscal impact of an increasing proportion of pensioners to workers, and of the number of very old adults needing complex and expensive health and care services, is a preoccupation for many governments. It is also a concern for the individual wellbeing of vulnerable older adults, where the fiscal problem is dealt with through a dilution of services or the introduction of market reforms, as these may limit access by those least able to pay. From the perspective of solidarity, too, concerns are increasingly raised about intergenerational friction as the future of welfare for young people appears far less certain than that of their older counterparts (Hüttl, Wilson, & Wolff, 2015).

Globalisation has also impacted welfare, as developments in ICT, transport and financial liberalisation have accelerated the integration of international markets and the relocation of jobs to economies where labour is cheaper and regulations are more flexible. The argument goes that as governments compete to retain or attract foreign direct investment by keeping taxes and wages low, their capacity to fund the welfare state declines. Opinions differ as to whether globalisation actually affects the welfare state, that is, whether it results in less welfare expenditure, or whether it actually raises expenditure because benefits and services are increased to compensate those losing out to globalisation (Meinhard & Potrafke, 2012). A recent meta-review of the evidence suggests that while globalisation has not eroded welfare state activities, it has been a major cause of increased inequality within many countries (Potrafke, 2015) where top incomes have increased markedly and lower wages have all but stagnated for years.

Concern with *inequality* has thus risen markedly in recent years among scholars and international organisations (see for instance Stiglitz, 2015; Atkinson, 2015; Milanovic, 2016), especially since the 2008 financial crisis. The rise in inequality has been described by many as the 'scourge' of the times because of its effect on individual wellbeing, social cohesion and political stability. Even if the EU has among the lowest rates of inequality in the world, one common measure – the S80/S20 ratio – shows the income share of the richest 20% in the EU28 to be 5.2 times that of the poorest 20% (Eurostat, 2018b), the share of those on lowest incomes having declined since the financial crisis (European Investment Bank, 2018). The 'Easterlin Paradox' refers to findings by Easterlin (1973) who found, studying 30 national surveys, that even where overall incomes increase, people do not necessarily feel better off if their situation relative to social standards remains the same or deteriorates. Ensuring that the benefits of growth extend to all remains a challenge on many countries' policy agenda.

Labour market changes have also affected wellbeing. Since the late 20th century, labour markets in most advanced economies have seen a major shift from manufacturing to service employment, enabled by offshoring and by rapid technological developments, and by rising consumption of services as people become more affluent. The decrease in manufacturing jobs has meant that many of those losing such jobs have taken up employment in lower paid service sectors. Service employment tends to be more polarised than manufacturing, between the highly productive and well paid sectors like communications and finance, and the low productivity service sectors where working conditions are often precarious. The vulnerability of those with lower skill levels, and of youth with little work experience, was made evident by the 2008 financial crisis which saw unemployment rise particularly among these groups. When unemployment peaked in 2013, 23.5 per cent of EU28 youth were unemployed (compared to 10.9 per cent of the total EU28 working age population), raising concerns over intergenerational fairness and the long-term welfare of today's youth. Modest economic recovery since 2014 has seen unemployment rates decline. However, the labour market position of the low skilled is still of concern. In 2016, the EU28 employment rate for low skilled workers was 54.3 per cent, compared to 84.8 per cent of the high skilled (European Union, 2017b), challenging welfare states to raise the skill levels of jobseekers and facilitate their entry to employment.

Changing gender roles have also challenged the traditional welfare state which was based upon a male breadwinner-female homemaker model with many women lacking an individual income and with social security benefits deriving from the labour market status of their spouse. Over the past twenty five years, the female employment rate has risen while that of men has remained largely static, standing at 71.9% for men and 61.4% for women in 2017 (European Union, 2017b) though these aggregate figures disguise significant differences between countries. Gender gaps in the labour market persist, both in terms of employment and pay, leading Esping Anderson (2009) to describe gender equality as an 'incomplete revolution'. Yet for welfare at least, gender role changes have had a revolutionary impact, requiring for instance the individualisation of benefits so that working women become eligible in their own right; social security credits for caring periods; family-friendly measures and anti-discrimination legislation. The impact of increased female employment upon the availability of care for children and older adults is another major challenge which only seems set to increase as the population ages further. Another important gendered challenge is the support of lone parents and their children. For many of the 9.2 million lone parents in the EU (of whom 85 per cent are women) achieving adequate living standards, economic independence and work-life balance is particularly difficult. While one quarter of the EU28 population faces the risk of poverty, this is true of almost half of all lone mothers and one third of all lone fathers (European Institute for Gender Equality, 2017).

Large-scale *migration* into advanced economies has also become increasingly relevant to welfare. In Europe, this peaked in 2015 and 2016 when over one million migrants from outside the EU – many fleeing wars and persecution and others in search of economic security – arrived in Europe. While some argue that the scale of migration is such that it burdens the welfare system of host countries and provokes ethnic intolerance, there is also some evidence that when the net contribution of migrants is taken into account, the balance tends to be positive, both in fiscal terms as well as in meeting labour market shortages (see for instance OECD, 2014). Though many migrants make important labour market contributions, across Europe they continue to be over-represented in poverty and deprivation statistics. Almost half the non-EU migrants were at risk of poverty or exclusion in 2016, which is more than double the rate for EU nationals. Severe material deprivation was also more prevalent, affecting 15.5 per cent of non-EU migrants compared to 7.4 per cent of nationals (Eurostat, 2018c). One fifth of employed migrants experience in-work poverty, that is, their household income still falls below the poverty threshold (60% of average household income) despite the fact that one or more persons in the household is in paid employment. Migrants tend to have lower life satisfaction; they face difficulties in finding adequate housing and employment; and are more vulnerable to crime and racism. Ethnic intolerance in many countries has further complicated the task of those welfare states to define and manage their ethical obligations to migrants, particularly to those who do not qualify for asylum.

Lastly, *public attitudes* also affect welfare, as public perception of the legitimacy of welfare (especially for particular groups) influences political decisions on benefits and services. In a comparative study, Brooks and Manza (2006) find that public support clearly affects the resilience of the welfare state. Svallfors (2010) brings together a number of findings from various national datasets in the late twentieth century, to note that while people are generally supportive of welfare states, this applies much more to universal services like pensions and healthcare than to targeted social assistance where respondents expressed concerns over 'welfare cheating' and inefficient bureaucracy. More recently Roosma, van Oorschot and Gelissen (2014) study 2008/9 data from 25 European countries and largely confirm these findings, noting that while most people support welfare state provisions, they have 'normative' concerns over the "moral flaws of benefit recipients" (p. 504) and 'administrative' concerns over the imperfect targeting of benefits and services. Countering such arguments, Bregman (n.d.) contends that "poverty is not a lack of character; it is a lack of cash". In another work, he discusses the cognitive effects of poverty, and how the 'scarcity mentality' of the poor means that they are more preoccupied with immediate survival than with planning for the longer term. This preoccupation, he suggests, often results in what seem to be poor decisions, but which are more of a symptom, than a cause, of their poverty (Bregman, 2017). Avoiding the vilification of the poor in public and political discourse is important to the solidarity which underpins the sustainability of the welfare state.

CRITICAL DEBATES IN WELFARE

The challenges outlined above, especially in the context of the post-2008 crisis, are often cited in defence of welfare reform. In many countries welfare reforms, which accelerated since the 1980s, have included the introduction of market principles in welfare provision; a tightening of eligibility criteria; and the stalling or even reduction of the levels of social benefits and services. When viewed through the lens of traditional social policy principles such as adequacy, affordability, equity and effectiveness, these developments have rekindled or extended a number of critical debates in social policy. A selection of four of these is briefly presented below.

The first debate to be considered concerns the notion of *citizenship* as a basis for access to social benefits and services, which has become increasingly salient in a time of large-scale migration. In 1949, T. H. Marshall wrote his classic three-stage account of the development of citizenship rights, defining citizenship as "a status bestowed on those who are full members of a community [who are] equal with respect to the rights and duties with which the status is endowed" (Marshall, 2014, p. 32). In his account, the eighteenth century saw the establishment of civil rights – those individual liberties such as free speech and worship, the right to work and own property, and to enjoy equal treatment under the law. In the 19th century, no doubt spurred by the French Revolution, citizenship was extended to include the political rights to vote and stand for office. Citizenship was further extended in the twentieth century to include social rights, or what Marshall defined as a "whole range, from the right to a modicum of economic welfare and security to the right to share to the full in the social heritage and to live the life of a civilised being according to the standards prevailing in the society" (2014, p. 28). The law courts are most closely linked to civil rights, and parliaments to political rights, while the effective exercise of these rights depends in turn on the education and social service systems. For Marshall, the three sets of rights are mutually complementary and indivisible.

Although still widely cited, Marshall's work has been criticised. From the right of the political spectrum, criticism has been levelled at the fact that citizenship theory has lacked a corresponding account of citizens' obligations (see for instance, Mead, 1986). Feminists have criticised the fact that while citizenship theory has focused on equal rights in the public sphere, it has traditionally been far harder for women to enjoy these rights due to inequalities in the private sphere, where women undertake the bulk of unpaid care, lacking access to a personal income and sometimes to equal treatment at law (see for instance, Walby, 1994). Perhaps the most pressing debate pertains to the way citizenship serves to limit migrants' access to services and benefits on the same terms as nationals. On the one hand, some argue that citizenship and nationality are closely linked, and that the sustainability of the welfare state depends on public willingness to contribute to it, which in turn requires a sense of shared identity (Freeman, 1986). Others, however, argue that globalisation requires a broader basis for citizenship than nationality, and that a renewed ethics of welfare is needed to increase migrants' access to social rights (Dean, 2011). Further, as Lister (1997) points out when discussing the 'exclusionary tensions' of citizenship, it is important to bear in mind the particular vulnerability of migrants' dependents – their spouses and children – as they face compounded inequalities on the basis of both race and gender, and often rely on derived rather than individualised rights.

The second debate concerns the *social investment* approach which has characterised social policy in Europe since the turn of the new millennium (Hemerijck, 2013). This approach focuses particularly on education and training, job search assistance and childcare, because investing in people's capacities to learn and to work at every life stage is believed to have positive effects on social inclusion, labour market participation and economic efficiency. Social policy is thus seen as a productive investment rather than a burden, which has brought welcome balance to the 'welfare dependency' arguments of the late twentieth century. This view of social policy as a 'productive factor' was given added weight by the European Commission's 2013 Social Investment Package, intended to guide member states to effectively address their post-crisis social challenges (European Commission, 2013b).

However, there has been some criticism of social investment. This relates particularly to its strong emphasis on the 'activation' of the unemployed (through more stringent benefit conditions and job search and training obligations), while paying far less attention to job quality and to improving the situation of those who are furthest from the labour market (Leoni, 2016). Critics also suggest that reframing social expenditure as an investment may divert spending away from the very poorest, where it may not generate the 'returns' expected of an investment. Cantillon (2011) contends that social investment must not be allowed to overshadow the enduring need for social redistribution through adequate levels of social security. This remains an important point even if Kuitto's (2016) study of 23 countries in the 2000s did not find evidence that social investment has displaced traditional social security thus far. The potential of social investment seems to vary across countries. As Kazepov and Ranci (2017) discuss in the case of Italy, for all to benefit from social investment, a number of broader contextual conditions must be in place, such as provisions for gender equality, inclusive labour markets and responsive education systems.

The third debate pertains to the *mixed economy of welfare*, or the respective roles of the statutory, commercial, voluntary and informal sectors in the organisation of welfare. As Powell (2007) notes, there is no one best welfare mix, and the mix varies across time and space. Since the late twentieth century, arguments have been made both for and against a greater role for each of the different sectors. The field of care services offers a key example of the welfare mix debate, particularly in respect of the role of families and the private sector in this field.

Until the 1980s, care did not come under the scrutiny of policymakers because "care, as an emotion and as labour, was ... seen as private and feminine" (Rummery & Fine, 2012, p. 321). Demographic developments have changed this, and placed care squarely on the policy agenda, particularly long-term care. The volume of care work formerly undertaken by women has become increasingly evident, as higher female employment rates and population ageing both increase care needs and make them more visible. Recognising this, as well as the fact that not everyone has family members on whom to depend for care and support, led Lister (1994) to propose the concept and practice of defamilialisation – a greater role for the state in meeting care needs, intended to enable people to maintain good living standards irrespective of their access to family support.

Over recent years, many countries have expanded statutory care services for the very young and older adults, but not everyone agrees with this approach and ideas about the state's proper role in providing care differ. On the one hand, for instance, it has been argued that the state has unduly encroached on the private sphere and should – respecting the principle of subsidiarity – empower families to perform their caring obligations themselves through adequate legislative and financial support. Writing of Italy, Di Nicola (2015) argues how a logic of defamilialisation diminishes the value of care, turning into a commodity the most important aspect of family life and hence "empty[ing] the family of all meaning, turning it into a unit of cohabiting adults that have nothing in common except achieving an economy of scale that makes cohabitation financially advantageous" (p. 202). On the other hand, and writing of Spain, Deusdad, Javornik, Mas Giralt and Marbàn Flores (2017) lament the refamilialisation of care after the 2008 crisis, stating that cutbacks in long-term care have had negative effects on people in need and "significant consequences for gender equality as women's opportunities to access independent income are skewed" (p. 194). The debate around responsibility for care simmers on, particularly in Southern Europe where families have traditionally been the main providers of care to their members.

The increased provision of care by the commercial sector has also generated controversy. Arguments for an enhanced private sector role in welfare typically include increased consumer choice, quality and the ability to operate with greater efficiency than a large-scale bureaucracy. Equally, opponents contend that the introduction of market principles into welfare impacts negatively upon important principles like equity, affordability and democratic scrutiny. Baldock (2003) makes a broad case for the way public services strengthen a shared sense of solidarity and civic life. Others have also argued that increased choice is a fiction because people whose needs are greatest rarely have the information or resources to choose between service providers. Nor is it clear that the quality of private care is always superior. As operators seek to compete on cost and thus to remain affordable to consumers, or to remain competitive in bidding for public contracts, quality may suffer and service users may have little redress or recourse to alternatives. Further, because care is a costly business, many smaller operators find it hard to survive. As Scourfield (2007) notes, because larger operators benefit from economies of scale they tend to progressively increase their market shares, reducing the choices open to service users. A sound regulatory framework and prioritisation of those with greatest needs are important dimensions of accessible and good-quality private care.

The fourth and last debate, around the *divisions of welfare,* is an old one that has been revived and extended in recent years, to illustrate that resources are not only redistributed through the social welfare system but also through other less visible means, and often in greater amounts, to those whose needs are less. The term 'divisions of welfare' was coined by Richard Titmuss (1958), in response to early claims of excessive expenditure on welfare benefits. Titmuss argued for a broadening of social policy analysis to encompass not only social benefits but also fiscal and occupational ones. Fiscal welfare is delivered through the tax system and refers to revenue forgone by the state, for instance, tax credits on private schooling, on private pensions or on mortgage interest. Occupational welfare is delivered through one's employment, for instance, sick pay and subsidised childcare but also non-taxable benefits like health insurance, company cars and mobile telephony costs.

All three divisions of welfare redistribute resources; however, while social welfare aims to benefit those with lowest incomes, fiscal and occupational welfare tend to be regressive as they confer greater benefits to those on higher incomes. Focusing on fiscal welfare, Sinfield (2007) discusses how forgone revenue does not appear in public accounts and is subject to far less scrutiny than social benefits, despite the fact that in the UK at least, income tax relief actually exceeded social welfare expenditure in 2005/6. For Sinfield, the fact that "most elements of tax welfare continue to ... widen inequalities – and do so relatively invisibly ... is a very compelling reason to take a broader framework for social policy analysis than 'the welfare state'" (2007, p. 142).

More recently, Farnsworth (2012) argues that corporate welfare, or the ways in which the state supports business, should also be more open to scrutiny and 'conceptually embedded' in social policy analysis. While corporations have always benefited indirectly from state intervention (in terms, for instance, of a healthier and better educated workforce), they also benefit more directly through various forms of state subsidies, such as the financial bailouts after the 2008 crisis. Like fiscal welfare, corporate welfare is a contested subject. As Farnsworth shows, it is criticised on both the right and left of the political spectrum. The Right argues that when politics and business mix, this distorts markets, prolongs the survival of non-viable businesses and increases dependence on the state, all of which they believe to harm competitors, consumers and taxpayers. The Left, on the other hand, sees corporate welfare as reducing resources for those who need them most while favouring those élites with good political connections.

There may be times when a strong case can be made for state support to industry, for instance, where numerous jobs or new skills would be created, or where closure would imperil the livelihoods of many or even of a whole region. However, the effectiveness of such state support in the medium- or longer-term is unclear and rarely made public, if evaluated at all. At the very least, though, recognising the reality of state support to private enterprise challenges the notion that redistribution only benefits disadvantaged minorities and, as Farnsworth (2012) suggests, strengthens rather than weakens the case for an improved private sector contribution to the welfare state.

CONCLUSION

This chapter has provided an outline of the development of welfare states together with some of the main contemporary challenges and debates in this field. The social and economic impact of welfare over the past century is incalculable and it is hard for most of us to imagine a society without, for instance, universal schooling and health care, and social security benefits at critical points in one's life. The logic of welfare – the collective pooling of resources to face universal risks – has secured widespread support for the welfare state, making solidarity an integral part of individual and social notions of wellbeing. However, the viability, adequacy and effectiveness of welfare are challenged by a number of developments, not least population ageing and migration, and changes in the labour market and gender roles. Inequality within countries is on the rise, and good welfare benefits and services remain important to the wellbeing of certain groups such as older adults on low income or in need of long-term care, the low skilled, inexperienced youth, lone parents and their children, and migrants and their dependents. Addressing these challenges requires just political choices, careful policy design based on value clarity and robust evidence; service user involvement; and strong regulatory frameworks.

ACKNOWLEDGEMENT

With gratitude to Dr Charles Pace for our early discussion about this chapter.

REFERENCES

Atkinson, A. (2015). *Inequality*. Cambridge, MA: Harvard University Press.
Baldock, J. (2003). On being a welfare consumer in a welfare society. *Social policy and society, 2*(1), 65–71.
Baldwin, P. (1990). *The politics of social solidarity. Class bases of the European welfare state 1875–1975*. Cambridge: Cambridge University Press.
Boswell, J. (1988). *The kindness of strangers*. New York, NY: Pantheon Books.
Bregman, R. (2017). *Utopia for realists and how we can get there*. London: Bloomsbury.
Bregman, R. (n.d.). *Poverty isn't a lack of character. It's a lack of cash*. Retrieved May 24, 2017, from https://thecorrespondent.com/6777/poverty-isnt-a-lack-of-character-its-a-lack-of-cash/260541765-09059a71
Brooks, C., & Manza, J. (2006). Why do welfare states persist? *The Journal of Politics, 68*(4), 816–827.
Cantillon, B. (2011). The paradox of the social investment state: Growth, employment and poverty in the Lisbon era. *Journal of European Social Policy, 21*(5), 432–449.
Dean, H. (2011). The ethics of migrant welfare. *Ethics and Social Welfare, 5*(1), 18–35.
Deusdad, B., J. Javornik, R., Mas Giralt, R., & Marbán Flores, R. (2017). Care in the wake of the financial crisis: gender implications in Spain and the United Kingdom. In F. Martinelli, A. Anttonen, & M. Mätzke (Eds.), *Social services discrupted – Changes, challenges and policy implications for Europe in times of austerity*. Cheltenham: Edward Elgar.
Di Nicola, P. (2015). Care work between defamilialisation and commodification. *Italian Sociological Review, 5*(2), 189–205.
Easterlin, R. (1973). Does money buy happiness? *The Public Interest, 30*(Winter), 3–10. Retrieved April 17, 2017, from http://www.nationalaffairs.com/storage/app/uploads/public/58e/1a4/b73/58e1a4b738c04566289875.pdf
Esping Anderson, G. (2009). *The incomplete revolution – adapting to women's new roles*. Cambridge: Polity Press.
European Commission. (2013a). *The European Union explained – Employment and social affairs – Promoting jobs, inclusion and social policy as an investment*. Retrieved from http://ec.europa.eu/social/main.jsp?catId=738&langId=en&pubId=7545&furtherPubs=yes
European Commission. (2013b). *Towards social investment for growth and cohesion* (COM(2013) 83 final). Retrieved April 18, 2017, from http://ec.europa.eu/social/main.jsp?langId=en&catId=1044&newsId=1807&furtherNews=yes
European Institute for Gender Equality. (2017). *Poverty, gender and lone parents in the EU*. Retrieved June 11, 2018, from http://eige.europa.eu/lt/rdc/eige-publications/poverty-gender-and-lone-parents-eu
European Investment Bank. (2018). *Inequality in Europe*. Luxembourg: EIB.

Eurostat. (2018a). *Government expenditure on social protection.* Retrieved June 11, 2018, from http://ec.europa.eu/eurostat/statistics-explained/index.php/Government_expenditure_on_social_protection

Eurostat. (2018b). *S80/S20 income quintile share ratio by sex and selected age group – EU-SILC survey.* Retrieved June 11, 2018, from http://ec.europa.eu/eurostat/data/database

Eurostat. (2018c). *Migration integration statistics – at risk of poverty and social exclusion.* Retrieved June 11, 2018, from http://ec.europa.eu/eurostat/statistics-explained/index.php/Migration_integration_statistics_-_at_risk_of_poverty_and_social_exclusion

European Union. (2015). *EU policy making and growing inequalities.* Luxembourg: Publications Office of the European Union.

European Union. (2017a). *The 2018 ageing report.* Luxembourg: Publications Office of the European Union.

European Union. (2017b). *Employment and social developments in Europe 2017.* Luxembourg: Publications Office of the European Union.

Farnsworth, K. (2012). Bringing corporate welfare in. *Journal of Social Policy, 42*(1), 1–22.

Flora, P., & Heidenheimer, A. J. (1981). *The development of welfare states in Europe and America.*

Freeman, G. P. (1986). Migration and the political economy of the welfare state. *The Annals of the American Academy of Political and Social Science, 485,* 51–63.

Garland, D. (2014). The welfare state: A fundamental dimension of modern government. *European Journal of Sociology, 55*(3), 327–364.

Hantrais, L. (2007). *Social policy in Europe* (3rd ed.). London: Palgrave.

Heins, E., & de la Porte, C. (2015). The sovereign debt crisis, the EU and welfare state reform. *Comparative European Politics, 13*(1), 1–7.

Hemerijck, A. (2013). *Changing welfare states.* Oxford: Oxford University Press.

Hüttl, P., Wilson, K., & Wolff, G. (2015). *The growing intergenerational divide in Europe* (Bruegel Policy Contribution 2015/17). Retrieved June 5, 2018, from http://bruegel.org/2015/11/the-growing-intergenerational-divide-in-europe/

Kazepov, Y., & Ranci, C. (2017). Is every country fit for social investment? Italy as an adverse case. *Journal of European Social Policy, 27*(1), 90–104.

Kuitto, K. (2016). From social security to social investment? *Journal of European Social Policy, 26*(5), 442–459.

Lister, R. (1994). 'She has other duties' – Women, citizenship and social security. In S. Baldwin & J. Falkingham (Eds.), *Social security and social change: New challenges to the beveridge model.* Hemel Hempstead: Harvester Wheatsheaf.

Lister, R. (1997). A feminist synthesis of citizenship. *Feminist Review, 57,* 28–48.

Manow, P., & van Kersbergen, K. (2014). Religion and the western welfare state. In C. Pierson, F. G. Casstles, & I. K. Naumann (Eds.), *The welfare state reader* (3rd ed.). Cambridge: Polity Press.

Marshall, T. H. (2014). Citizenship and social class. In C. Pierson, F. G. Casstles, & I. K. Naumann (Eds.), *The welfare state reader* (3rd ed.). Cambridge: Polity Press.

Mead, L. (1986). *Beyond entitlement: The social obligations of citizenship.* New York, NY: The Free Press.

Meinhard, S., & Potrafke, N. (2012). The globalisation-welfare state nexus reconsidered. *Review of International Economics, 20*(2), 271–287.

Milanovic, B. (2016). *Global inequality. A new approach for the age of globalisation.* Cambridge, MA: Harvard University Press.

Offe, C. (1982). Some contradictions of the modern welfare state. *Critical Social Policy, 2*(5), 7–16.

Organisation for Economic Cooperation and Development, "Is migration good for the economy?" *Migration Policy Debates,* May 2014. Retrieved 4 April 2017 from https://www.oecd.org/migration/mig/OECD%20Migration%20Policy%20Debates%20Numero%202.pdf

Pierson, C. (2006). *Beyond the welfare state* (3rd ed.). Cambridge: Polity Press.

Pierson, P. (1996). The new politics of the welfare state. *World Politics, 48*(2), 143–179.

Potrafke, N. (2015). The evidence on globalisation. *The World Economy, 38*(3), 509–552.

Powell, M. (Ed.). (2007). *Understanding the mixed economy of welfare.* Bristol: Policy Press.

Roosma, F., van Oorschot, W., & Gelissen, J. (2014). The weakest link in welfare state legitimacy: European perceptions of moral and administrative failure in the targeting of social benefits. *International Journal of Comparative Sociology, 55*(6), 489–50.

Rummery, K., & Fine, M. (2012). Care: A critical review of theory, policy and practice. *Social Policy and Administration, 46*(3), 321–343.

Scourfield, P. (2007). Are there reasons to be worried about the 'caretelization' of residential care? *Critical Social Policy, 27*(2), 155–180.

Sinfield, A. (2007). Tax welfare. In M. Powell (Ed.), *Understanding the mixed economy of welfare*. Bristol: Policy Press.

Stiglitz, J. (2015). *The price of inequality*. London: Penguin.

Svallfors, S. (2010). Public attitudes. In F. G. Castles, S. Leibfried, J. Lewis, H. Obinger, & C. Pierson (Eds.), *The Oxford handbook of the welfare state*. Oxford: Oxford University Press.

Titmuss, R. (1958). *Essays on the welfare state*. London: George Allen & Unwin.

Walby, S. (1994). Is citizenship gendered? *Sociology, 28*(2), 379–395.

Woods, T., & Canizares, A. (2005). *How the Catholic Church built western civilisation*. Washington, DC: Regnery History.

INDEX

A
Acceptance
  by others, 11
Age
  and wellbeing, 150
Agency
  and disabled people's campaign for change, 133
  and wellbeing, 141
Aristotle, 1. *See* Eudaimonia
Attachment
  attachment framework, 67
  caregiver behaviour, 68
  emotional regulation, 68
autonomy
  individual, 139
Autonomy
  as important to disabled people's movement, 139
  promoted by professionals working in domestic violence, 120
  relational, 139

B
Belonging, 18
  and vulnerable youth, 106
  belongingness hypothesis, 7, 11
  need to belong, 10, 11

C
Capabilities approach, 2
Capitalism
  and leisure, 112
Care
  as example of mixed economy of welfare, 167
  defamilialisation, 167
  ethics of care, 137
  family, 138
  impact of care ethic upon leisure, 111
  impact of rising female employment, 164
  personal, 138
  refamilialisation, 168
  social, 138
  tension between protection and autonomy, 138
Children
  risk of poverty in Malta, 73
  understanding children's behaviour, 68
Choice
  and chaos, 138
  and control, 140
  and control in personal budgets, 139
  to stay in abusive relationship, 124
Citizenship
  as basis for benefits, 166
  contribution of leisure, 112
  criticism of tripartite model, 166
  Marshall, T. H., 166
  young people, 99
Cognitive psychology, 10
Community
  attributes and wellbeing, 151
  impact upon young people, 99
Cooperation
  benefits of, 11

D
Demography
  effects of second demographic transition, 65

INDEX

Disability
　affirmative model of, 135
　as neither simple nor unitary, 140
　definition of impairment vs
　　disability, 135
　disablism, 135
　genetic technology, 136
　intellectual, 139
　medical model, 134
　relational model of, 135
　social model of, 134
　tragic view, 136
Disabled people
　core goals, 133
　positioning as citizens, 133
Disempowerment
　as result of violence, 117
Diversity
　and empowerment process, 124
Domestic violence
　consequences for poorer
　　women, 71
　definition, 71
　effect on children, 71
　statistics for Malta, 71

E
Ecological framework, 68
Economics
　definition, 145
　fundamental assumptions of, 146
Education
　and wellbeing, 150
Emotional intelligence
　assessment of, 30
　common elements, 26
　definition, 24, 26
　evolution of concept, 24
　four-branch model, 26
　models, 25
Emotional regulation
　in adversity, 21
　resilience, 28

Employment
　family-friendly support, 74
　impact of dual earner couples on
　　family wellbeing, 73
　minimum wage and poverty, 73
　women in employment, 72
Empowerment
　as reclaiming one's life after
　　violence, 117
　at collective level, 125
　at individual level, 121
　definition, 120
　importance of informal networks, 123
Environment
　and wellbeing, 150
Eudaimonia, 1
European Union
　social agenda, 162
Exclusion
　effects of, 12

F
Financial crisis
　impact on labour market, 164
　of 2008, 161
Flourishing
　elements of, 40

G
GDP
　gross domestic product, definition
　　of, 147
　in Malta, 151
　weakness in measuring wellbeing,
　　147
Gender
　and wellbeing, 150
　criticism of citizenship theory, 166
　impact of changing roles on welfare
　　state, 164
　lone parents, 164
Globalisation
　impact on welfare, 163

Goals
  accountability to, 146
  congruence of, 40

H
Happiness
  as policy goal, 2
Health
  and wellbeing, 150
Hedonism, 1

I
Illiteracy
  costs of, 84
Illness, 7
Inclusion
  need to promote, 19
Income
  and life satisfaction, 72
  income adequacy, 72
Inequality
  rise of, 163
Intervention
  by government for social outcomes, 146
  forms of, 146
Isolation
  effects of, 12

L
Labour market
  activation policy, 162
  contribution of migrants, 164
  critique of activation, 167
  family-friendly measures, 164
  impact of changes on welfare, 163
Learning
  stimulated by affective mechanisms, 12
Leisure
  as contesting social norms, 113
  as multidimensional, 109
  as 'time out' from controls, 112

  benefits for society, 110
  body modification, 113
  darker side, 112
  deviant leisure, 113
  fluidity of class distinctions, 109
  impact of gender, 111
  important across lifespan, 110
  meaning differs by social context, 110
  positive emotional impact, 110
  violence in sports, 112
Life satisfaction
  measurement of, 147
Literacy
  as human right, 83
  benefits of, 83
  changes in recent years, 85
  negative impact of poor literacy, 83
Longevity
  linked to social integration, 15
  strength of relationships, 16

M
Marital status
  and wellbeing, 150
Marriage
  crude marriage rates, 70
Meaning
  and flourishing, 2
  derived from print, 82
  in deviant leisure, 114
  in suffering, 41
  search for, 41
Migrants
  migrant children's risk of poverty, 73
Migration
  and citizenship, 166
  difficulties faced by migrants, 165
  impact on welfare state, 164
  peak in 2015, 164
  vulnerability of dependents, 166
Motivation, 8, 9

INDEX

N
Neoliberalism
    start of, 161

P
Pain
    physical, 7, 12, 13
    social, 7, 12, 13
Parents
    positive parenting, 75
Participation
    as fundamental to empowerment, 127
    of youth, 104
Patriarchy
    definition of, 118
Politics
    role of social Catholicism in birth of welfare state, 160
    role of socialism in birth of welfare state, 160
Poverty
    cognitive effects of, 165
    effect on parenting behaviour, 74
    effects on children, 74
    risk of lone parents, 164
    statistics in Malta, 73
Professionals
    lack of youth trust in, 103

R
Redistribution
    arbitrariness, 138
Regulation
    as necessary in field of care, 168
Relationships
    as important to persons with disability, 139
    as vital to life goals, 140
    between parents and children, 72
    conflict in, 14
    couple relationships, 70
    egalitarian, 65
    link to life satisfaction, 71
    maintenance, 12
    quality within families, 67
    relationship security, 68
    spontaneous inclination to form, 12
    their effect on emotions, 12
Religion
    as institutional, 36
    christianity and charity, 160
    declining church attendance, 36
    religious strain, 43
Resilience
    definition, 28
    in relationships, 67
Retrenchment
    start of, 161
Rights
    balance between right to protection and right to risk, 140
    civil rights of citizenship, 166
    social rights of citizenship, 166
    women's needs as claimable rights, 125
Risk
    lifecourse risks, 160

S
Self-esteem, 7–10, 18
    effects of, 8
    Maslow, 9
Shame
    as lethal emotion, 123
Social Anxiety Disorder, 10
Social Comparison Theory, 9
Social connections
    health benefits, 15
    health risks when absent, 16
    types of, 14
Social integration, 14
    positive effects, 15
Social intelligence, 18
Social interaction
    need for interpersonal skills, 18

INDEX

Social investment, 162
   as contested, 166
   prerequisites, 167
Social justice
   in capabilities approach, 3
Social support, 14
   as buffer against stress, 14
Social value
   in nonproductive work, 146
Sociometer, 10, 11
Solidarity
   as EU principle, 162
   as strengthened by public services, 168
   logic of solidarity in welfare state, 160
Spirituality, 36
   and psychological problems, 43
   as distinct from religion, 36
   as transcendence, 36
   correlates of spiritual coping, 43
   dimensions of, 38
   human beings as spiritual, 37
   meaning-making, 36, 37
   relationship, 37
   secular, 37
   spiritual health, 41
Statistics
   alcohol use in Malta, 75
   cohabitation, 70
   crude divorce rates, 70
   domestic violence in Malta, 71
   life expectancy, 75
   literacy in Malta, 85
   marital separations, 70
   same sex couples, 70
Stress, 7
   caused by negative interactions, 15
Subsidiarity
   as EU principle, 162
Support
   important aspects to persons with intellectual disabilities, 139
   paid services, 140

Systemic framework
   family subsystems, 66

U
Unemployment
   impact on wellbeing, 150

V
Values
   congruence, 39
   valuing all human life, 136
Violence
   consequences of intimate partner violence, 117
   turning points for women, 120
Voluntary sector
   as seen by youth, 103
Vulnerability
   as social state, 100
   effects, 101

W
Welfare
   as concern of economics, 145
   as productive factor, 167
   social assistance, 160
   social insurance, 160
Welfare State
   austerity measures, 162
   core contradiction of, 161
   corporate welfare, 169
   divisions of welfare debate, 168
   expenditure, 162
   fiscal welfare, 168
   mixed economy of welfare, 167
   occupational welfare, 168
   origins of, 160
   public attitudes to, 165
   public concerns over, 165
   reforms, 161, 165
   retrenchment, 138
   role of private sector in care, 168
   three main phases of, 160

INDEX

Wellbeing, 7–9, 18
- and cross cultural comparisons, 154
- and economic activity, 147
- areas for government promotion, 151
- as defined by care practitioners, 137
- as defined by client, 137
- as flourishing, 28
- as having purpose in life, 141
- biopsychosocial-spiritual model, 44
- cannot be conferred by carers, 141
- common manifestations of, 27
- dimensions of, 41
- domains of spiritual wellbeing, 42
- effect of domestic violence, 72
- eudaimonia, 8
- eudaimonic, 39
- eudaimonic approach, 27
- factors affecting, 148, 149
- family, 66
- flourishing, 40
- health in Malta, 75
- hedonic, 38
- hedonic approach, 27
- importance of social feedback, 11
- indices of, 147
- in Malta, 152
- measurement of, 2
- multidimensionality, 66
- predictors of, 40
- psychological, 39
- psychological approach, 28
- social, 11, 138
- social dimension, 28
- spiritual wellbeing scale, 42
- subjective, 8, 27, 39
- surveys of, 148

Y

Youth
- attributes, 99
- moral panic, 99
- scapegoating, 100
- voices of, 102